RURAL TRANSITION IN AZERBAIJAN

Rural Economies in Transition

Series Editors

Much of the world's rural population lives in transition countries that are attempting to transform their economies from the centrally planned socialist system to a market-oriented system. The Rural Economies in Transition series evaluates the deep impact these transformations are having in Central and Eastern Europe, the former Soviet Union, and Asia. Based on original empirical work by international teams at the cutting edge of research, each volume presents the results of one complete empirical study devoted to a single country or region. The editors have designed the series to provide agricultural, development, and political economists, as well as scholars in other disciplines, with authoritative and up-to-date factual information about rural transition. The editors welcome manuscript submissions from scholars engaged in original empirical research in the field.

Private Agriculture in Armenia, by Zvi Lerman and Astghik Mirzakhanian
Romanian Agriculture and Transition toward the EU, edited by Sophia Davidova and Kenneth J. Thomson
Transition, Institutions, and the Rural Sector, edited by Max Spoor
Greening Industrialization in Asian Transitional Economies: China and Vietnam, edited by Arthur P. J. Mol and Joost C. L. van Buuren
Agriculture in Transition: Land Policies and Evolving Farm Structures in Post-Soviet Countries, by Zvi Lerman, Csaba Csaki, and Gershon Feder
Building Market Institutions in Post-Communist Agriculture: Land, Credit, and Assistance, edited by David A. J. Macey, William Pyle, and Stephen K. Wegren
Russia's Food Policies and Globalization, by Stephen K. Wegren
Cooperation in the Romanian Countryside: An Insight into Post-Soviet Agriculture, by Rachel Sabates-Wheeler
Reinventing the Cuban Sugar Agroindustry, edited by Jorge F. Pérez-López and José Alvarez
Integrated Development of Agriculture and Rural Areas in Central European Countries, edited by Sophia Davidova, Kai Bauer, and Michael Cuddy
Measuring Social and Economic Change in Rural Russia: Surveys from 1991 to 2003, by David J. O'Brien and Valery V. Patsiorkovsky
Russia's Agriculture in Transition: Factor Markets and Constraints on Growth, edited by Zvi Lerman

RURAL TRANSITION IN AZERBAIJAN

Zvi Lerman and David Sedik

LEXINGTON BOOKS
A division of
ROWMAN & LITTLEFIELD PUBLISHERS, INC.
Lanham • Boulder • New York • Toronto • Plymouth, UK

Published by Lexington Books
A division of Rowman & Littlefield Publishers, Inc.
A wholly owned subsidiary of The Rowman & Littlefield Publishing Group, Inc.
4501 Forbes Boulevard, Suite 200, Lanham, Maryland 20706
http://www.lexingtonbooks.com

Estover Road, Plymouth PL6 7PY, United Kingdom

British Library Cataloguing in Publication Information Available

Library of Congress Cataloging-in-Publication Data

Lerman, Zvi, 1941-
Rural transition in Azerbaijan / Zvi Lerman and David Sedik.
p. cm. — (Rural economies in transition)
Includes bibliographical references and index.
ISBN 978-0-7391-4316-2 (cloth : alk. paper) — ISBN 978-0-7391-4318-6 (electronic)
1. Land reform—Azerbaijan. 2. Agriculture and state—Azerbaijan. 3. Rural development—Azerbaijan. 4. Agriculture—Economic aspects—Azerbaijan. 5. Poverty—Azerbaijan. 6. Azerbaijan—Rural conditions. 7. Azerbaijan—Politics and government—1991- 8. Azerbaijan—Economic conditions—1991- I. Sedik, David J. II. Title.
HD1333.A98L47 2010
333.3'14754--dc22

2009049862

™ The paper used in this publication meets the minimum requirements of American National Standard for Information Sciences—Permanence of Paper for Printed Library Materials, ANSI/NISO Z39.48-1992.

Printed in the United States of America

Contents

Introduction

AZERBAIJAN, WITH ITS TWO Trans-Caucasian neighbors—Armenia and Georgia—are examples of successful land reform: the three countries implemented a sweeping and irreversible shift to individual farming, which in turn has led to impressive recovery in agriculture. The agrarian transition in these small CIS countries contrasts with that in Russia, Ukraine, and Kazakhstan, where land privatization has been accompanied by policies encouraging the persistence of large corporate farms and agricultural recovery has been much less impressive.

The underlying objective of land reform in all transition countries is not only to encourage growth and improve productivity in the agricultural sector as a whole, but also (and perhaps mainly) to increase the incomes and the well-being of their large rural populations, which rely on agriculture for a substantial part of the family budget. From this perspective, land reform may have a significant impact on poverty alleviation issues which are at the core of the agenda in many international organizations. This book accordingly evaluates the record of land reform in Azerbaijan, with special focus on its impact on rural household incomes and rural family well-being. It is part of the conceptual basis for advancement of international policy support programs in some regions of CIS, and especially in Central Asia.

This approach explains the title of our book, *Rural Transition* rather than the more conventional "agricultural transition." The study examines the institutional and policy changes that went into agrarian reform in Azerbaijan and analyzes to what degree they were responsible not only for the robust growth in agriculture, but also for the fall in rural poverty and the general improvement in rural incomes observed since 1996.

Azerbaijan's successful agrarian reform can be used as an important example for the other countries in the region, and documenting the experience of Azerbaijan can be of enormous assistance in showing what robust agrarian reforms can in fact deliver. Certainly, land reform is not the only reform needed in these countries in order to spur growth. The example of land reform in Azerbaijan illustrates that many complementary reforms in agriculture are required as well. However, land reform is a basis for further reforms. Careful documentation and analysis of the example of agrarian reform in Azerbaijan is an important part of a policy agenda for rural poverty alleviation in the region.

Structure of the Book

Our objective is to provide an overview of rural transition in Azerbaijan since independence, while at the same time linking it to a long-term perspective of agricultural development. We accordingly start with some historical notes on Azerbaijan (chapter 1) and then proceed to unfold the broad canvas of 40 years of agricultural development, starting roughly in the middle of the Soviet regime in the 1960s (chapter 2). Our account of rural transition in Azerbaijan begins during the Soviet period, in the era of Brezhnev and Kosygin (1964–82), continues through the era of Gorbachev (1985–91), and then recounts the institutional changes and their consequences over the years of transition in independent Azerbaijan. The need for reform is highlighted in chapter 3 against the backdrop of the gradual collapse of the Soviet economic system in the late 1980s, still before the dissolution of the USSR, and the failure to reconstruct a viable institutional basis for market agriculture in the early 1990s, immediately after independence. This chapter also describes the two waves of Azerbaijan's reforms—the pre-1996 reforms and the Aliyev reforms. chapter 4 presents data on sectoral changes in agriculture, mainly since 1996, including the positive impact of Aliyev reforms on agricultural performance. chapter 5 uses farm- and household-level survey data to examine the impact of reforms on rural family incomes and rural poverty. Some conclusions and policy recommendations are collected in chapter 6, where we argue that agricultural growth and recovery are dependent on successful policy reforms, and in particular the transition from traditional large-scale farms to substantially smaller family farms. A statistical annex after chapter 6 presents tables with selected time series from official statistical data. The references and the main sources of information (both printed and electronic) appear at the end.

The long-term perspective of rural and agricultural development in Azerbaijan since the 1960s that we elaborate in chapter 2 is unconventional for a study devoted primarily to an account of institutional change and its effects on agricultural growth, rural incomes, and poverty after 1995. However, our approach reflects a fundamental concern about the experience of the poor, small republics of the Transcaucasus and Central Asia. Having lived as part of the Russian and then Soviet Empire for nearly 200 years, these countries did not choose to end the Soviet economic system themselves. Starting with Gorbachev, they suddenly found that their familiar economic and political environment was reshaped from afar and then ended without their having much to do with it. The end of the Soviet regime in Azerbaijan left the country with no policy-making capacity, since agricultural policy during the Soviet era had always been made in Moscow.

Data Sources

The data for this study represent an integration of two strands: official statistics from the Azerbaijan Department of Statistics in Baku and data collected in a number of special surveys. The official statistics are primarily from the two main yearbooks published annually in Azerbaijan: the general statistical yearbook and the agricultural yearbook. In many cases these standard publications were supplemented with data kindly provided by Sefayddin Yusifov from the agricultural unit in the Department of Statistics. Thus, his time series of land balance data enabled us to construct the distribution of land between corporate and individual farms over the years, which is one of the unique contributions of our study. In addition to these official sources of independent Azerbaijan, we have also relied on statistical yearbooks from the Soviet period (when Azerbaijan was officially known as the Azerbaijan Soviet Socialist Republic or AzSSR). Another invaluable source is the database of the State Statistical Committee of CIS, an organization located in Moscow that maintains consistent time series since 1980 for all 12 CIS countries.

Much of the information for comparing asset and welfare issues in Azerbaijan comes from the second strand of data—three household surveys carried out in 1995, 2001, and 2003. These surveys were quite different in their sample size, their focus, their questions, and their sampling strategy (table A). Such profound differences prevented us from comparing most of the results over time, since such comparisons are particularly sensitive to survey design. Thus,

TABLE A
Rural Household and Farm Surveys in Azerbaijan: 1995, 2001, and 2003

Survey	*Year*	*Type of Survey*	*Rural Respondents*	*Stratification*	*Representativeness*
World Bank Azerbaijan Survey of Living Conditions (ASLC)	1995	LSMS-type household survey	972 households	Baku, outside of Baku, and internally displaced people, excluding occupied areas	Nationally representative
Household Budget Survey (HBS) of the State Statistical Committee of Azerbaijan	2001	Household budget survey	3,623 households	8 economic zones and Baku	Representative at each stratification level
World Bank Survey of Farms	2003	Survey of farms of three main organizational forms	703 households, 65 peasant (family) farms, 15 corporate farms	Districts Khachmaz, Shemaki, Imishly, Sabirabad, Lankaran, Masally, Khanlar, Tovuz	Representative within the selected regions, the main farming areas of Azerbaijan

we could make no judgments as to changes in average incomes, expenditures, or poverty levels based on these three instruments because of differences in the sampling structure, in the income and expenditure aggregates, and in the method of recall. However, all three surveys contained similar questions on land and livestock holdings. These statistics are probably least affected by differences in the questionnaire design and method of gathering data, and we therefore use some of these figures judiciously. In addition, the 2003 survey contained a number of inquiries on land received as a result of the land reform. We used these statistics to draw correlations between land received and a number of other issues.

Acknowledgments

This book builds on work carried out over a number of years by the authors on rural transition, poverty, and land reform in the countries of Europe and Central Asia. In particular, the idea for the book started after one of the authors (David Sedik) completed work on a background paper on rural poverty in Azerbaijan and a study of land reform in the region based on survey data. For permission to use our earlier works we thank Michael Mills and Nora Dudwick of the World Bank. We also thank Kostas Stamoulis and Benjamin Davis of FAO for their review and guidance on the analysis of rural poverty indicators in Azerbaijan.

In Azerbaijan we particularly thank Messrs. Seyfaddin Yusifov and Yashar Pasha of the State Statistical Committee in Baku for their kind assistance in advising us on data issues, as well as in collecting and supplying us with invaluable official statistical data. We also thank Mr. Amin Ismayilov of the State Land Committee for similar advice and for assistance in collecting invaluable official data on land in Azerbaijan. Last, we thank Mr. Islam Ibragimov of the Ministry of Agriculture for his assistance in our work on land reform in Azerbaijan.

1

Azerbaijan: The Country and the People

AZERBAIJAN'S ECONOMIC POLICIES over the past century were shaped by four major factors: the long colonial rule, first under the Russian Empire and then the USSR; a varied ethnic composition that contributed to prosperity through the benefits of "multicultural" entrepreneurship, but also led to intense civil strife; rapid population growth in a small country with essentially limited resources; and last, but not least, relative abundance of crude oil. The historical overview in this chapter highlights the first three factors and sets the stage for the discussion of rural transition in Azerbaijan that follows. The importance of oil is brought up later, in chapter 2, in the context of Azerbaijan's economic development.

Geography

Azerbaijan is located in the eastern part of the South Caucasus region, on the shore of the Caspian Sea, which forms the country's east border. It borders on Iran in the south, Russia in the north, Georgia in the northwest, and Armenia in the west. An arm or Armenia physically separates the Nakhichevan exclave in the southwest from the rest of the country (map 1).

This autonomous republic, comprising about 6% of Azerbaijan's total land area, was created in 1924, following a 1921 referendum that sweepingly endorsed the region's affiliation with Azerbaijan. Another western province, Nagorno-Karabakh (created in 1924 as an autonomous oblast within Azerbaijan with about 5% of the country's territory), is currently under self-rule by

MAP 1
Azerbaijan and its Transcaucasian neighbors. Source: UNICEF [http://www.unicef.org/infobycountry/azerbaijan_background.html].

its ethnic Armenian population and has de facto seceded from Azerbaijan. This is the outcome of a protracted armed conflict with Armenia, which erupted in 1988, when the Nagorno-Karabakh National Council voted for unification with Armenia, and ended with a ceasefire in 1994. Under the terms of the ceasefire, Armenia continues to occupy 20% of Azerbaijan's territory—the five ethnic-Armenian raions in Nagorno-Karabakh proper plus six ethnic-Azerbaijani raions surrounding Nagorno-Karabakh. The so-called Lachin corridor creates contiguous territory between Armenia in the west and Nagorno-Karabakh further east. Although the ceasefire has now held for more than ten years, Azerbaijan has never recognized the de facto secession of Nagorno-Karabakh and the occupation of the surrounding districts, nor is Nagorno-Karabakh officially recognized by any state in the world (including Armenia). The future of Nagorno-Karabakh and the occupied territories is the subject of ongoing negotiations between the two countries.

The heart of Azerbaijan is a wide valley along the river Kura, flowing from Georgia in the northwest to the Caspian Sea, and its right-hand tributary Araks (or Araz). The central valley is framed by three mountain ranges that occupy about half of the country: the edge of the Greater Caucasus Ridge in the north, the slopes of the Lesser Caucasus in the southwest, and the Talysh Mountains jutting from Iran in the southeast. The Lankaran Lowlands extend north to south in a thin strip between the Talysh Mountains and the Caspian Sea (map 2).

The climate varies from subtropical and dry in central and eastern Azerbaijan ("semiarid steppe") to subtropical and humid in the southeast, temperate along the shores of the Caspian Sea, and cold at the higher mountain elevations. Baku, on the Caspian, enjoys mild weather, averaging 4°C in January and 25°C in July. Because most of Azerbaijan receives scant rainfall—on

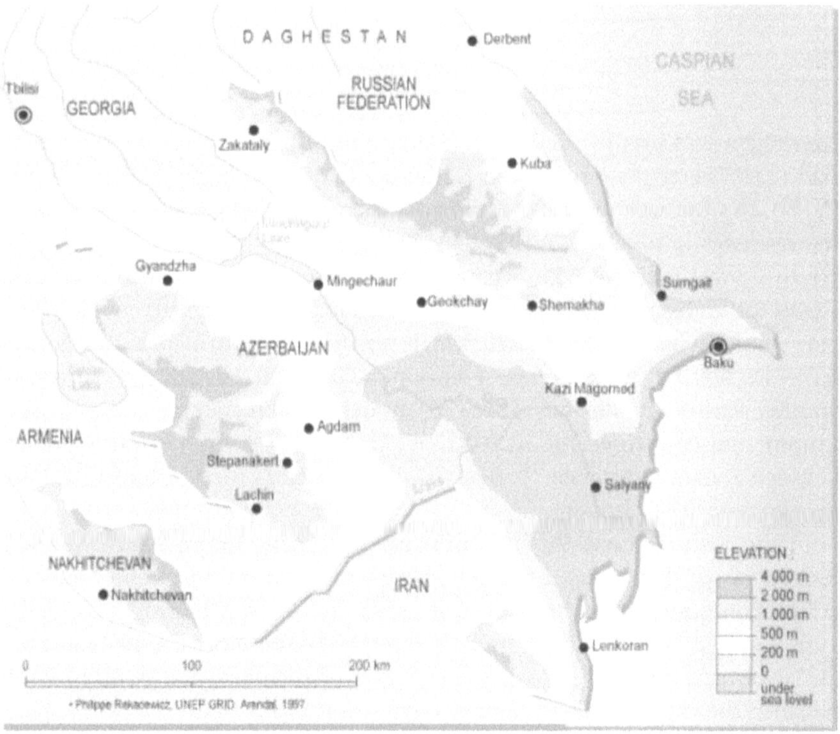

MAP 2
Azerbaijan topographic map. Cartographers: Philippe Rekacewicz, Emmanuelle Bournay (July 1997). Source: UNEP/GRID-Arendal Maps and Graphics Library [http://maps.grida.no/go/graphic/azerbaijan_topographic_map].

average 152 to 254 mm annually—agriculture requires irrigation. Heaviest precipitation occurs in the highest elevations of the Caucasus and in the Lankaran Lowlands in the far southeast, where the yearly average exceeds 1,000 mm (Curtis, 1994).

With land area of 86,600 sq. km, Azerbaijan is one of the small CIS countries: only Armenia, Georgia, and Moldova are smaller (the three former Soviet republics on the Baltic Sea—Latvia, Lithuania, and Estonia—are also smaller than Azerbaijan, but they are not part of CIS). However, Azerbaijan's rapidly growing population of 8.7 million (2008 data) puts it in the middle of the population ranking: only 5 of the 12 CIS countries—Russia, Ukraine, Uzbekistan, Kazakhstan, and Belarus—have a larger population than Azerbaijan (State Statistical Committee of CIS, 2008). Ethnically, Azerbaijan is the only Turkic-speaking country in the South Caucasus, alongside its non-Turkic neighbors Armenia and Georgia.

History

Azerbaijan was part of the Persian Empire until the early 1700s, when Russian czars (Peter the Great, then Catherine the Great) began expansion into the South Caucasus. By 1806, Czarist Russia controlled Georgia and most of the khanates in northern Azerbaijan. Russia's expansionist intentions in the South Caucasus triggered a war with Persia, which ended in 1813 with the Treaty of Gulistan officially dividing Azerbaijan between Russia (northern part) and Persia (southern part, which remains an Iranian province to this day—see box 1.1). The Treaty of Turkmanchay signed in 1828 at the end of another Russo-Persian war (1826–28) awarded Nakhichevan to the Russian Empire and confirmed the Araz River (Araks in Armenia) as the boundary between Russia and Persia. At that point, Persia had ceded all its South Caucasus territories to Russia.

In the 19th century, Russian influence over daily life in Azerbaijan was less pervasive than that of indigenous religious and political elites and the cultural and intellectual influences of Persia and Turkey. During most of the 19th century, the Russian Empire extracted commodities from Azerbaijan and invested little in the economy. However, the exploitation of oil in Azerbaijan at the end of the 19th century—the world's first oil well was drilled just south of Baku in 1848–49—brought an influx of Russians into Baku, increasing Russian influence and expanding the local economy. Although ethnic Russians dominated the oil business and government administration in the late 1800s, many Azerbaijanis became prominent in particular sectors of oil production, such as oil transport on the Caspian Sea. Armenians also gained

Box 1.1. A Brief History of South Azerbaijan

The Araz River was established as the border between the Russian Empire in South Caucasus and Iran by the Treaty of Turkmanchay in 1828. "Russian" Azerbaijan (coinciding with today's Republic of Azerbaijan) was in the Caucasus, north of Araz, while "South Azerbaijan" was in northwestern Iran, south of Araz, between the Caspian Sea in the east and the border with Turkey and Iraq in the west. South Azerbaijan (or Azarbaijan in the accepted Iranian pronunciation) comprises three provinces: Ardebil in the east, on the Caspian Sea, Tabriz in the center, and Uromiyeh in the west, on the Turkish–Iraqi border. The population in these three provinces is predominantly ethnic Azeri and it is estimated at 10 million (more than in the Republic of Azerbaijan). The physical barrier imposed by the Araz River between the North and the South has become a literary symbol of national separation, nurturing a culture of "longing" for unification. Iranian geographers often use the name Arran for Northern Azerbaijan, after one of the Caucasus provinces of the Persian Empire.

At the end of World War I, after the defeat of Turkey in November 1918, British forces advanced from Iran in the south to occupy the "Russian" North Azerbaijan. Then the link between the two parts of Azerbaijan was severed again in April 1920, when the Red Army retook North Azerbaijan. Toward the end of World War II the Soviet Union, with the consent of the Western Allies, occupied South Azerbaijan and created in 1945 the Democratic Republic of Azerbaijan. This autonomous republic collapsed in 1946 when the Iranian Army took over after the retreat of the Red Army from northern Iran. Many of the South Azeri intelligentsia escaped to the North, where they fuelled a movement for reunification of North and South Azerbaijan.

A violent manifestation of nationalist ferment erupted at the end of 1989, when North Azerbaijan was in the throes of domestic violence between the Azeris and the Armenians triggered by the Nagorno-Karabakh conflict. Azeris rioted along the Iranian border, especially in Nakhichevan, destroying border checkpoints and crossing into Iranian South Azerbaijan to meet their compatriots. Azerbaijani intellectuals appealed to the Soviet Politburo for relaxation of border controls between Soviet and Iranian Azerbaijan, comparing the "tragic" separation of the Azerbaijani nation to the divisions of Korea or Vietnam. Moscow sent the army into Azerbaijan to quell the disturbances, and the Soviet forces cooperated with Iranian authorities to secure the Azerbaijan–Iran border. These actions of the central Communist authorities further alienated the population from Moscow's rule and accelerated the movement toward independence.

The use of the Azeri language in Iran was banned in the 1950s under Shah Mohammed Riza Pahlevi. The restriction was formally abolished after the Islamic revolution of 1979, but the Azeri population has not enjoyed much cultural freedom since the consolidation of the Ayatollah Khomeini's regime in 1983. The attitude in Tehran toward the national aspirations of the Azeri population is decidedly inimical.

importance as merchants and local officials of the Russian monarchy. In 1905 social tensions erupted in riots and other forms of death and destruction as Azerbaijanis and Armenians struggled for local control, resisting Russian rule (Curtis, 1994).

After the 1917 Bolshevik Revolution in Russia, the Baku Bolsheviks—a grouping of mainly Russians and Armenians—declared a Marxist republic in Azerbaijan. Muslim nationalists (the Musavat Party) separately declared the establishment of the Azerbaijan People's Democratic Republic in May 1918, after Georgia and Armenia had declared independence. The Muslim forces, with substantial backing from the Ottoman Turkish army, marched into the capital in September 1918, meeting little resistance from the Bolsheviks. Azerbaijan was occupied by Ottoman Turkish troops until the end of World War I in November 1918. British forces then replaced the defeated Turks and remained in Azerbaijan for most of that country's brief period of independence, which lasted from May 1918 through April 1920. Service (2005, p. 198) notes that "before the pan-Turkic Musavatist party came to power in Baku in 1918 there had formally been no such place as Azerbaijan."[1]

The Red Army invaded Azerbaijan in April 1920.[2] Lenin justified the invasion by the importance of Baku oil to the new Bolshevik state, still embroiled in a civil war. The Red Army met with little resistance, because the Azerbaijani forces were heavily involved in suppressing separatism among the Armenian majority in the Nagorno-Karabakh area of south-central Azerbaijan. In September 1920, Azerbaijan signed a treaty with Russia unifying its military forces, economy, and foreign trade with those of the emerging Soviet Union, although the fiction of Azerbaijani political independence was maintained.

When the Soviet Union was formally established in 1922, Azerbaijan, Armenia, and Georgia were combined in a single political entity—the Transcaucasian Soviet Federated Socialist Republic (TSFSR).[3] The three subunits ceded their nominal powers over foreign policy, finances, trade, transportation, and other areas to the central authority of the new republic. In 1936 the Stalin Constitution abolished the TSFSR, and the three constituent parts were proclaimed separate Soviet socialist republics within the USSR.

The invasion of 1920 began a 71-year period under total political and economic control of the state that became the Soviet Union, or USSR, in 1922. The borders and formal status of Azerbaijan underwent a period of change and uncertainty in the 1920s and 1930s, and thereafter remained stable through the end of the Soviet period in 1991.

During Stalin's era (1926–53), Azerbaijan suffered, as did the other Soviet republics, from forced collectivization and political purges. Yet during the same period, Azerbaijan also achieved significant gains in industrialization and literacy levels, which were impressive in comparison with those of other Muslim states of the Middle East at that time. After Stalin Moscow's intrusions were less sweeping but nonetheless authoritarian. Khrushchev, Brezhnev, and Gorbachev all actively intervened over the years in leadership nominations in the ruling Azerbaijan Communist Party, appointing and dismissing party heads to suit considerations in Moscow.

The weakening of central Soviet power in the late 1980s led to the emergence of a nationalist opposition to the Azerbaijan Communist Party. In the fall of 1989, the nationalist opposition—the Azerbaijan Popular Front (APF)—led a wave of protest strikes expressing growing political opposition to Communist rule. The Communist authorities bowed to opposition pressure, and in September 1989 the Azerbaijan Supreme Court passed a resolution of Azerbaijan's sovereignty proclaiming its right to secede from the Soviet Union after a referendum. This resolution was declared invalid in November 1989 by the Presidium of the Supreme Soviet in Moscow, the legislative body of the Soviet Union.

In the same period, reacting to Nagorno-Karabakh's declaration of unification with Armenia in the fall of 1989, Azerbaijanis unleashed a wave of violence against Armenian residents of Baku and other population centers. The turmoil seemed to jeopardize Communist Party rule, and in January 1990 Moscow deployed military and security forces to suppress these riots. Moscow also began a crackdown on the opposition forces in Baku and other cities. These events widened the breach between Azerbaijan and the central power in Moscow on the eve of the Soviet Union's dissolution.

Azerbaijan began the process of achieving formal independence on October 18, 1991, when the Supreme Soviet in Baku passed a law on state independence. In December 1991, over 99% of voters cast ballots in favor of independence in a referendum on that issue. The constitution was duly amended to reflect the country's new status. In 1993 Azerbaijan joined the CIS as a full member.

Thus, after more than 200 years of being a Russian, and then Soviet, colony Azerbaijan faced the daunting task of creating the institutions of independent statehood. The country had no experience of independent political rule and no familiarity or practice of independent policy making. Local decision-making expertise and instruments of governance had to be developed expeditiously to replace the disappearing Soviet structures.

Population Growth and Land Scarcity

Azerbaijan is a Muslim country, but like other Muslim republics in the former Soviet Union it is an essentially secular society, still free from manifestations of religious fervor. The Azeris are a Turkic-speaking people, linguistically and ethnically close to Turkey. During the Czarist and the Soviet periods, Azerbaijan was a multiethnic society, with the Azeri people accounting for less than 80% of the population. The two main ethnic minorities were the Armenians and the Russians, which in 1979 accounted for 16% of the population (table 1.1). While the Armenians represented 8% of Azerbaijan's population according to the 1979 census, they were the absolute majority in Nagorno-Karabakh (76% of the province's population). Yet only 123,000 out of 475,500 Armenians lived in Nagorno-Karabakh in 1979. Thus, the Armenian minority was not concentrated in its ethnic enclave and some 350,000 Armenians, or 6% of Azerbaijan's population, were scattered in other parts of the country.

The high proportion of ethnic Armenians in Nagorno-Karabakh accounts for the separatist tendencies of this province since the 1920s, while the visibility of Armenians all over the country, and especially in the capital of Baku, probably triggered the anti-Armenian violence in the Soviet twilight years. The share of Armenians dropped from 8% of the total population in

TABLE 1.1
Ethnic Composition of Azerbaijan's Population 1979–99

	Thousands			*Percent*			*Nagorno-Karabakh 1979*	
	1979	*1989*	*1999*	*1979*	*1989*	*1999*	*'000*	*%*
Total population	6026	7021	7953	100.0	100.0	100.0	162.2	100.0
Azeris	4709	5805	7205	78.1	82.7	90.6	37.2	23.0
Russians*	502	425	171	8.3	6.0	2.1	1.3	0.8
Armenians	475	390	121	7.9	5.6	1.5	123.1	75.9
Dagestan nationalities	205	215	229	3.4	3.1	2.9	0.6	0.3
Other nationalities	135	186	227	2.2	2.6	2.9		

*Including Ukrainians.
Source: 1979 from Statistical Committee of AzSSR (1980); 1989–99 from Statistical Committee of Azerbaijan (2006a).

1979 to 1.5% in 1999 (the latest census available), and common wisdom attributes this decline to the strong anti-Armenian sentiments prevailing since the late 1980s. Yet the Russian and Ukrainian minorities also experienced a dramatic exodus between 1979 and 1999, dropping from 8.3% to 2.1% of the population without any ethnic unrest directed against them. The shift from a multiethnic society to a more homogeneous Azeri nation is thus probably a general feature of independence.

Azerbaijan's population increased from 6.2 million in 1980 to 7.2 million in 1990 and then to 8.7 million in 2008, displaying a long-term growth rate of 1.2% a year. Azerbaijan's growth rate declined over time, but has so far remained positive, contrary to the situation in many other CIS countries, including Azerbaijan's Transcaucasian neighbors Armenia and Georgia, where positive population growth in the last decade of the Soviet era 1980–1990 changed to negative growth after 1990 (figure 1.1). With respect to population growth Azerbaijan is more like the four Central Asian countries across the Caspian Sea—Kyrgyzstan, Tajikistan, Turkmenistan, and Uzbekistan, which have maintained high positive growth rates since 1980 (higher even than Azerbaijan's).

The differences in the growth rates of rural and urban population in Azerbaijan were quite small. Rural population growth closely tracked total population growth, both rising by about 40% between 1980 and 2005. Still, the last decade of the Soviet period 1980–90 was characterized by slightly faster growth of the urban population, whereas during the independence

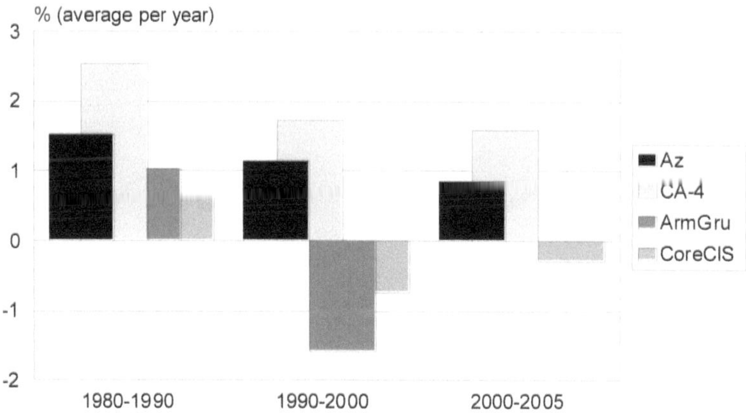

FIGURE 1.1
Population growth rates over time in Azerbaijan (Az) and other regions of the CIS. Legend: CA-4—Kyrgyzstan, Tajikistan, Turkmenistan, Uzbekistan; ArmGru—Armenia and Georgia; Core CIS—Russia, Ukraine, Kazakhstan, Belarus, Moldova. Source: Statistical Committee of CIS (2008).

TABLE 1.2
Annual Average Growth Rates of Total and Rural Population in Azerbaijan (Percent Per Year)

	Total Population	*Rural Population*
Entire period 1980–2005	1.24	1.37
Soviet period 1980–1990	1.52	1.47
Independent Azerbaijan 1990–2000	1.14	1.81
1990–2005	1.04	1.30

Source: Statistical Committee of Azerbaijan (2006a, 2006d).

period 1990–2005 the rural population grew at a slightly faster rate (table 1.2). The faster growth of the rural population was particularly noticeable during the first decade of independence 1990–2000, when Azerbaijan implemented most of the land reform measures, including large-scale distribution of land to rural families.

The share of rural population declined throughout the Soviet era, dropping from more than 50% in 1960 to 46% at the end of the 1980s (figure 1.2). This long-term trend was a reflection of Soviet industrialization and urbanization policies that acted to reduce the share of rural population in all former Soviet republics. The trend changed in 1989, when increasing economic hardships in urban areas combined with land distribution in the villages to boost rural population growth. The share of rural population accordingly rose from a low

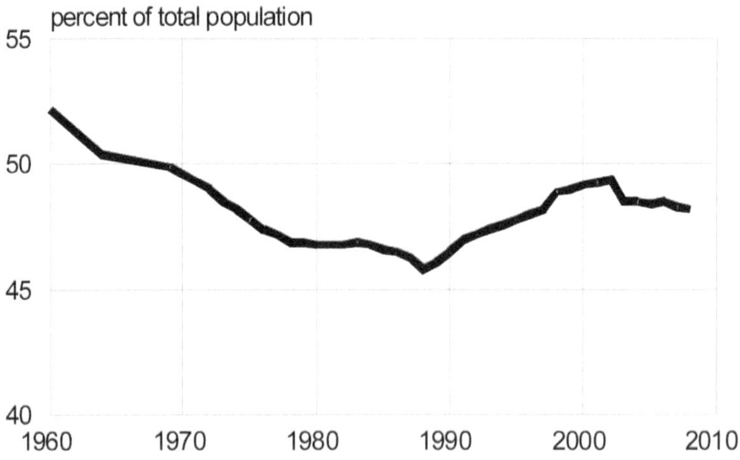

FIGURE 1.2
Share of rural population 1960–2008 (percent). Source: Statistical Annex Table A.1.

of 46% in 1990 to over 49% in the period between 1998 and 2002, dropping back to 48% thereafter (figure 1.2). Despite these interesting policy-induced changes in rural population growth over time, the fluctuations in the share of rural population since 1980 have been slight, within a narrow range between 46% and 49% (the vertical scale in figure 1.2 has been intentionally exaggerated to bring out these slight differences). Long term, the rural population in Azerbaijan accounts for just under half of the total population. Azerbaijan remains an agrarian society, in which the large rural population is reflected in high agricultural employment and a high share of agriculture in the economy (see chapter 2).

The rapid population growth in Azerbaijan is reflected in high population pressure on the naturally scarce resources of cultivable land in this mountainous country. The amount of arable land per rural resident in Azerbaijan is on the same general level as in Central Asia and its Transcaucasian neighbors, and an order of magnitude smaller than in the core CIS countries—Russia, Ukraine, Belarus, and Kazakhstan (table 1.3). Since irrigation is critically important for agriculture in Azerbaijan's semiarid climate, considerable efforts have been made since 1970 to increase the irrigated area, mainly by building canals that divert the surface flow from Kura and Araks rivers to the fields (see chapter 2, figure 2.3). The increase of cultivable area through irrigation

TABLE 1.3
Arable Land Per Rural Person in CIS Countries (2002)

	Arable Land Per Rural Resident, Ha	*% of Arable Land Under Irrigation (1990)*
Transcaucasus		
Azerbaijan	0.42	86
Armenia	0.43	62
Georgia	0.38	59
Central Asia (CA-4)		
Kyrgyzstan	0.41	79
Tajikistan	0.18	81
Turkmenistan (1996)	0.60	106
Uzbekistan (2001)	0.25	100
Core CIS		
Kazakhstan	3.32	7
Russia (2001)	3.05	5
Ukraine	1.99	8
Belarus	1.94	2
Moldova	0.86	17

Source: Statistical Committee of CIS (2008).

projects has generally kept pace with the population growth and as result the amount of arable land per capita remained constant all through the 1980s and the 1990s. Long term, the arable land per capita (counting both rural and urban population) decreased slightly from 0.26 hectares in 1970 to 0.22 hectares between 1980 and 2000 and 0.21 hectares in 2004–05 (Statistical Committee of Azerbaijan, 2006b).

The emphasis on irrigation has continued since independence, with the World Bank and Asian Development Bank providing loans for rehabilitation and expansion of irrigation networks. Because of its location at the lower reaches of Kura and Araks, Azerbaijan is at the receiving end of all industrial and agricultural effluents from its upstream neighbors (mainly Georgia). International donors, in addition to irrigation projects, have launched environmental health programs designed to reduce water pollution levels and improve access to clean drinking water for both rural and urban populations in Azerbaijan.

The Economic Regions of Azerbaijan[4]

Like other small CIS countries, Azerbaijan has a highly differentiated geography with a highly differentiated agriculture. The country is divided into ten economic regions, which include the cities and the rural districts (table 1.4, map 3). The Absheron region in eastern Azerbaijan includes the Absheron

TABLE 1.4
Economic Regions of Azerbaijan

	Geographic Location	*Number of Districts*	*Population 2005), %*	*Area, %*
Absheron*	East-center, Caspian shore	4	27.0	3.9
Guba-Khachmaz	Northeast	5	5.6	8.8
Dakhlik-Shirvan	North-center	4	3.2	7.0
Shaki-Zagatala	North-northwest	6	6.5	10.3
Ganja-Gazakh	Northwest	11	13.4	14.4
Karabakh**	Southwest	12	10.0	17.6
Aran (Mugano-Salyan)	Center	18	20.4	24.7
Lankaran	Southeast	6	9.4	7.0
Nakhichevan	Southwest, exclave	8	4.5	6.3

Source: Statistical Committee of Azerbaijan (2006a, 2006c), Government of Azerbaijan (2004).
*The capital city of Baku accounts for 22% of the country's population.
** Including Nagorno-Karabakh (five districts), the Kalbajar-Lachin region on the border with Armenia to the west (four districts), and the three districts of Terter, Agdam, and Fizuli to the east. The Kalbar-Lachin region accounts for 2% of the population and 7.5% of the area of Azerbaijan.

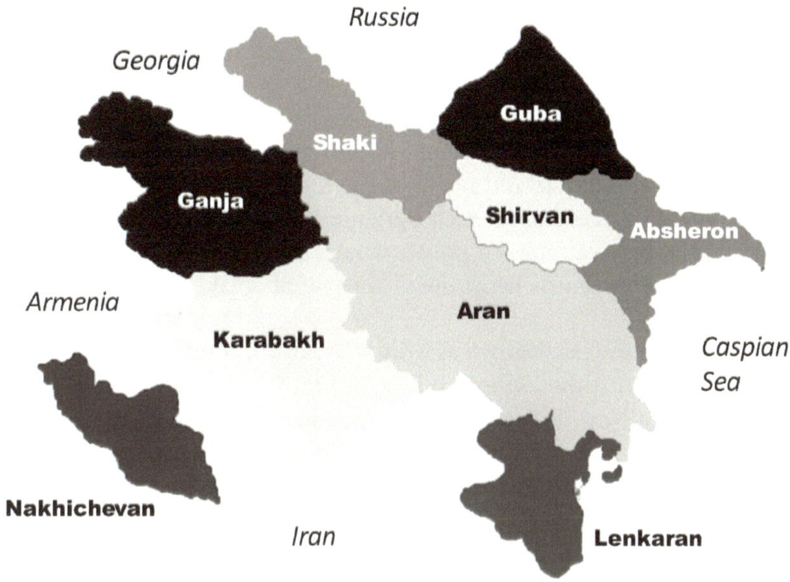

MAP 3
The economic regions of Azerbaijan. Source: Based on www.azregionaldevelopment.org.

Peninsula jutting into the Caspian Sea, with the capital city of Baku at its tip. This is the most populous region in the country, accounting for fully 27% of Azerbaijan's population (of which 22% is in Baku). Because of its advantageous geographic position, the Absheron region is crossed by freight routes connecting Azerbaijan and the whole of Transcaucasia with the North Caucasus and Central Asia. Highways run from the peninsula to every corner of the country. Its main natural wealth is mineral, including oil, natural gas, iodobromide waters, and limestone used in building and cement production. Absheron is the leader in industrial production in Azerbaijan, with industries that include oil refineries and processing plants, as well as iron and steel, non-ferrous metallurgical, and chemical industries. Although it is on the shores of the Caspian Sea, the Absheron region remains one of the most arid parts of Azerbaijan. As a result, it is agriculturally least developed among Azerbaijan regions, contributing very little to crop or livestock production (table 1.5). Absheron is the only region in Azerbaijan without its own sources of drinking water, which has to be brought in by pipelines.

The Guba-Khachmaz [Quba-Khachmaz] region lies to the north of Absheron stretching from the shores of the Caspian Sea into the Greater Caucasus mountains. Its coastal lowlands specialize in grain and vegetable production, while vast orchards surround the towns of Quba and Qusar. The mountain slopes are used for grazing. Special breeds of sheep are raised; their skins are used in the local fur industry.

The Dakhlik-Shirvan [Dagliq-Shirvan] region, an industrially and agriculturally developed part of Azerbaijan, is centered on the Shirvan Plain, just south of Guba-Khachmaz and north of the Kura River. Industry is generally engaged in the processing of such agricultural products as cotton, grapes, and fruit. The best varieties of pomegranates are grown in this region. The most important vineyards lie in the vicinity of Shamakhi, a town famed for its wines.

The Aran region (also known as Mugano-Salyan, comprising the Kur and Orta Kur regions) is the largest and second most populous region, stretching south of the Kura River within the boundaries of the Mili and Mugan plains at the center of the country. The soil and water endowment of Aran is highly favorable for agriculture, and it ranks as the leading agricultural region in the country. Aran specializes in cotton growing (under irrigation), producing nearly nine-tenths of the gross cotton output of Azerbaijan. The cotton-ginning plants, in addition to being on the Kura River, have the advantage of being located on railways and motor roads. Aran is also an important rice- and wheat-producing region, and it contributes close to 40% of livestock production in the country (table 1.5).

The Lankaran region in the southeast of Azerbaijan is well endowed by nature, and its warm climate is beneficial for subtropical crops, such as tea, rice, grapes, tobacco, and citrus trees. The region also produces spring and winter vegetables, but the main and most famous crop is tea (table 1.5), which is processed at local tea factories. Other industries are centered around food processing, furniture, silk, and wood. Colorful rugs and carpets are made in the Talysh Mountains.

The southwestern region includes Nagorno-Karabakh proper and the four districts around Lachin on the border with Armenia. It essentially faces Nakhichevan over the arm of Armenian territory that has separated the Nakhichevan exclave from "mainland" Azerbaijan since the early Soviet times. This region lies in the Greater Caucasus mountains, at an average altitude of 4,900 feet, and its broken relief impedes the development of transport, industry, and agriculture. Agricultural production is concentrated in the mountain valleys. Livestock constitutes a large percentage of the gross agricultural output, with sheep and pigs the main species. Cotton, grapes, tobacco, and grain are the major crops; wine-making, silk-making, and electrical engineering are the leading industries.

The Ganja-Gazakh [Ganja-Qazakh] region is situated in the center of Transcaucasia, near the junction of Azerbaijan, Armenia, and Georgia. The

TABLE 1.5
Agricultural Production by Economic Regions, in Percent (2005)

	Sown Area	*Wheat Production*	*Rice Production*	*Tea Production*	*Cotton Production*	*Cows*	*Milk Production*
Absheron	0.4	0.1	—	—	—	1.6	2.7
Aran	45	38	31		88	39	36
Dakhlik-Shirvan	7	9	—	—	1	6	6
Ganja-Gazakh	12	12	—	—	2	12	13
Guba-Khachmaz	8	11	—	—	—	7	9
Lankaran	8	10	69	93	—	13	13
Shaki-Zagatala	12	10	—	7		11	11
Karabakh	5	5	—	—	9*	5	5
Nakhichevan	4	5	—	—	—	4	5
Total	100	100	100	100	100	100	100

*Production in Agdam, Fizuli, and Terter districts east of the territories occupied by Armenia. No production data are available for the occupied districts.
Source: Data aggregated by economic regions from raion-level data in Statistical Committee of Azerbaijan (2006b).

region has conditions favorable both for human life and for agriculture. It is an important producer of both wheat and livestock. The city of Ganja is an industrial center, with food, engineering, chemical, and non-ferrous metallurgical industries. Naftalan is a health resort.

The Shaki-Zagatala [Shaki-Zaqatala] region lies in the north of the country, west of Quba-Khachmaz and Dagliq-Shirvan regions. It borders the Greater Caucasus range, which shelters it from cold northern winds. The numerous mountain rivers provide ample supplies of water, and the region is densely populated. Agricultural products include tobacco, aromatic plants (mint, basil, roses), corn (maize), various fruits, and tea. The area is also a major producer of hazelnuts and walnuts.

The Nakhichevan region—an exclave on the southwest separated by an arm of Armenia from the rest of Azerbaijan—is a typical semidesert, although irrigation has made it possible to cultivate grapes and grain. There are several sources of mineral water in the foothill areas.

* * *

Azerbaijan entered the post-Stalinist years as a small, poor, rural country with a long history of colonial rule, mixed ethnic composition, and relatively rapid population growth. In these respects Azerbaijan was little different from the other Soviet republics of the Transcaucasus and Central Asia. However, in the 20 years of Soviet rule from 1965 to 1985 Azerbaijan showed a remarkable record as an agricultural producer, without experiencing the slowdown from which the USSR as a whole suffered after 1973, toward the end of the Brezhnev era. Just how this remarkable growth was achieved during the Soviet period and how Azerbaijan fared in the years of transition to a market economy is the subject of the following chapter.

Notes

1. Service attributes this statement to the Russian translation of a book by the prominent Iranian geographer of Azeri origin Enayat Olla-Reza [Enayatollah Reza], published under the title *Azerbaidzhan i Arran* in Yerevan, Armenia (1993). The statement appears in the introduction to the Russian translation (p. 5) written by the Armenian scholar Garnik Asatryan, not by Olla-Reza himself.

2. For a fascinating vista of life in Azerbaijan from the oil boom at the end of the 19th century to its fall in 1920 see the novel *Ali and Nino* by Kurban Said (Overlook Press, 1999; Anchor, 2000). Originally written in German and published in Austria in 1937, the book was rediscovered and translated into English in 1970 by Jenia Graman. The first English-language edition was published in 1970 by Random House (USA) and Hutchinson (UK). Since its revival in 2000, the book has been translated into

dozens of other languages (see, e.g., http://azer.com/aiweb/an_covers/123_ali_nino_cover.html).

3. The Russian acronym is ZSFSR, where the initial Z stands for "Zakavkazskaia." The name and the abbreviation of the new entity were patterned on those for Russia, which was called the Russian Soviet Federated Socialist Republic, or RSFSR.

4. There is no uniformly accepted spelling for the regions and districts of Azerbaijan due to ambiguous transliteration from the Azeri alphabet to English. Here we follow the transliteration adopted by the State Statistical Committee of Azerbaijan. Alternative spellings are shown in square brackets. This section draws on materials from Encyclopedia Britannica Online (2007) and Government of Azerbaijan (2004).

2

Policy and Agricultural Development in Azerbaijan

A 40-Year Perspective

An explanation of rural change over 40 years must start with agriculture, as agriculture, along with food processing, traditionally provided the main source of earnings in the Soviet countryside and continues to do so in rural Azerbaijan today. The hypothesis of this book is that changes in policies—both during the Soviet period and after the dissolution of the USSR—have been the main factor determining agricultural growth. For the Soviet period the growth of agricultural production in the USSR was driven primarily by increasing rates of centrally planned agricultural investment, which were symptomatic of the higher volume of resources flowing into agriculture during this period. For the post-Soviet period agricultural growth in the former Soviet Union was driven by the wide array of reform policies implemented after 1991, and most notably by the striking transition from predominantly collective to individual agriculture across the CIS.

The Soviet agricultural model ensured robust growth in Azerbaijan and agriculture was a leading sector of the Azeri economy during the entire Soviet period. Azerbaijan, in contrast to the USSR as a whole, did not experience any slowdown of growth toward the end of Brezhnev's regime, between 1973 and 1985. On the contrary, both economic and agricultural growth in Azerbaijan accelerated in the early 1970s. The economic malaise that affected the USSR in the 1970s and intensified in the early 1980s was hardly felt in Azerbaijan. The economy of Azerbaijan, including agriculture, did not slow down until 1985, when the country began to feel the increasing uncertainty associated with Gorbachev's political changes.

The gradual decline in agricultural production observed during Gorbachev's regime turned into a transition-induced free fall after independence. Rapid decline in agricultural production ceased only after President Heydar Aliyev came to power and introduced a radical land reform in 1995–96. However, even the resumption of agricultural growth in 1995 could not restore agriculture to its former glory as a leading sector of the economy. Radical reforms in the agricultural sector in post-Soviet Azerbaijan were accompanied by equally important changes in investment policy in the oil and gas extraction sector leading to the "petrolification" of the Azeri economy after 1995. The role of agriculture in the Azeri economy declined steadily after 1995 to a fraction of its former glory, a normal phenomenon in a market-driven economy. In the ten years between 1996 and 2006 the oil extraction sector progressed from being only half the size of agriculture to seven times its size, producing over half of GDP in Azerbaijan.

In this chapter we follow the standard growth-accounting paradigm to demonstrate how the long-term patterns of agricultural growth in Azerbaijan are linked to changes in the use of resources, including the main factors of production as well as investment flows. We then examine the "petrolification" of the Azeri economy as the country's rediscovered natural wealth triggered a transformation from a largely agrarian society to an economy based on oil revenues. The rapid growth of the oil extraction sector has led to great concern about the dangers of the Dutch Disease for Azerbaijan. Surprisingly, we find no clear evidence to suggest that the "petrolification" of the Azeri economy has produced the symptoms commonly associated with the Dutch Disease, namely a real appreciation of the currency or the crowding out of other sectors of the economy.

Patterns of Agricultural Growth in Azerbaijan

An overview of Azerbaijan's agriculture between 1965 and 2008, spanning both the Soviet and the post-Soviet eras, shows four distinct patterns of development: rapid growth in the period 1965–85, stagnation changing to gradual decline from 1985 to 1991, catastrophic decline in 1991–96, and recovery since 1996 (figure 2.1). The trends in agriculture closely follow the macroeconomic trends as reflected in GDP growth, which reveals the same basic patterns, although GDP growth did not stop in 1984–85 and persisted for a few years more, until the effects of the war and civil unrest began to be fully felt. Furthermore, GDP growth accelerated sharply after 2004 due to the expansion of the petroleum sector and by 2008 it had overtaken agricultural growth by a substantial margin (this effect is not shown in figure 2.1 from

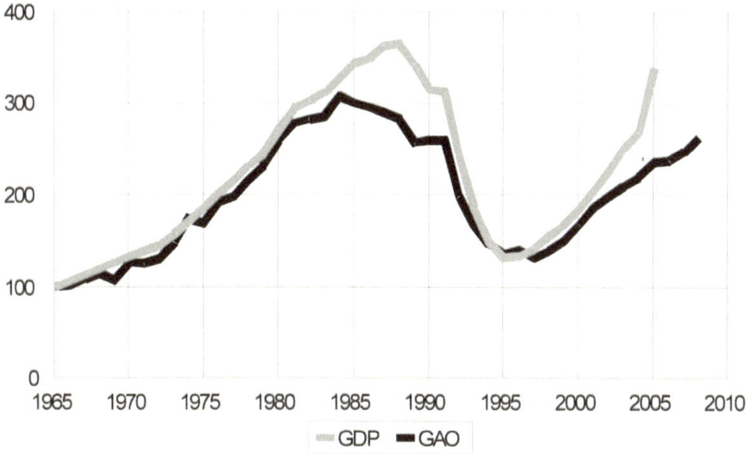

FIGURE 2.1
GDP and agricultural output (GAO) 1965–2008. Source: Statistical Committee of AzSSR (various years), Statistical Committee of Azerbaijan (various years).

considerations of vertical scale). Box 2.1 is a brief primer "for the uninitiated" on how to read figure 2.1 and similar figures in this book.

The four phases of agricultural development in Azerbaijan are clearly related to the policy environment. The first phase is the Soviet growth period from 1965 to 1985, which started under Brezhnev (1964–82) and continued

Box 2.1 How Agricultural Growth Is Measured

GAO, or gross agricultural output, is the standard aggregated measure of the value of production in agriculture. Expressed in index numbers, it gives a convenient variable for representing growth. Official statistical sources usually provide the year-to-year percentage changes in agricultural production, based on physical volumes or values expressed in constant prices. The year-to-year changes in GAO can be chained into a GAO index expressed cumulatively in percent of a particular base year. In figure 2.1 the base year is 1965, and the index numbers along the black curve express cumulative growth of GAO from 1965 to each particular year. In 1984 the GAO index reached 300 (i.e., the value of gross agricultural output in 1965 was three times its value in 1965); in 1995 the GAO index bottomed out at 130 (i.e., agricultural production was just 30% above its value 30 years previously, in 1965). The graph curve plotting the GDP index is constructed similarly and it essentially tracks overall economic growth, as distinct from agricultural growth.

during the brief regimes of Andropov (1982–84) and Chernenko (1984–85). The Soviet growth phase in 1965–85 was sustained by the stable supportive environment that characterized the post-Stalin attitude toward agriculture in the USSR as a whole and by extension also in Azerbaijan (box 2.2).

Box 2.2. Soviet Agriculture and Food Policies

The agricultural policies of Soviet Azerbaijan prior to 1991 have to be seen in the context of decisions by the Soviet leadership after Stalin's death in 1953 to move toward de-Stalinization of the economic system. In agricultural policy de-Stalinization meant raising agriculture from the bottom to near the top of the list of planner priorities. In practical terms this meant an attempt to raise the productivity of agriculture through an ambitious investment program and an effort to improve Soviet diets, primarily through increasing milk and meat consumption (Millar, 1990).

Under Stalin, food policy was based on the principles of national self-sufficiency and on the near-forced transfer of food supplies from the countryside to the cities. The Soviet population was entirely dependent on domestic production (there were no food imports until as late as 1963–64) and urban food supplies were determined by state procurement. The state purchased agricultural commodities from collective farms, the dominant organization for food production in this period, at state-determined procurement prices, and delivered food to the cities for sale in shops at state-determined retail prices. Since the regime's policy was to keep retail food prices low, procurement prices were correspondingly low. In a collective farm a peasant's pay was his share of the net returns of the farm. Low procurement prices meant that his pay was either nil or insignificant. In the end, state procurement of food from collective farms was little more than confiscation during the Stalin era.

Soviet food policy in the post-Stalin years 1960–85 was shaped by decisions to reverse the Stalinist policies of severe exploitation of the peasantry and to increase consumption of food and particularly meat as a symbol of a better life for Soviet citizens. The regime accomplished these aims through three policy foci. The first concerned raising food production through increased investment in the sector. By the early 1970s the Soviet farm sector was receiving 25% of gross fixed investment in the Soviet economy, up from 16% in the 1950s and 20% in the 1960s. The second focus of post-Stalin policies concerned improving the incentives of Soviet farms for production and marketing, mainly by raising agricultural procurement prices for commodities delivered to the state and lowering the tax burden on farms. The third focus aimed at easing the restrictions on agricultural workers and the rural population. Mandatory procurement from household plots was dropped (under Khrushchev and Brezhnev), in 1966 farm wages were decoupled from farm performance and collective farm workers were guaranteed a minimum monthly income, and in 1975 peasants in collective farms received for the first time internal passports that allowed them to travel within the USSR (Hanson, 2003). Another beneficial effect of the enormous attention given to agriculture in this period by Soviet leaders was an impressive rise in the relative wages of agricultural workers and employees. Wages of agricultural workers in state farms grew from about two-thirds of the economy average in 1960 to near parity with the rest of the economy in 1985 (table B2.2). Collective farm wages also rose significantly in that period.

TABLE B2.2
Average Money Wage in the USSR, 1960–89

	1960	*1970*	*1980*	*1985*	*1989*
All economy (current rubles)	81	122	169	190	240
Industry/all economy, %	114	109	110	111	110
State farms/all economy, %	67	83	88	96	97
Collective farms/all economy, %	n.a.	61	70	81	n.a.

Source: Statistical Committee of USSR (1987), p. 431; Statistical Committee of USSR (1991), p.76.

The post-Stalin leadership's emphasis on agriculture and food production was understandable, but the dilemmas faced by their control over distribution did not change from the Stalinist period. Soviet food policies in both periods were designed to isolate urban consumers from food costs. They accordingly involved great difficulties of balancing growth in urban incomes and food supplies, on the one hand, with growth in rural procurement prices and production incentives, on the other. The policy of stable food prices more than anything came to be associated with the legitimacy of the socialist regime in the eyes of Soviet consumers (despite the resulting food shortages). The disintegration of the precarious balance between urban and rural economies in the 1980s led to widespread discontent.

The second period from 1985 to 1991 covers the episode of unsuccessful reforms under Gorbachev, which failed to halt the "growth slowdown" experienced by the USSR economy after 1973, at the end of Brezhnev's regime (Hanson, 2003, p. 98, 128–163). Agriculture in the USSR generally stagnated during Gorbachev's period, growing at an average of only 1–2% per year

(Statistical Committee of the USSR, 1991). In Azerbaijan, agriculture entered a phase of gradual decline in 1985, attributable specifically to Gorbachev's anti-alcohol campaign that shattered Azerbaijan's wine exports and demolished its vineyards. The Gorbachev period of reforms ended in the political and economic dissolution of the USSR, and the negative growth of the third period after 1990 reflects the transition decline that hit Azerbaijan together with all the former Soviet republics (Lerman, Csaki, and Feder, 2004, p. 168). During the 1990s the countries that formerly made up the USSR went their separate policy ways with some recovering sooner than others. On average, agriculture in the CIS countries resumed moderate growth after 1998, which to us signals the beginning of the fourth phase—the recovery phase.

Under Gorbachev it became fashionable to refer to the pre-1980 years as "the period of stagnation," referring to the growth slowdown that afflicted the end of the Brezhnev era. Azerbaijan, however, did not experience any stagnation or slowdown before 1980. In fact, the Soviet period between 1965 and 1980 was characterized by a rapid increase of agricultural production in Azerbaijan, with gross agricultural output (GAO) in 1980 reaching nearly three times the 1965 level. Stagnation began in the early 1980s, as agricultural growth slowed down during 1980–85 and then changed to decline between 1985 and 1991—the year when the Soviet Union dissolved and Azerbaijan became independent. Azerbaijan entered independence in 1991 with GAO at 250% of the 1965 level. This in itself was below the 300% mark achieved in 1984–85, but the initial shock of transition triggered a rapid decline in agricultural production (and in the economy as a whole): by 1996 GAO had dropped to about 120% of the 1965 level. The latest phase since 1996 has been characterized by resumption of growth, with GAO in 2008 reaching 260% of the 1965 level.

Changes in Factor Use

The Soviet growth period from 1965 to 1985 witnessed an impressive increase in the resources allotted to agriculture in Azerbaijan. The horsepower capacity of farm machinery more than doubled between 1965 and 1985 (Statistical Committee of Azerbaijan, 2001, vol. 1, p. 252). The number of people employed in agriculture increased by 50% between 1965 and 1985 (figure 2.2), irrigated arable land grew during the same period by 25% from about 800,000 hectares to nearly 1 million hectares through expansion of irrigation systems (figure 2.3), and total cultivated area under field crops and perennials increased by 30% from 1.4 million hectares in 1965 to 1.8 million hectares in 1985 (figure 2.4).

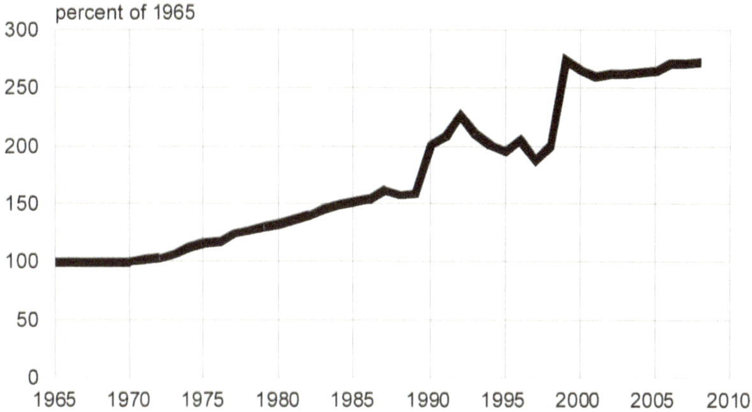

FIGURE 2.2
Agricultural labor 1965–2008 in percent of 1965. Source: Statistical Committee of AzSSR (various years) for 1965–80, Statistical Committee of CIS (2008) for 1980–90, Statistical Committee of Azerbaijan (2006d, 2009b) for 1990–2007; series spliced at 1980.

In response to the broad policy goal set by central government in Moscow, which called for increases in livestock consumption as a sign of rising living standards under socialism (box 2.3), Azerbaijan increased the livestock herd by 50% from 2 million standard head in 1965 to nearly 3 million head in 1985 (figure 2.5; this includes large horned cattle, sheep and goats, pigs, and poultry appropriately weighted). The increase in livestock numbers in Azerbaijan

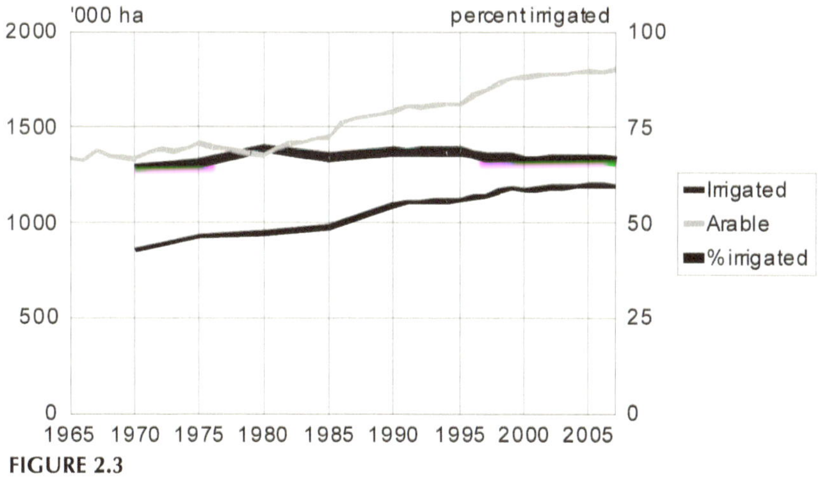

FIGURE 2.3
Arable and irrigated arable land 1965–2007 (thousand hectares and percent of arable land). Source: Statistical Committee of Azerbaijan (2006b, 2009b).

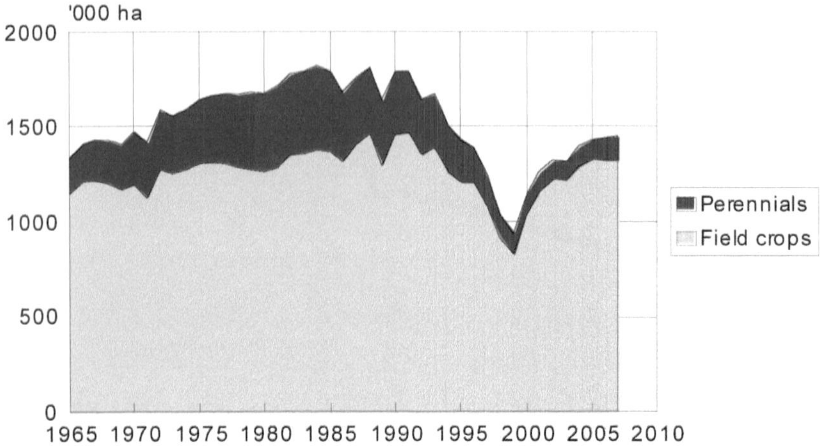

FIGURE 2.4
Area under field crops and perennial plantations 1965–2007. Source: Statistical Committee of Azerbaijan (2006b, 2009b).

far exceeded that in its two Transcaucasian neighbors and in the European Soviet republics, lagging only behind the livestock growth rates in Tajikistan, Uzbekistan, Lithuania, and Belarus (Statistical Committee of USSR, 1969, 1988).

The rates of growth in these factors of production, however impressive on their own, pale in comparison with the increase in the use of mineral fertilizers. Fertilizer deliveries to Azerbaijan's agriculture increased steeply (figure

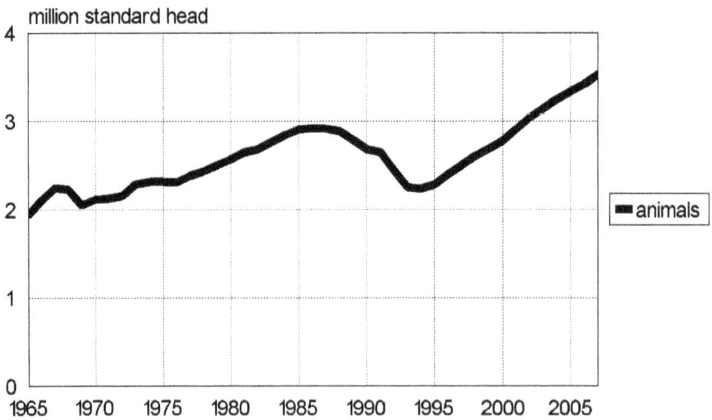

FIGURE 2.5
Livestock herd 1965–2007 (thousand standard head). Source: Statistical Committee of Azerbaijan (2006e, 2009b).

Box 2.3. The Party's Goal of Increasing Meat Consumption Per Capita

At the January 1961 Central Committee Plenary Meeting Nikita Khrushchev stated that the USSR would overtake the United States in production of meat per head. Though this claim seems unrealistic now—Soviet GDP per capita in 1960 was only 35% of that in the United States (see Maddison, 1995, cited in Hanson, 2003)—at the time it reflected the belief of the Soviet regime that the high growth rates of the late 1950s, which exceeded those in the United States, would persist. The emphasis on food consumption continued after Khrushchev's fall. Leonid Brezhnev sought to improve the Soviet standard of living primarily through bettering the population's diet. For consumers these policies meant a shift in consumption patterns from reliance on bread and potatoes to higher meat consumption (Liefert and Swinnen, 2002).

The drive to increase livestock consumption in the USSR enjoyed a measure of success. Consumption of livestock products in the Soviet Union, including Soviet Azerbaijan, did increase in this period. Even during the last decade of the Soviet regime, in 1980–89, meat consumption per capita grew by almost 20% (thick black curve in figure B2.3). Still, meat consumption per capita in the USSR never came close to that in the United States (table B2.3). This was to be expected, because Soviet GDP per capita never reached more than 30%–35% of that in the United States (Hanson, 2003, p. 244). Measured in relation to GDP per capita, however, Soviet meat consumption at the end of the 1980s was quite a

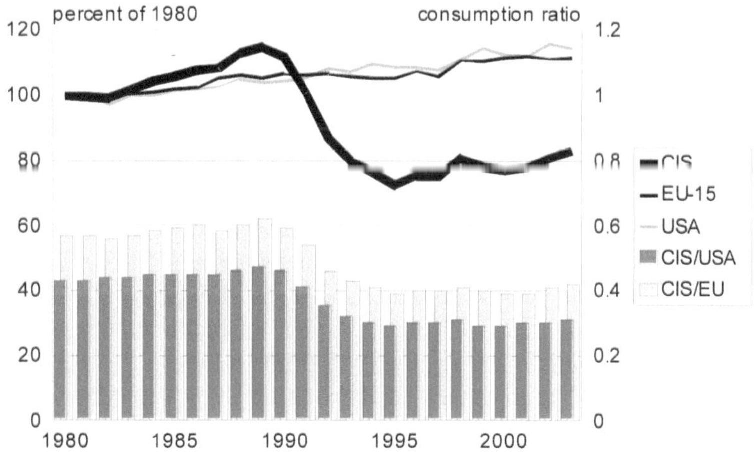

FIGURE B2.3
Meat consumption per capita in CIS, EU-15, and USA 1980–2003. Source: EU-15 and USA from FAO (2007); CIS from Statistical Committee of CIS (2008).

TABLE B2.3
Per Capita Consumption of Meat in CIS, EU-15, and USA 1980–2003 (kg Per Year)

	CIS	*EU-15*	*USA*	*CIS/EU-15*	*CIS/USA*
1980–1989	49.2	84.0	109.5	0.58	0.45
1990–1995	40.8	86.8	115.7	0.47	0.35
1996–2003	36.4	90.2	120.9	0.40	0.30

Source: CIS from Statistical Committee of CIS (2008); EU-15 and USA from FAO (2007).

bit higher than in countries with similar GDP per capita. Non-planned economies with GDP per capita up to US$3,500 (1995 dollars), which is the relevant range for all former Soviet republics on the eve of transition, reported annual meat consumption of about 16 kg per capita, compared to 45 kg per capita for the USSR. Thus, despite lagging behind the US, the Soviet Union was characterized by "overconsumption of meat" relative to its level of GNP per capita (Sedik, 1993; Sedik, Sotnikov and Wiesmann, 2003).

The contraction of the livestock herd in the former Soviet Union during the transition—a market response to the persistent lack of profitability in the livestock sector—produced a sharp decline in meat consumption per capita (thick black curve in figure B2.3). By 1995 meat consumption per capita in CIS had dropped to 40% of the 1990 level. Thereafter meat consumption per capita stabilized, resuming its moderate long-term growth. Overall, the per capita meat consumption in 2003 was 20% below the 1980 level and 30% below the 1990 level. The per capita meat consumption in the Western market economies (EU-15 and the United States) followed a steady upward course, rising by 12%–15% between 1980 and 2003 (see the thin lines in figure B2.3).

2.6: note the logarithmic scale on the vertical axis, which was necessary to accommodate the large changes in quantities). Steep increases registered both in absolute quantities of fertilizers (by nearly a factor of 6, from 58,000 ton active substance in 1965 to 314,000 ton in 1985) and in rates per hectare of arable land (quintupling from 38 kg/ha in 1965 to 180 kg/ha). The total growth of fertilizer deliveries in Azerbaijan outstripped the growth for the USSR as a whole (where fertilizer deliveries grew by "only" a factor of 4 between 1965 and 1985). Throughout the entire period fertilizer deliveries per hectare in Azerbaijan were higher than the average for the USSR (where deliveries per hectare increased from 28 kg/ha in 1965 to 113 kg/ha in 1985). The fragmentary data available on fertilizer consumption rates (as distinct from delivery rates) indicate that at the end of the 1980s Azerbaijan was consuming 50% more fertilizer per hectare than the rest of the Soviet Union and twice as much

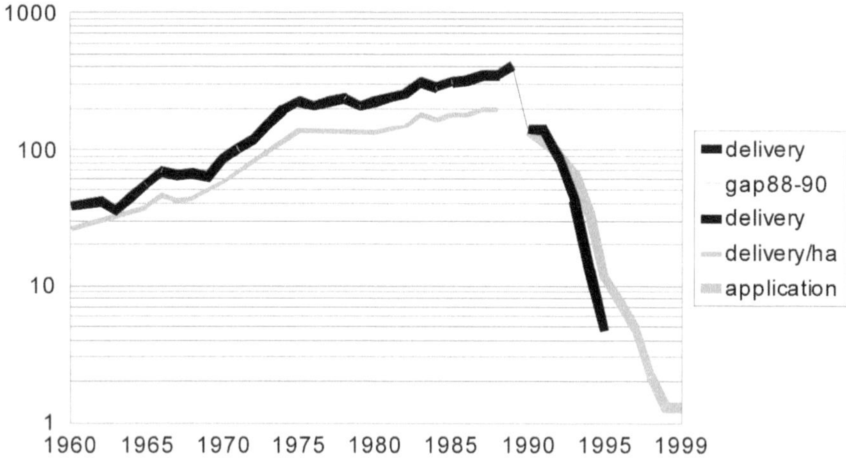

FIGURE 2.6
Fertilizer delivery and application 1960–99. Source: Statistical Committee of AzSSR (various years), Statistical Committee of Azerbaijan (2006b).

as the United States (but for some reason only two-thirds of the consumption rate in France; see table 2.1).

The pattern of changes in resource use after 1985 was no longer monotonic. While irrigated area continued expanding, fertilizer deliveries and consumption collapsed completely. Agricultural labor continued increasing, but it now grew in two distinct waves: a sharp increase in 1989-92 reflecting the influx of refugees displaced by the Nagorno-Karabakh war and civil unrest, and another sharp increase in 1996–98 reflecting the new reform policies that led to rapid individualization of agriculture. The livestock herd dropped by more than one-quarter between 1986 and 1993, and then resumed its long-term growth, again in response to individualization policies (the labor-rich household sector is the

TABLE 2.1
Consumption of Fertilizer Per Hectare of Land Under Annual and Perennial Crops (kg/ha, Average for 1987–88)

	Average Consumption, kg/ha
Azerbaijan	198
USSR	120
United States	95
France	307

Sources: Shend (1993); FAO (2007).

traditional driver of the labor-intensive livestock sector in all CIS countries). Thus, the straightforward positive relationship between agricultural production and resource use that characterized the Soviet growth period 1965–85 is not observed during the subsequent phases of agricultural development in Azerbaijan, suggesting a technological change in agriculture during the post-Soviet period (see the section *Agricultural Productivity* for a rigorous analysis of this phenomenon using production functions).

Part of the reason for high rates of growth both in investment and in factor use in Azerbaijan (particularly fertilizer use) was the rapid buildup of livestock inventories between 1965 and 1985 (see figure 2.5). The Party's desire to increase consumption of meat (box 2.3) was one of the driving forces for sectoral change in Azerbaijan's agriculture. The share of livestock production in GAO increased from around 20% in the 1970s to nearly 40% in 1985, and Azerbaijan shifted from a predominantly crop-producing country to an agriculture with a much more balanced product mix. The feed base needed to be expanded quickly in order to feed the large increase in animal inventories. In Azerbaijan, this involved primarily an increase in area sown to feed crops, whose share in total cropped area grew from about 15% in 1965 to 25% in 1985 (figure 2.7).[1]

In parallel with the increase of feed-producing areas, we also observe an increase in vineyards, apparently driven by market demand for Azerbaijan's wine and brandy from other Soviet republics. The expansion of feed crops and vineyards came at the expense of the area in grains, which decreased continuously through 1985. The structure of sown area during the Soviet growth period 1965–85 was moving away from grains toward animal feed and vineyards.

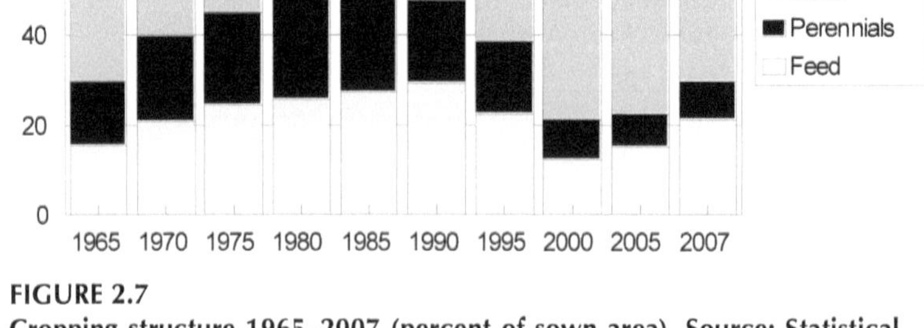

FIGURE 2.7
Cropping structure 1965–2007 (percent of sown area). Source: Statistical Committee of Azerbaijan (2006b).

The cropping pattern began to change in the opposite direction after 1985, and especially during independence. Vineyards were savagely uprooted, first in compliance with Gorbachev's anti-alcohol campaign of 1985 (box 2.4) and then in response to shrinking export opportunities for wine and brandy in the post-Soviet space. The area under feed crops was reduced following the dramatic decline in livestock inventories after 1990, and crop production shifted back into grains. The increase in area under vegetables since 2000 (figure 2.7) is a manifestation of the transition to individual farming, as labor-intensive vegetable growing is particularly favored among smallholders. The growing role of vegetables came at the expense of the area cropped to cotton (the main technical crop in figure 2.7), which is not a favorable commodity for smallholders in the CIS.

Box 2.4. Gorbachev's Anti-Alcohol Campaign

One of the most dramatic changes in Soviet history is the attempt to restrict the consumption of alcohol by Mikhail Gorbachev during his anti-alcohol campaign beginning in May 1985. Despite the laudable intentions of Gorbachev supported by the entire Politburo, the anti-alcohol measures met with considerable opposition. Officials of the central planning authority Gosplan, Ministry of Trade, the processing industry, and agricultural producers had always defended the cause of alcohol as best they could, arguing that restrictive measures would cost the state budget billions of rubles, ruin the grape growers, and close down much of the capacity of the wine-making industry (Richardson, 1999).

This dire scenario seems to have come true in Azerbaijan. Wine and spirits were one of the main products of Azerbaijan's food industry, sustaining burgeoning exports to other Soviet republics. Wine production increased five-fold from 2 million decaliters in 1965 to more than 10 million in 1985, with brandy production recording similar gains (most of the wine and spirits were exported). The growth in wine and alcohol production was driven by a dramatic expansion of vineyards, which grew from 50,000 hectares in 1960 to 280,000 hectares in 1984, just before Gorbachev's anti-alcohol campaign was launched. The increase in the area of vineyards boosted grape production, which rose from 90,000 ton in 1960 to 2.1 million ton in 1984. The growth in production outstripped the growth in vineyard areas as the yields more than tripled from about 3 ton/ha in 1960 to 10 ton/ha in 1984.

And then came May 1985 with Gorbachev's anti-alcohol campaign. Within a single year, the area of vineyards in Azerbaijan shrank by 25% and grape production dropped by nearly 30% (figure B2.4a). The sharp declines continued, and in 1990, on the eve of transition, viticulture and grape production had dropped to 60% of their peak in 1984. Since 2000,

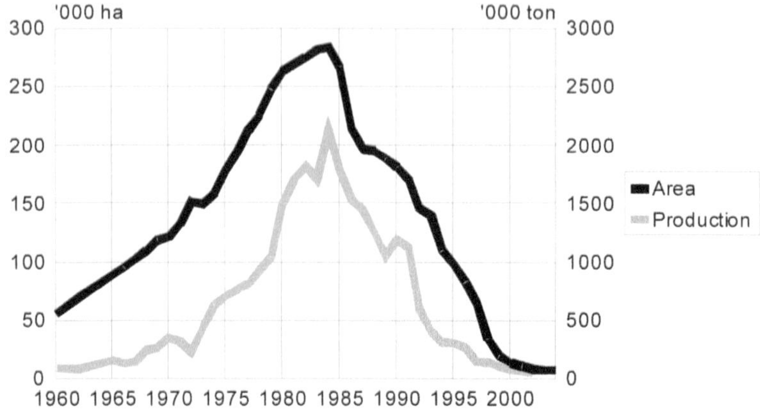

FIGURE B2.4A
Area of vineyards and grape production. Source: See figure 2.8

viticulture in Azerbaijan is a pale shadow of its past glory: the country has less than 10,000 hectares of vineyards and produces less than 60,000 tons of grapes—one-fifth of the quantity produced in 1984.

The behavior of wine and brandy production was more complex: by 1986, within a single year, it had dropped from the 1980–81 peak back to the 1965–70 levels. After 1986, however, it recovered nicely, almost returning to the 1980–81 peak by 1990 (figure B2.4b). The real collapse came after 1990, when production of wine and spirits practically disappeared compared to Soviet-era levels (with or without Gorbachev), presumably because of the disappearance of the traditional wine export markets and the general dislocations in industry after independence.

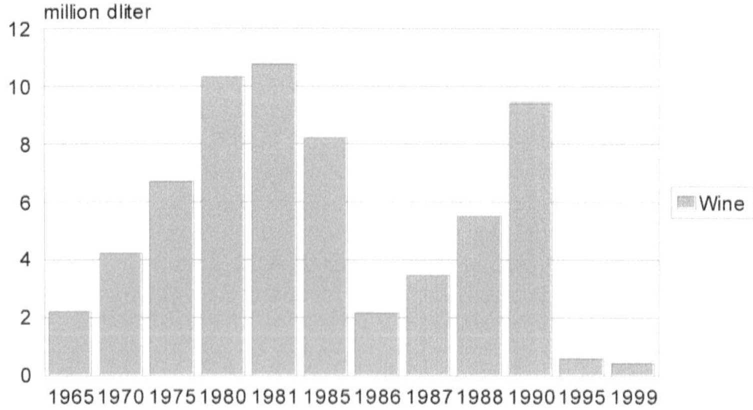

FIGURE B2.4B
Wine production. Source: See figure 2.8

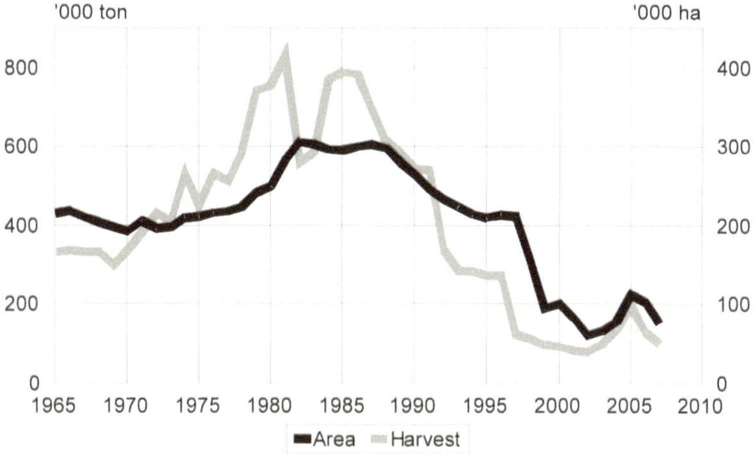

FIGURE 2.8
Cotton production and area under cotton 1965–2007. Source: Statistical Committee of Azerbaijan (2006b, 2009b).

The changing role of cotton in Azerbaijan is an interesting story in itself. During the 1980s Azerbaijan was one of the four major cotton producers in the USSR, ranking after Uzbekistan, Turkmenistan, and Tajikistan by production volumes. The cotton production curve closely followed the curve of areas cropped to cotton (figure 2.8; the correlation coefficient is 0.85). The area under cotton replicates the characteristic pattern of agricultural development in Azerbaijan shown in figure 2.1: an increase of 50% during the Soviet growth period between 1965 and 1982, leveling out during the Gorbachev regime between 1982 and 1988, and rapid decline after 1989.

Cotton areas collapsed from a peak of 300,000 hectares in the 1980s to 61,000 hectares in 2002, a decline of 80%. Cotton production in the same period dropped from 700,000–800,000 ton to a mere 80,000 ton, a drop of about 90%. It is only since 2003 that both cotton areas and cotton production have shown certain signs of recovery, perhaps repeating the overall recovery of Azeri agriculture with a five-year delay and in particular responding to the post-privatization support policies introduced in 1998–2001 (see chapter 3). Cotton production in Azerbaijan fell much more during the transition than among other former Soviet producers. While in the 1980s Azerbaijan was producing at about 10%–15% of Uzbekistan's cotton output, after 1995 Azerbaijan's cotton production dropped to 2%–5% of Uzbekistan. Kazakhstan, a minor cotton producer in the Soviet period, has actually overtaken Azerbaijan and is now producing four times as much of this commodity.

Agricultural Productivity

While the use of factors of production increased significantly during 1965–85, agricultural output (in constant prices) appears to have increased faster, resulting in significant increases in partial productivity of both land and labor. Agricultural output grew by 183% between 1965 and 1985, outstripping the growth in all major factors of production (except fertilizer deliveries). This suggests real gains in productivity during the 20-year period 1965–85. Indeed, figure 2.9 shows that the productivity of land and the productivity of labor (calculated as the ratio of the value of agricultural output in constant 2000 manats to cultivated land and to the number of employed in agriculture, respectively) increased practically at the same rate between 1965 and 1981; thereafter their trends diverged as the productivity of land continued to increase, while the productivity of labor began to decline. Over the entire 20-year period 1965–85, the productivity of both land and labor roughly doubled (table 2.2).

The observed increase in partial productivity of land and labor during 1965–85 is confirmed by estimation of the production function for Azerbaijan agriculture using the time series of sectoral data for the corresponding period. In a Cobb-Douglas production function regressing agricultural output on land and labor, the two inputs have statistically significant positive coefficients (adding the livestock herd to the model resulted in a statistically not significant coefficient for this regressor; fertilizer and farm machinery were not included, because no sufficient data are available for these variables after 1990). Moreover, the estimated coefficients of land and labor (1.30 and 1.62, respectively) sum to more than 1, which points to increasing returns to scale in 1965–85. In other words, a 1% increase in land or labor during this period

TABLE 2.2
Changes in Output, Resource Use, and Productivity 1965–85 and 1985–90 (Percent)

	1965–85 (20 years)	*Mean Annual Rate of Growth*	*1985–90 (5 years)*	*Mean Annual Rate of Growth*
Agricultural output	+183	+5.34	−15	−3.12
Cultivated land	+34	+1.46	0	0
Agricultural labor	+52	+2.11	+32	+5.66
Livestock	+50	+2.04	−8	−1.62
Farm machinery (HP)	+114	+3.88	+19	+3.59
Fertilizer deliveries	+460	+9.00	−54	−14.4
Productivity of land	+112	+3.83	−15	−3.14
Productivity of labor	+86	+3.16	−35	−8.30

Source: Calculated from sources in figures 2.1, 2.2, 2.5.

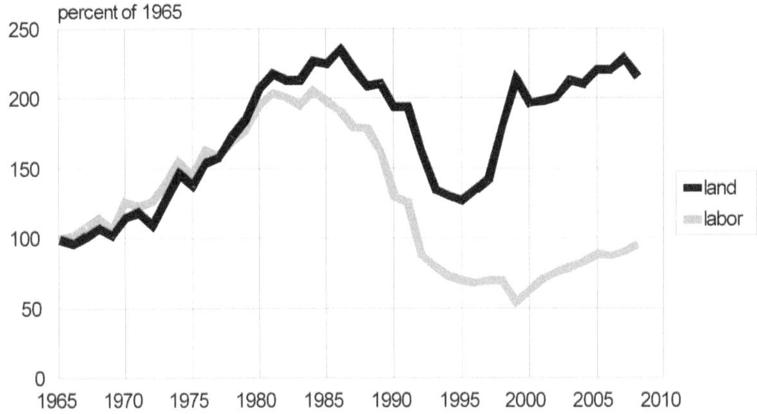

FIGURE 2.9
Partial productivity of agricultural land and labor (1965=100). Source: Calculated from sources in figures 2.1, 2.2, 2.4.

produced more than a 1% increase in agricultural output, which explains the observed increase in partial productivity of land and labor in figure 2.9.

The production function describes the technology of input use in agriculture. The estimated coefficients of the Cobb-Douglas model are the factor shares, and in the standard Solow growth calculus they can be applied to the annual growth rates of each input (land and labor in our model) to calculate the annual growth rate of the aggregated basket of inputs. This aggregated input growth is equal to the output growth explained by the production technology. If the observed, actual output growth is greater than the output growth explained by the inputs, the residual is interpreted as positive technical change leading to an increase in total factor productivity (TFP). If the observed output growth is less than the input growth, the negative residual points to a decrease in TFP over time. The analysis of Azerbaijan data during the period 1965–85 shows that agricultural output increased by 5.34% per year, while the inputs aggregated using the production function coefficients grew by 5.10% per year (table 2.3). This gives a growth of 0.24% per year in TFP. The corresponding positive technical change was probably brought about by a flow of productive investments in agriculture during the Soviet period (see section on investment below).

The increases in factor use slowed down considerably during the last years of the Soviet regime 1985–90, leading to stagnation and ultimately decline in agricultural output (see table 2.2). Only agricultural labor continued to increase at a steep rate, as civil unrest in the cities and the war with Armenia fuelled waves of migration to the relative safety of villages. On the other hand, the war had an obvious adverse effect on cultivated areas, the livestock herd,

TABLE 2.3
Production Function Analysis of the Soviet Agricultural Growth Period 1965–85 in Azerbaijan

	Estimated Mean Annual Rate of Growth (1965–85)	*Production-Function Coefficients*	*Weighted Input Growth*
1. Agricultural output	5.34		
2. Cultivated land	1.46	1.30	2.36
3. Agricultural labor	2.11	1.62	2.74
4. Aggregated inputs			5.10
5. Annual change in productivity (1 − 5)			0.24

and fertilizer deliveries. Declining agricultural output combined with stagnation of cultivated areas led to a decrease in partial productivity of land (−15% between 1985–90), whereas rapidly increasing agricultural labor produced an even steeper decline in partial productivity of labor (−35% over the same five years).

The production function analysis reported above for the growth period 1965–85 was extended to cover the three main phases of agricultural development in Azerbaijan—Soviet growth, transition decline, and post-reform recovery. Estimation was carried out using three inputs—land, labor, and livestock, because livestock was found to have a statistically significant impact on production in the two later periods. Table 2.4 summarizes the different patterns of change in agricultural output and the three main inputs by period.

During the decline period 1986–96, which began in the last years of the Soviet era and accelerated after independence, the shrinking agricultural output was driven by the shrinkage of cultivated area and the decrease of the livestock herd, both of which have statistically significant coefficients in the production

TABLE 2.4
Average Growth Rates of Agricultural Output and Main Inputs for the Three Periods of Agricultural Development in Azerbaijan (Annual Percent)

	Soviet Growth 1965–1985	*Decline 1986–1996*	*Recovery 1997–2007*
Agricultural output	5.6	−7.1	6.5
Cultivated land	1.5	−1.9	1.6
Labor	2.1	+2.9	3.8
Livestock	2.0	−2.0	3.5

Source: Calculated from sources in figures 2.1, 2.2, 2.5.

function for this period (recall that the coefficient of livestock was not statistically significant in the production function for the Soviet growth period 1965–85). The effect of labor during the decline phase was not statistically significant (contrary to its effect in the period 1965–85), as labor continued to increase despite the decrease in output and other factors of production (see figure 2.2). Finally, during the recovery period 1997–2008, the relationship of agricultural output with cultivated land and labor was positive but not statistically significant; the relationship with livestock, on the other hand, was positive and statistically significant. All three input coefficients—for land, labor, and livestock—were statistically significantly different from the corresponding coefficients for the Soviet growth period (table 2.5).

The production technology of the recovery period 1997–2008 is thus markedly different from the production technology of the Soviet growth period 1965–85: the strong dependence on land and labor that characterized the Soviet growth era gives way to strong dependence on livestock as a factor of growth, presumably because the livestock herd largely shifted from collective farms to the individual sector during the early 1990s. The disappearance of statistically significant dependence on labor is an indication of labor redundancies that emerged in rural areas as a result of refugee inflows and urban-to-rural migration in response to urban unemployment pressures and the opportunities presented by land privatization.

The production technology of the decline period 1986–96 displays clear transition features between the two growth periods (table 2.5). While the coefficient of cultivated land is significantly different from zero (both output and land decline), it is not statistically different from the coefficient of the Soviet growth period (when both output and land increased). The coefficient of agricultural labor becomes statistically not significant (as in the recovery period), while the coefficient of livestock becomes statistically significant

TABLE 2.5
Production Function Coefficients for the Three Periods of Agricultural Development

	Soviet Growth 1965–1985	*Decline 1986–1996*	*Recovery 1997–2008*
Intercept	−14.92*	−18.91*	−7.56^
Cultivated land	1.434*	1.431*	0.289^
Labor	1.677*	0.056^	0.298^
Livestock	0.106*	1.975^*	1.348^*

Note: The three-input production function was estimated with dummy coefficients for the three periods. The table reports full coefficients recalculated from the estimated dummy coefficients.
* Statistically significantly different from 0 (at 10% level).
^ Statistically significantly different from the coefficient in the Soviet growth period 1965–85.

(also as in the recovery period). Moreover, the coefficients of both labor and livestock are significantly different from the corresponding coefficients in the Soviet growth period.

The comparison of the coefficients in table 2.5 clearly supports our previous claim that agricultural development in Azerbaijan is divided into three distinct phases: the Soviet growth period 1965–85, the stagnation and decline period 1986–96, and the recovery period 1997–2008 related to the achievements of land reform. The three phases are reflected in the statistically significant differences between the corresponding production function coefficients of the three periods.

Investment in Agriculture

Investment was an important policy instrument used during the Soviet era to foster agricultural growth. After the death of Stalin the Party leadership expressed frequent concern about the performance and efficiency of agriculture, and stressed the importance of raising investment in agriculture as a way to stimulate growth in production (Hanson, 2003). Investment is a source of growth in all economies, but in a market economy the decision of how much and in which sector to invest is made by individual entrepreneurs, investors, and businesses. The volume and area of investment are therefore not a policy instrument of the government. In the centrally planned economy the array of policy instruments available to planners was quite different. The Krushchev and the Brezhnev leaderships spoke at length on the necessity to increase the priority of agriculture in the Five-Year Plans during their reigns, and dramatically increased the farm sector's share in total investment under four consecutive Five-Year Plans from 1961–65 through 1976–80 (table 2.6).

The portion of total investment earmarked for agriculture grew rapidly in this period in order to fund construction of large feeding lots, hog and poultry complexes, feed mixing plants, and grain storage facilities. Investment in the agricultural sector grew more quickly than in other sectors, so that the portion of total investment devoted to agriculture rose from 16% in the 1950s to 24% in the 1970s and early 1980s (table 2.6), and that at a time when agriculture accounted for only 15% of Soviet GDP (Statistical Committee of USSR, 1972).

Increased investment in Soviet agriculture was concentrated in on-farm facilities. Though investment in upstream suppliers of fertilizers, pesticides, and farm machinery production, as well as downstream slaughterhouses and processing facilities, would seem to be a necessary complement to expansion of farm production facilities, table 2.6 indicates that on-farm investment

TABLE 2.6
Investment in Agriculture the USSR and in Azerbaijan During the Soviet Period (% of Total Investment)

	USSR		Azerbaijan	
Five-Year Plan	*Farm Level Investment*	*Entire Agro-Industrial Complex*	*Farm Level Investment*	*Entire Agro-Industrial Complex*
1946–1950	12.9	—	11.6	—
1951–1955	16.3	—	14.6	—
1956–1960	16.8	—	16.5	—
1961–1965	18.6	19.8	16.2	—
1966–1970	21.3	23.4	17.8	—
1971–1975	24.0	26.5	22.5	27.0
1976–1980	24.5	27.0	25.0	33.9
1981–1985	24.3	26.9	24.2	34.4
1986–1989	—	—	23.2	30.3

Sources: USSR from Statistical Committee of USSR (1982, pp. 365, 373; 1987, pp. 324, 373); Azerbaijan from Statistical Committee of Azerbaijan (2001, vol. 1, pp. 295, 302, 309).

consistently accounted for over 90% of total investment in the agro-industrial complex in the USSR.

In Azerbaijan, investment in agriculture increased rapidly, particularly in the 1970s, indicating the sector's increasing importance. Table 2.6 illustrates the initial increase in the importance of agriculture in total investment under Khrushchev (1956–64) and the further increases under Brezhnev (1965–85). Moreover, in the 1970s and the 1980s investment in up- and downstream facilities in Azerbaijan accounted for considerably more of total investment in the agro-industrial complex (20%, rising to 30%) than is the case for the entire USSR (stable at less than 10%). Agricultural growth responded well to increases in investment in the 1970s, but, despite rising investment, slowed markedly in the second half of the 1980s (see figure 2.1).

The investment instrument was at least partly effective in stimulating growth of GAO, if not necessarily efficient. Though we do not have constant price data for the entire Soviet growth period, data from two Five-Year Plans—1971–75 and 1981–85—show a correlation between growth in agricultural investment and GAO growth at the republic level (figure 2.10; note that Azerbaijan had by far the highest growth of investment and the highest growth of GAO in this period). The emphasis of the Soviet leadership on investment thus reflected conscious political decisions to increase the total resources allocated to agriculture in the interest of achieving growth.

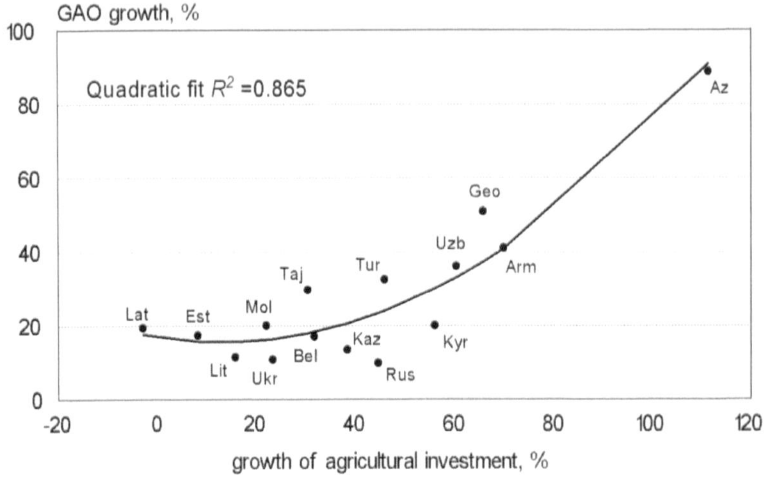

FIGURE 2.10
GAO growth vs. growth of agricultural investment 1971–75 to 1981–85, by republic (in constant 1973 prices). Source: Statistical Committee of the USSR, 1988, pp. 27–32, 385.

Increasing investment shares were symptomatic of a general increased level of resources allocated to agriculture during the Soviet growth period. The increase in resources allocated to agriculture and the growth in agricultural production that resulted had the effect of raising the portion of national income deriving from agriculture in all republics. This produced the peculiar situation of an increase of the importance of agriculture in the Soviet economy as a result of economic growth—precisely the opposite of the situation observed in market economic development (table 2.7).

TABLE 2.7
The Growth of Agricultural Investment and Increasing Role of Agriculture in the Economy Between 1970 and 1985

Indicator	*Year*	*Azerbaijan*	*High Investment Growth**	*Medium Investment Growth***	*Low Investment Growth****
Agricultural Investment	1970	100	100	100	100
	1985	211	163	138	114
GAO	1970	100	100	100	100
	1985	189	137	121	116
Agriculture in NMP (%)	1970	19	24	25	22
	1985	33	31	30	29

*Turkmenistan, Tajikistan, Uzbekistan, Georgia and Armenia, Kyrgyzstan (simple averages).
**Moldova, Kazakhstan, Belarus, Lithuania (simple averages).
***Ukraine, Estonia, Latvia, Russia (simple averages).
Sources: Statistical Committee of USSR (1987, pp. 123, 215; 1989, pp. 426; 1991, p. 12).

It is often noted in the literature (see, e.g., Easterly and Fischer, 1995; Lerman et al., 2003) that the rapid growth in the Soviet Union during the pre-Gorbachev period 1965–80 was primarily extensive growth, associated mainly with increases in the use of factors of production rather than increases of productivity. Easterly and Fischer (1995), in particular, argue that the massive capital investments in the USSR produced inadequate returns. The available data are insufficient to test this claim for agriculture and we can only try to compare the growth of agricultural output in Azerbaijan with agricultural investment over time.

During the 20 years from 1966 to 1985 the average annual investment in Azerbaijan's agriculture more than tripled (in constant prices). Figure 2.11 presents the investment amounts in agriculture (in constant prices) as reported in official statistical sources by five-year periods (gray bars corresponding to successive Five-Year Plans) and the share of agricultural investment in total investment (black curve). Agriculture was obviously receiving increasing attention as a target sector for investment until about 1980, when its share in total investment peaked at 25%. After that agriculture's share decreased as other sectors began to attract a greater share of total investment, although the absolute investment amounts in agriculture continued to increase sharply all through the 1980s.

The information on average annual investment and the value of agricultural output made it possible to obtain rough estimates of the marginal return on investment (ROI) in agriculture since 1960. The marginal ROI in agriculture was calculated as the ratio of the average annual increase in

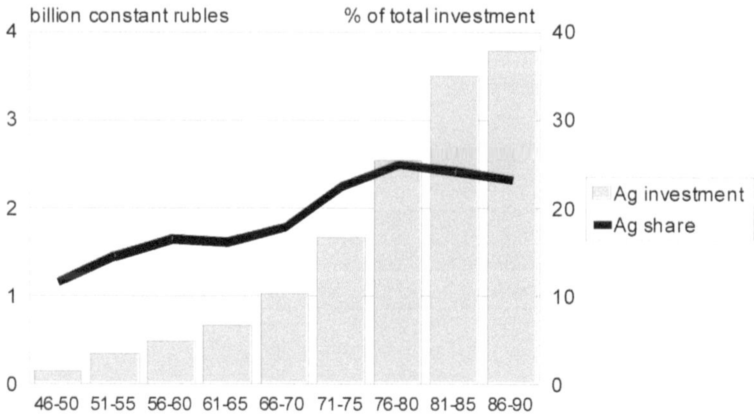

FIGURE 2.11
Investment in agriculture in Soviet Azerbaijan by Five-Year Plans 1946–50 through 1986–90: Absolute amounts (bars) and share in total investment (curve). Source: See table 2.7.

agricultural output (in constant 1983 prices) to the average annual investment in agriculture (also given in constant prices, but of an unspecified base year). Unfortunately, the numerical values of this ratio do not provide a conventional rate of return in percent, because the numerator (annual change in GAO) and the denominator (annual investment flows) are expressed in constant rubles of different years. However, the trend of this ratio over time is perfectly meaningful, and table 2.8 shows that the marginal return on investment in agriculture was increasing between 1960 and 1980 (from a notional value of 0.9 in the five-year period 1961–65 to 1.9 in 1976–80).

This is another clear indication of increasing returns to scale in Azerbaijan's agriculture, reinforcing the previous discussion of the production function (see the section *Agricultural Productivity*): each additional unit of investment funds produced a greater increase in agricultural output as the capital base of agriculture grew. This trend may have provided a political and practical justification for the rapid increase in agricultural investment over time. The increasing returns to investment in Azeri agriculture seem to indicate that Easterly and Fischer's argument about inadequate returns to capital investment in the Soviet economy as a whole did not apply to Azeri agriculture during the Khrushchev and Brezhnev periods.

The situation changed dramatically toward 1985, when Gorbachev's anti-alcohol campaign produced sharp declines in grape production (see box 2.4) and triggered a general slowdown in agricultural growth. Investments continued pouring into agriculture as previously, but the new political reality suppressed the previously rapid growth of output. This resulted in a substantial drop in marginal ROI in 1981–85—the five-year period that absorbed the brunt of the declines associated with the anti-alcohol campaign. After 1985, agricultural slowdown changed to outright decline due to the pervasive disruptions caused by the war with Armenia and civil unrest. This decline in

TABLE 2.8
Marginal Return on Investment in Agriculture in Azerbaijan, 1961–90

Period	*Investment in Agriculture, Average Per Year*	*Change in GAO, Average Per Year, %*	*Marginal Return on Investment*
1961–65	135	−3.1	0.92
1966–70	204	26.6	0.97
1971–75	332	33.9	1.51
1976–80	505	51.0	1.89
1981–85	700	15.8	1.34
1986–90	757	−13.6	−0.24

Source: Authors' calculations from sources for table 2.7.

output is reflected in negative return on investment in 1986–90 (when investments continued to flow into the sector at the same or even slightly higher level than previously).

From Agriculture to Oil: The "Petrolification" of the Azeri Economy

Soviet Azerbaijan was largely an agrarian country, and during the last decade of the Soviet era the share of agriculture in net material product (NMP, the equivalent of GDP in socialist national accounts) hovered around 30% (figure 2.12). If we add the share of the food processing industry to this figure, the value of agriculture and its related food processing industry accounted for over 40% of NMP during this period.

Agriculture dominated the manufacturing sector as well. Food processing was by far the largest industry in Azerbaijan before independence, accounting for 25% of industrial production in 1980. It was also the most rapidly growing industry in Azerbaijan, increasing its output by 9.4% per year (calculated between 1958 and 1987). By comparison, the production of electricity, a rough indicator of the overall growth of the economy, increased by only 6% per year. Within the food processing sector, canned foods (primarily fruits and vegetables) and wine grew fastest (figure 2.13). Fruits and vegetables (including canned fruits and vegetables) were the most export-oriented food industries in Azerbaijan in the years between 1987 and 1989.[2]

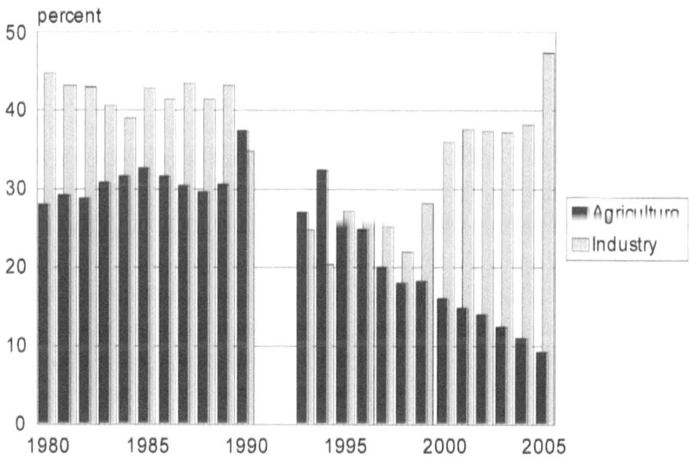

FIGURE 2.12
Share of agriculture and industry in GDP (NMP for 1980–90). Source: GDP from Statistical Committee of Azerbaijan (2006a), NMP in current prices from Statistical Committee of CIS (2008).

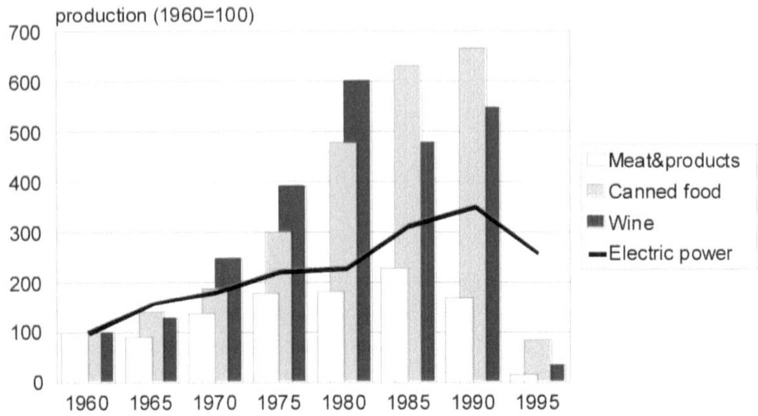

FIGURE 2.13
Food processing industry production in Azerbaijan, 1960=100. Source: Statistical Committee of Azerbaijan (2001, vol. 2, pp. 188–189, 407).

The role of agriculture in the economy began to decline after independence, with the industrial sector recording proportional gains. In 1995, industrial and agricultural output were evenly matched (see figure 2.12), each sector contributing about 25% of GDP (the remaining 50% came from transport, construction, and services).[3] Ten years later, in 2004, agriculture contributed slightly over 10% of GDP, whereas the share of industry was close to 40%.

The role of the oil industry in the economy increased sharply after 1995, primarily at the expense of agriculture and the non-oil industrial sector. The share of the oil industry almost doubled from 16% of GDP in 1995 to about 30% in 2002 and then soared stratospherically to over 50% of GDP in 2006 (table 2.9). The share of agriculture almost halved from 25% of GDP in 1995 to 14% in 2002, shrinking further to less than 10% in 2006. The share of non-oil industries shrank from 13% in 1995 (almost on a par with the oil industry at that time) to less than 10% in 2002–08.

Figure 2.14 shows the changes in the sectoral structure of Azerbaijan's economy, with the oil industry virtually displacing the non-oil industries (the black band at the top) and sharply cutting into agriculture (the dark gray band at the bottom). The share of the other sectors (construction, transport, services) did not decrease during most of the period and in 2002–04 they accounted for 50% of GDP, roughly the same (and even slightly higher) than in 1995. However, the sharp increase in the share of the oil sector after 2004 led to a sharp drop in the share of the service sector, whose role decreased to 35% of GDP in 2006–08.

TABLE 2.9
Sectoral Structure of the Economy 1995–2006

Year	*Agriculture*	*Oil Industry*	*Non-Oil Industries*	*Other Sectors*	*All Economy*
1995	25	16	13	45	100
1996	25	14	15	46	100
1997	20	15	12	53	100
1998	18	14	10	59	100
1999	18	20	9	52	100
2000	16	27	6	51	100
2001	15	30	6	50	100
2002	14	29	9	49	100
2003	12	28	10	50	100
2004	11	29	9	51	100
2005	9	39	8	43	100
2006	7	51	6	36	100
2007	6	54	6	34	100
2008	6	52	5	37	100

Source: Statistical Committee of Azerbaijan (various years); see table A.4.

Oil Extraction in Azerbaijan

To put the recent "petrolification" of the Azeri economy in perspective, it is useful to examine the long-term development of oil extraction in Azerbaijan since the time when it was a province of the Czarist Russian Empire. In

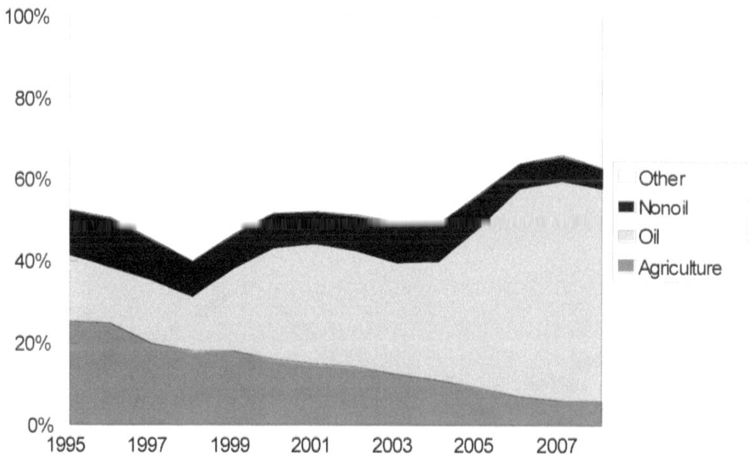

FIGURE 2.14
Sectoral structure of GDP 1995–2008 (% of gross value added). Source: Ministry of Economic Development (2001), Statistical Committee of Azerbaijan (2007).

fact, Azerbaijan was the first country in the world where oil wells were drilled and oil began to be extracted in the middle of the 19th century. Production increased rapidly and in 1901, for example, Azerbaijan produced 11.4 million tons of oil, more than the United States. At that time, Azerbaijan accounted for more than half of world production. As the 20th century progressed, however, Azerbaijan's role in oil production decreased as the industry developed in other regions of the USSR and elsewhere in the world (Encyclopedia Britannica, 2004). The production of Azeri crude declined precipitously after 1900 through a combination of disruptions caused by strikes of revolutionary-minded oil workers and severe depletion of the original "four Baku oil fields" (figure 2.15). Instead of developing new oil fields in Azerbaijan, Soviet capital moved to the new Groznyi wells in Chechnya, north of the Caucasus Range.

The changing role of Azerbaijan as an oil producer is best demonstrated in relation to USSR and Russia. In the early 20th century, Azerbaijan's share in crude oil production of the Russian Empire declined from 87% in 1909 to 73% in 1913 (Ministry of Finance, 1914). In 1940, on the eve of World War II and at the beginning of Stalin's Third Five-Year Plan, Azerbaijan was still producing 71% of USSR crude oil; a quarter of a century later, in 1967, its share was down to 7.5% of USSR crude production, although the absolute volume of 22 million ton was the same as in 1940 (Soviet Encyclopedia, 1967). In the post-Soviet period (since 1992), Russia produces over 80% of CIS crude output. Kazakhstan is second with 10% of all CIS countries, while

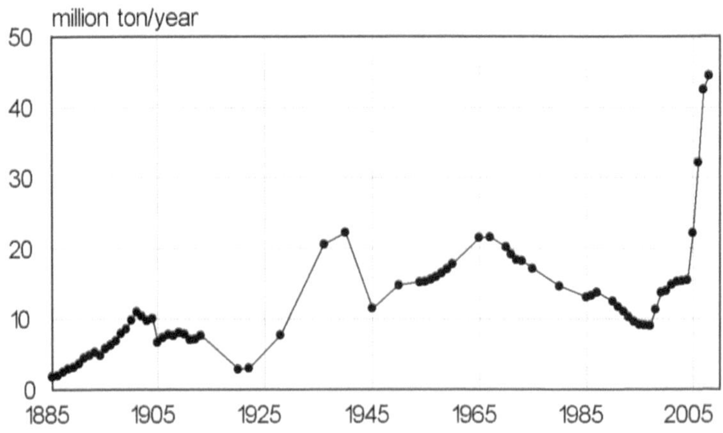

FIGURE 2.15
Crude oil production 1885–2008. Source: 1885–1912 from Ministry of Finance (1914); 1913–2008 from Statistical Committee of AzSSR (various years) and Statistical Committee of Azerbaijan (various years).

Azerbaijan contributes only 3% of the total (Energy Information Administration, 1999).

Figure 2.15 shows that Azerbaijan's oil production collapsed during World War I, increased spectacularly after 1920, collapsed again during World War II (1940–45), and achieved a tremendous recovery after World War II, with crude output in 1965 restored to the 1940 peak level of 22 million tons. After 1965, however, Azerbaijan's oil production began a long downward slide, mainly due to inevitable depletion of the traditional land deposits. During a quarter of a century between 1965 and 1990, the output of Azeri crude oil fell by a staggering 42% from 22 million tons to 12.5 million tons. The decline during the early years of independence, between 1991 and 1997, is actually a continuation of this downward trend that started in 1965, long before such deterioration could be blamed on economic disruptions at the end of the Soviet era.

Oil production resumed its growth after 1998, and rose gradually until 2005, when it jumped at an astounding rate of 40% per year for three years running (tapering off only in 2008). Annual output of oil in Azerbaijan, at 44 million tons in 2008, exceeds Soviet peak levels of over 20 million tons in 1940 and 1965. However, projections suggest that the current phase of Azerbaijan's oil boom will be short lived and oil production from existing fields will begin to decline in 2012, just as it declined after 1965 (Economist Intelligence Unit, 2007). According to latest estimates, Azerbaijan's proven crude oil reserves are around 7 billion barrels, more than a ten-fold increase from 600 million barrels in 2002 (Index Mundi, 2008).

Is There a Dutch Disease in Azerbaijan?

The term "Dutch Disease" was coined by *The Economist* (1977) to describe the decline of the manufacturing sector in the Netherlands after the discovery of North Sea natural gas in the 1960s. The literature on Dutch Disease refers to the danger that a natural resources boom may lead to the loss of competitive position of domestically produced tradable goods, thus contributing to deindustrialization of the nation's economy. The term is used in reference to Azerbaijan because of the development of significant offshore oil deposits in this country after 1995. Increases in the world price of crude oil after 2000 added to the boom in oil and gas extraction in Azerbaijan, thus increasing concerns that the economy may suffer from the Dutch Disease.

The Dutch Disease may pose a serious risk for transition economies such as Azerbaijan, which have yet to establish globally competitive industry. The long-run growth of these economies depends on the development of a diversified production base with a competitive manufacturing sector. The risk is particularly high for Azerbaijan, since (unlike Russia) its oil boom is projected to be short lived. Though a boom in a natural resource sector involves risk, it can also contribute greatly to short- and long-run growth of the economy. A booming oil sector adds to GDP growth and it has the potential to generate three significant benefits: (1) tax revenues that can be used by the government to improve domestic infrastructure relevant for broader economic development; (2) domestic capital to spur the development of globally competitive industry; and (3) spillover managerial expertise that can be employed outside of the oil sector. It falls to the government to design appropriate macroeconomic and reform policies to avert the possible deleterious effects of a resource boom and to make wise use of the resource windfall.

The loss of competitiveness of domestic manufacturing in models of the Dutch Disease in resource-rich economies derives from two effects, a resource shift effect and a real exchange rate effect. Both effects combine to crowd out the non-oil traded goods sector of the economy, namely manufacturing and agriculture, but for different reasons. The resource shift effect refers to increases in the demand for inputs in the booming sector, taking labor and capital away from other sectors. The exchange rate effect arises because the discovery of a new resource or (in the case of Azerbaijan) the newfound ability to exploit that resource generally leads to an increased inflow of foreign currency in the form of new export revenues or increased foreign investment in the resource sector. The increase in the supply of foreign currency in the country results in an appreciation of the domestic currency: the abundant dollars become cheaper, which means that the exchange rate declines as each unit of domestic currency buys less dollars. If this appreciation overtakes domestic inflation, then the real exchange rate also appreciates, which adversely affects the competitiveness of manufactured or agricultural exports. Indeed, export goods valued at 1,000 Azeri manats sold outside Azerbaijan for $100 when the exchange rate was 10 manats to $1, but the same goods with real value of 1,000 Azeri manats (adjusted for inflation) would sell abroad for $125 when the real exchange rate appreciates to 8 manats to $1. The higher dollar price of Azeri goods would clearly make them less competitive on world markets, leading to production declines in manufacturing and agriculture (see box 2.5 for Azerbaijan's record of inflation and exchange rates).

Notwithstanding the possible harmful long-run effects of a resource sector boom, rapid growth of the oil sector undoubtedly adds to the growth of GDP. For Azerbaijan this can be seen most clearly by considering table 2.9 that shows the portion of GDP attributable to the oil sector. Rapid growth in the oil extraction sector accounting for between 30% and 50% of GDP certainly spurs the growth of the economy overall. The question posed by the Dutch Disease literature is whether the resource sector boom is managed

Box 2.5. Inflation and Exchange Rate in Azerbaijan

The early years of Azeri independence were characterized by galloping inflation of over 1,000% annually. Remarkable stabilization was achieved after 1995, but a certain acceleration of inflation (to about 10%–15% annually) has been observed since 2004 (figure B2.5a).

The first manat (AZM) was introduced in 1992, replacing the Russian ruble at a rate of ten rubles to one manat. The rate of exchange at the end of 1992 stood at 41.5 manats per US dollar. The galloping inflation in 1992–95 led to the collapse of the manat against the US dollar, with the rate of exchange rising a hundred-fold to around 4,000 manat per US dollar in 1994–95. The real exchange rate in this period depreciated sharply, dropping by nearly 80% of the 1992 base. Since 1995, the nominal exchange rate has remained fairly stable, fluctuating in a wave-like pattern between 3,800 and 4,800 manat per US dollar. The real exchange rate followed basically the same wave-like pattern, rising between 1997 and 2000 (depreciation of the real manat), falling between 2001 and 2004 (appreciation of the real manat), and then rising again into 2008 (see table A.18). The real depreciation of the manat since 2004 is a reflection of the accelerating inflation in recent years combined with the government's policy of keeping the nominal rate fixed (figure B2.5b). Overall, despite two episodes of appreciation (1995–97 and 2001–04), the real exchange rate has remained fairly steady during the last 12 years, and its level in December 2006

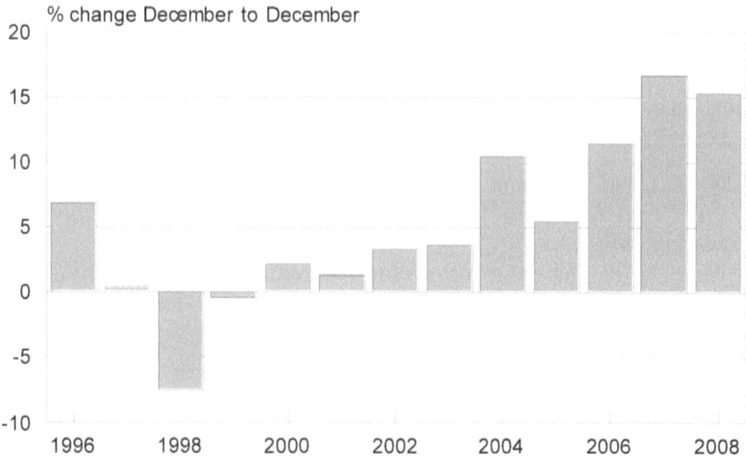

FIGURE B2.5A
Annual inflation rates 1996–2008. Source: National Bank of Azerbaijan. (statistical annex table A.17).

is comparable to that in December 1995 (see table A.18). On January 1, 2006, a new ("national") manat (AZN) was introduced at a value of 5,000 old manat.

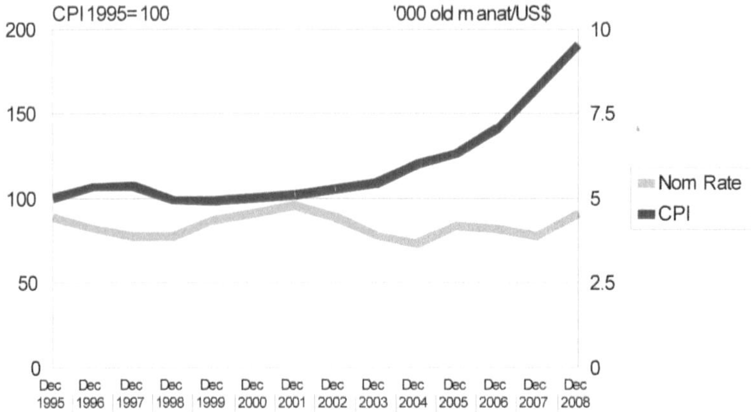

FIGURE B2.5B
Nominal exchange rate and Consumer Price Index 1995–2008. Source: National Bank of Azerbaijan (statistical annex table A.18)

wisely, harnessing its positive growth effects with due attention to possible deleterious exchange rate effects. Both theoretical and empirical analyses of the Dutch Disease highlight the need to pay particular attention to development of a diversified and competitive manufacturing base to counteract the negative effects.

Our discussion of the real exchange rate effect and the resource shift effect suggests that there are two possible diagnostic symptoms of Dutch Disease:

(1) Appreciation of the real exchange rate as a result of large foreign exchange inflows.
(2) One of the fast-growing sectors crowds out other sectors (e.g., oil crowds out agriculture and non-oil industries).

To see whether Azerbaijan shows symptoms of Dutch Disease we first examine two time series on real exchange rate and real growth by sector. The real exchange rate dropped precipitously by a staggering 80% from 1992 to 1997, showing a very strong real appreciation of the manat. This huge initial appreciation probably reflected a one-time adjustment of the exchange rate from an essentially non-equilibrium situation of the Soviet period to the new market equilibrium, caused predominantly by exchange rate decontrol in the early years of independence. Thereafter the real exchange rate has remained relatively stable, although there was some appreciation following the implementation of a stabilization program under IMF auspices in January 1995.[4]

On the whole, examination of the real exchange rate does not support the presumption of Dutch Disease in Azerbaijan. Since 1995 the real exchange rate in Azerbaijan has alternated between short periods of appreciation and depreciation. The thin curve in figure 2.16 shows that the manat underwent real appreciation between 1995 and 1997, this was followed by real depreciation of the manat through 2000, and the period between 2000 and 2004 was again characterized by real exchange rate appreciation (also see the record of inflation and nominal exchange rates in box 2.5). These fluctuations of the manat between real appreciation and real depreciation continued while oil extraction was steadily rising (thick black curve in figure 2.17). Finally, in 2005–08 the manat experienced real depreciation while extraction of oil in Azerbaijan literally took off. Overall, oil extraction seems to be associated with depreciation, and not appreciation, of the real exchange rate in Azerbaijan (the correlation coefficient between the two series is positive and statistically significant over the entire period 1995–2008).

Let us now turn to the evidence of "crowding out." Figure 2.14 shows a definite crowding out of agriculture and non-oil industries. However,

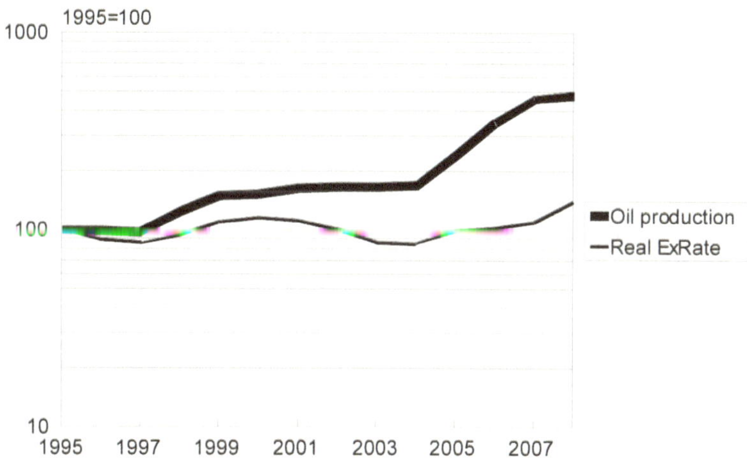

FIGURE 2.16
Real exchange rate and oil extraction indexes 1995–2008. Source: Real exchange rate index from National Bank of Azerbaijan (2009); oil production index calculated from Statistical Committee of Azerbaijan (various years) with latest updates from Statistical Committee of Azerbaijan (2009a).

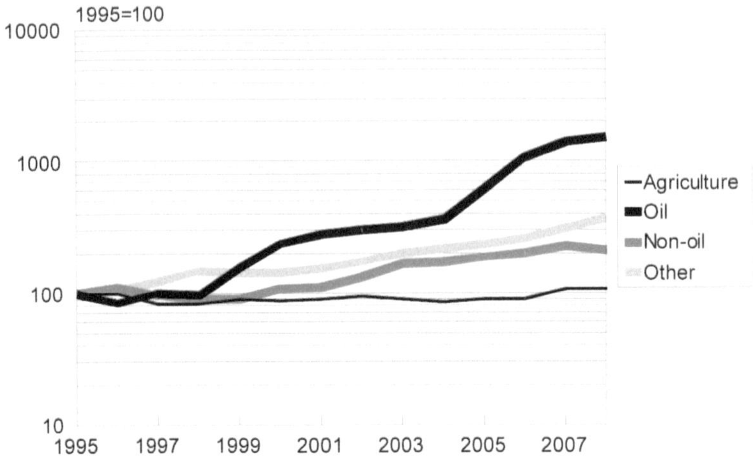

FIGURE 2.17
Sectoral GDP growth, 1995=100. Source: Statistical Committee of Azerbaijan (various years).

this figure shows percentages, and what counts is the value of (real) GDP by sector. Since no statistical estimates of real GDP by sector are available, we use the real GDP index and the sectoral structure percentages to estimate "sectoral" growth indexes. This is far from satisfactory, because the sectoral structure percentages are based on current prices, but there is no other choice. The resulting estimates in figure 2.17 show that agriculture is stagnating,[5] the oil sector is skyrocketing, but non-oil industries and other sectors are also growing as part of the overall growth of the economy, though growth in the non-oil sector seems to have slowed since 2004. Thus, the hypothesis that the oil sector is crowding out other sectors in the strict sense of an actual decline is not supported by the evidence. Of course, the other sectors do not grow as fast as the oil sector, but this is no surprise. The oil sector could still be suppressing growth rates in other sectors through its demand for factors of production (resource shift effect). However, the oil sector in Azerbaijan uses very little labor—less than 1% of the country's labor force. It is therefore unlikely that growth in the oil extraction sector is having a major impact on domestic labor markets as the vehicle for crowding-out effects.

Our examination of Dutch Disease in Azerbaijan relies upon a strict interpretation of the symptoms: appreciation of the real exchange rate and crowding out in the sense of an actual decline in non-oil sectors. We find no convincing evidence of either of these symptoms of Dutch Disease in Azerbaijan. Certainly, this does not mean that the Dutch Disease is not relevant to Azerbaijan, as our strict interpretation does not cover the important issue

TABLE 2.10
Resource Dependence in Selected Countries

	Azerbaijan (2000)	*Kazakhstan (2000)*	*Mexico (1999)*	*Iran (1999)*	*Norway (1999)*
Oil and gas in % of exports	85.2	46.8	7.3	69.4	0.3
Oil and gas in % of total government revenue	36.2	27.5	29.3	45.9	0.2
FDI in oil and gas in % of total FDI	80.5	69.7	n.a.	n.a.	n.a.

Source: European Bank for Reconstruction and Development (2001).

that Azerbaijan's economy is dominated by the oil sector (table 2.9) and the country is exceptionally dependent on oil as a source of export revenue and as a source of foreign direct investment (table 2.10).

From a Soviet Colony to Independence: What Azerbaijan Has Become in the 21st Century

In Azerbaijan the time path of gross agricultural production (GAO) shows four distinct periods: rapid growth in the period 1965–85, stagnation changing to gradual decline from 1985 to 1991, catastrophic decline in 1991–96, and recovery since 1996. These four periods correspond quite closely with four agricultural policy regimes in Azerbaijan: the Soviet growth period fuelled by increasing investment, the Gorbachev years of liberalization and uncertainty, which ended with the dissolution of the USSR, the early years of independence, and the Aliyev years starting in 1996. The close correspondence between the GAO growth path and policy regimes suggests that changes in policies—during the Soviet period and after the dissolution of the USSR—have been the main factor determining agricultural growth in Azerbaijan.

The four phases of agricultural development in Azerbaijan echo on the whole the general growth pattern of the USSR and its post-1991 successor the CIS. Yet economic and agricultural growth in Soviet Azerbaijan differed in a number of specific features from the pattern of the USSR, which mainly reflected the experience of Russia as the dominant Soviet republic. First, the economic malaise that affected the USSR as a whole in the 1970s and which intensified in the early 1980s was hardly felt in Azerbaijan. On the contrary, both economic and agricultural growth accelerated in the early 1970s and Azerbaijan's economy did not slow down until 1985. Second, the slowdown of agricultural growth in the USSR between 1973 and 1985, at the end of the

Brezhnev era, was generally attributed to declining growth in factors of production and stagnation in total factor productivity in the 1970s (Diamond, Bettis, and Ramsson, 1983). In Azerbaijan, on the other hand, increases in fertilizer deliveries, in labor, and in farm machinery stimulated growth and furthermore led to positive growth in total factor productivity. Far from being the sick sector of the Azeri economy, agriculture was the growth leader in Soviet Azerbaijan. Third, Azerbaijan enjoyed healthy returns on investment in agriculture during the Soviet period, while the returns on investment in the USSR were disappointing as increased investment in agriculture under Khrushchev and Brezhnev failed to stop the slowdown in agricultural growth.

The Soviet agricultural model in Azerbaijan ensured robust growth through 1985 and the end of the Soviet growth period began with decisions made far away in Moscow through no fault of Azerbaijan. Gorbachev's anti-alcohol campaign of 1985 triggered a catastrophic decline in grape and wine production, two of the fastest growing subsectors in agriculture and food processing. The fall in agricultural production that followed continued until independence, when the gradual reduction turned into a free fall. Rapid decline in agricultural production ceased only after President Heydar Aliyev came to power and introduced a radical land reform in 1995–96.

The recovery of agriculture in Azerbaijan in response to Aliyev's reforms could not restore the sector to its former glory, primarily due to the "petrolification" of the Azeri economy after 1995. Despite healthy agricultural growth, the role of agriculture in Azerbaijan declined steadily after 1995, while the oil extraction sector was growing rapidly. In the ten years between 1996 and 2006 the oil extraction sector progressed from being only half the size of agriculture to seven times its size, producing over half of GDP in Azerbaijan. Today Azerbaijan is no longer an agrarian economy: it is an economy with extreme concentration in the oil extraction sector with all the attendant benefits and risks. Surprisingly, we find no clear evidence to suggest that the "petrolification" of the Azeri economy has produced the symptoms commonly associated with the Dutch Disease, namely a real appreciation of the Azeri manat or the crowding out of other sectors of the economy.

Notes

1. Contrary to Azerbaijan, other Soviet republics responded to increased livestock inventories by intensifying the use of grain for animal feed. The portion of grain used for feed in the USSR rose from a little over 20% to 60% in this period. While additional investments over a longer period were expected to increase grain yields to the

point where domestic supplies would be sufficient to cover demand for both animals and humans, in the shorter run the USSR resorted to large grain imports to fill the feed gap. By the late 1980s the USSR was the largest grain importer in the world.

2. USDA/ERS (1997). Data on exports of wine are not available.

3. The change in statistical variable from Soviet-era NMP until 1990 to internationally recognized GDP after 1992 may have affected the numerical values but not the trend on the two sides of the gap in figure 2.12.

4. An appreciation of the currency after stabilization is consistent with the experience of other CIS transition countries (Rosenberg and Saavalainen, 1998, p. 16).

5. The curve for agriculture in figure 2.17 is agriculture's sectoral gross value added calculated as a portion of GDP from national accounts. This is different from gross agricultural output (GAO) that represents the gross value of agricultural production from agricultural accounts.

3

The Design and Implementation of Land Reform

UNDER GORBACHEV IT BECAME fashionable to refer to the period of Soviet history before 1985—the era of Brezhnev, Andropov, Chernenko—as the "era of stagnation." In contradistinction to this Moscow-centric view of economic history, it was precisely during this period that Azeri agriculture enjoyed robust growth and rising rural living standards. Such was the accomplishment of the post-Stalin Soviet leadership, which set two main goals for agriculture in the USSR: first, increasing livestock consumption as a proof of rising living standards under socialism and, second, stopping the exploitation of the peasantry that had taken place under Stalin. The Soviet regime enjoyed a definite success in achieving both of these goals in Azerbaijan. Though Azerbaijan was one of the poorer republics, incomes grew slowly and there was near full employment and certain stability. Consumption of livestock products increased, though per capita meat consumption remained only a little over half that of the average Soviet citizen. The monthly wages in agriculture, which had been substantially less than the average republic wage at the beginning of this period, seemed to catch up by 1985. Rural families were allowed relative freedom of action on their household plots, leading to much faster growth of agricultural production in the individual sector than in the collective and state farm sector, although the latter was the exclusive recipient of all state investments. In sum, the decades of the 1970s and 1980s in Azerbaijan saw an undeniable relative increase in living standards of the rural population compared to urban.

In Azerbaijan, then, the motivation for economic reform did not stem from the acknowledged failure of Soviet agriculture in the Brezhnev years. There was little reason for the leadership of Azerbaijan to change the Soviet system based on the pre-1985 results. The motivation for reform came only after 1985, for this is when the Soviet agricultural and political systems in Azerbaijan began to falter. Initially modest falls in agricultural production that began to appear in 1985 with the general weakening of the Soviet system changed to truly dramatic declines after independence in 1991, when hyperinflation and general transition disruptions were followed by mounting farm losses, accumulation of farm debt, and falling real wages in agriculture. The accelerating decline after 1985, and especially after 1991, clearly pointed to the need for radical systemic reforms. Still, land and farm legislation showed no substantial departures from Gorbachev-style reforms until as late as 1995, although many former Soviet republics (including Azerbaijan's neighbors in Armenia and Georgia) adopted a fairly radical reform agenda starting in 1991–92.

The period of policy drift came to an end in 1995—two years after Heydar Aliyev had become Azerbaijan's third president (see table 3.1 for a chronol-

TABLE 3.1
The First Presidents of Independent Azerbaijan

Period in Office	*President*	*Details*
9/91–5/92	Ayaz Mutalibov	Formerly First Secretary of the Azerbaijan Communist Party (1990–91), becomes the country's first president in elections boycotted by the opposition; resigns after a massacre of Azerbaijanis fleeing from Nagorno-Karabakh and the establishment by Armenian forces of the Lachin corridor linking Armenia to Nagorno-Karabakh through Azerbaijani territory.
6/92–6/93	Abulfaz Elchibey	Leader of the nationalist Popular Front Party (PFP), elected president in contested elections. Incompetent handling of the Nagorno-Karabakh conflict, inadequate management of the economy, and perception of widespread corruption among government officials culminated in an armed insurrection (the "coup of June 1993"), forcing Elchibey to resign and flee to his native Nakhichevan (where he died in 2000).
6/93–10/03	Heydar Aliyev	Head of Azerbaijan KGB (1967–69), First Secretary of the Azerbaijan Communist Party (1969–82), Deputy Prime Minister of the USSR and the first Muslim to become a full member of the Politburo (1982–87); forced by Gorbachev to leave the Politburo on charges of corruption and incompatibility ("one of the great Communist dinosaurs"); returned to his native Nakhichevan in 1990 and was appointed parliament chairman in 1991; recalled to Baku as acting president in June

Period in Office	President	Details
		1993 in a deal with coup leaders and confirmed as president in October 1993 election. "He then ruled the country for a decade with a rod of iron—encouraging foreign investment while discouraging political pluralism" (BBC.COM obituary). Elected for a second term in October 1998. Collapsed while giving a speech on live television in April 2003 and stood down from the presidency before the October 2003 election. Died December 12, 2003.
10/03–	Ilham Aliyev	The son and heir apparent of Heydar Aliyev. Appointed Prime Minister and thus presidential successor in August 2003, as Heydar Aliyev's health was rapidly failing. Won the presidential election of October 2003.

ogy of the first presidents of independent Azerbaijan). Aliyev provided the political will that gave impetus to the process of land reform in Azerbaijan. He personally pushed through the groundbreaking 1995–96 land and farm reform laws, and when reform implementation was unsatisfactory, promoted further legislation (starting in 1998) that provided post-privatization support to farms and eliminated institutional foot-dragging by the state bureaucracy. The results were an astonishingly rapid shift of farm structure in Azerbaijan from collective to individual agriculture. In three short years between 1995 and 1998 the share of arable land controlled by corporate farms—the successors of collective and state farms—declined from 90% to 20%, and since 2001 sown land in corporate farms has remained at a negligible 2% of cultivated area (down from 90% up to 1995).

The Need for Reform: The Soviet Agricultural System Comes Apart 1985–95

A retrospective look at agricultural development clearly shows that the Soviet system in Azerbaijan began to break down in 1985, a good six years before the declaration of independence and the dissolution of the USSR. The long period of robust agricultural growth peaked out in 1984 and the trend changed from growth to decline the following year (figure 3.1). By 1990–91, the index of agricultural production had dropped 15% below its 1984 peak (table 3.2) due to a combination of factors related to central Soviet politics and the local situation in Azerbaijan. Central Soviet politics in that period were characterized by general uncertainty and weakening of the system

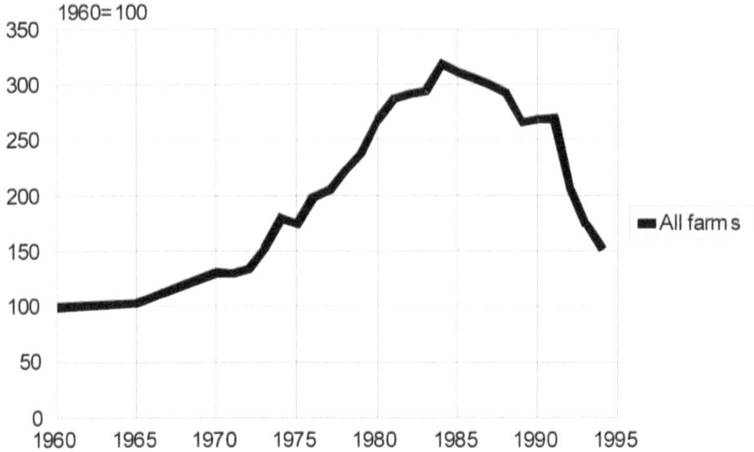

FIGURE 3.1
Growth and decline of gross agricultural output (GAO) 1960–94. Source: See figure 2.1.

under Gorbachev, whereas locally Azerbaijan suffered from increasing violence between Azeris and Armenians throughout the country, reflecting what had become a full-fledged war in Nagorno-Karabakh. Gorbachev's central policies tried to arrest or remedy the incipient decline in all of the USSR, but Azerbaijan was too busy with its internal problems to focus on the need for corrective economic reforms within the ailing Soviet system. The decline in agriculture accelerated and took on catastrophic proportions for Azerbaijan after the dissolution of the Soviet Union in 1991, when the pressures of war were exacerbated by galloping inflation, disruption of input supplies through traditional state channels, and loss of export demand from former Soviet partners. This acceleration of decline after independence is clearly seen in figure 3.1, where the gross agricultural output (GAO) curve drops precipitously after 1991. Thus, between 1990 and 1995, agricultural production in Azerbaijan fell by a further 47%, dropping to 44% of the 1984 peak (table 3.2). The magnitude of the decline clearly pointed to the need for radical systemic reforms.

The fall in agricultural output after 1991 was almost exclusively a consequence of production declines in corporate farms, rather than in the individual sector—household plots and peasant farms (table 3.2). By 1995 production in agricultural enterprises—former state and collective farms representing perhaps more than anything else the Soviet agricultural model—had fallen to 23% of the 1984 level, while the output from the individual sector—the antithesis of socialist ideology—was virtually at the same level as in 1984.

TABLE 3.2
Privatization of Agricultural Production: Indices of Gross Agricultural Output by Farm Type (1984=100)

Year	*All Farms*	*Corporate*	*Individual*
1984	100.0	100.0	100.0
1985	97.8	95.7	102.5
1990	84.5	72.8	118.4
1991	84.8	69.4	129.5
1992	64.6	49.7	108.4
1993	54.7	37.9	104.2
1994	47.7	29.3	102.5
1995	44.4	23.4	106.7
1996	45.7	21.7	117.1
1997	42.9	13.2	131.5
1998	45.5	5.7	164.4
1999	48.8	2.8	186.1
2000	54.7	1.7	213.1
2001	60.7	1.6	237.6
2002	64.6	1.8	252.5
2003	68.2	3.0	263.0
2004	71.4	3.7	273.4
2005	76.7	3.9	294.3
2006	77.4	3.8	298.6
2007	80.5	5.3	306.4
2008	85.4	6.4	322.6

Source: Statistical annex table A.6.

Individual production had continued to increase between 1984 and 1991 and then dropped by about 25% between 1991 and 1995. This fall was in part due to the overall effects of economic disruption but, perhaps more significantly, it was the outcome of the downward statistical bias associated with the omission in 1995 of the output from at least some of the territories occupied by Armenian forces (about 20% of Azerbaijan's territory in Nagorno-Karabakh and its surrounding region). Considering this bias, the reported fall in individual sector production seems quite modest indeed.

The fall in production of corporate farms was not the only symptom of the disintegration of the Soviet agricultural system in Azerbaijan. Another symptom involved a dramatic increase in the proportion of unprofitable agricultural enterprises, from 8% in 1990 to nearly two-thirds in 1996 and up to 87% in 1998 (table 3.3). Profitability of agricultural enterprises worsened as farm managers failed to adjust their management style to the new economic reality, which was characterized inter alia by galloping inflation and rapidly deteriorating terms of trade.

TABLE 3.3
Farm Profitability, Inflation, and Terms of Trade in Agriculture

Year	*Unprofitable Corporate Farms (%)*	*Inflation—Year-to-Year Change in Consumer Prices (%)*	*Year-to-Year Change in Agricultural Commodity Prices (%)*	*Year-to-Year Change in Manufactured Product Prices (%)*	*Terms of Trade in Agriculture*
1990	7.9	—	—	—	1.000
1991	n.a.	106.6	58	135	0.672
1992	n.a.	912.3	766	1303	0.415
1993	n.a.	1129.1	611	1040.7	0.259
1994	32.0	1663.5	1331	1058.4	0.320
1995	47.0	411.8	388	1765.3	0.084
1996	62.1	19.9	14	98	0.048
1997	75.0	3.7	−15	11.8	0.037
1998	86.7	−0.8	1	−12.4	0.042
1999	70.5	−8.5	−1	−6.1	0.044
2000	52.5	1.8	−0.4	27.4	0.035
2001	35.7	1.5	4.2	1.8	0.036
2002	29.0	2.8	5.4	−2.3	0.038
2003	25.3	2.2	4.3	16.1	0.034
2004	17.1	6.7	16.3	12.9	0.036
2005	11.4	9.6	8.0	18.6	0.032
2006	12.3	8.3	12.8	17.7	0.031
2007	10.1	16.7	10.8	8.0	0.032

Notes: N.a. not available; terms of trade in the last column is calculated as the ratio of the index of prices received by agricultural producers to the index of prices paid for farm inputs.
Sources: Percent of unprofitable farms from Statistical Committee of Azerbaijan (2006b, 2009b); inflation and price data from Statistical Committee of CIS (2008).

As inflation rates hit 1,000% per year in 1992–94, agricultural producers faced increasing prices both for products they sold and for farm inputs they had to purchase. However, prices of farm inputs rose much faster than farm commodity prices, because the breakdown of the Soviet system of artificially low fixed prices for farm inputs unleashed a price scissors effect. Thus, the price index of manufactured goods (approximating the prices of farm inputs) rose by a factor of 81,000 between 1990 and 1995, while the index of prices received by agricultural producers rose in the same period merely by a factor of 7,000 (these cumulative numbers are calculated from the corresponding year-by-year price changes in table 3.3). As a result, the terms of trade in agriculture, defined as the ratio of the index of prices received by agricultural producers to the index of prices paid for farm inputs, dropped dramatically from a relative level of 1 in 1990 to 0.08 in 1995—a fall of 92% (in subsequent years the terms of trade stabilized at around 0.03–0.04 as hyperinflation was brought under control).

The deterioration in financial performance of corporate farms continued even after stabilization of the Azeri currency. By 1998, with inflation firmly in check, the proportion of unprofitable corporate farms had increased to 87%. Thus, independently of inflation, corporate farms in this period suffered increasing losses, which undermined their ability to pay their suppliers and workers, resulting in a severe fall both in agricultural production and in rural wages. Though there are no statistics on farm-level debt for this period, we know from other CIS countries with similar profitability deterioration that increasing farm losses were always accompanied by mounting debt to suppliers, increasing wage arrears, and severe declines in farm production (see Lerman, Csaki, and Sotnikov (2000) for five CIS countries).

Yet another source of difficulties for Azeri agricultural enterprises was the breakdown in trade relations between the countries of the former USSR. In the late 1980s Azerbaijan exported one-third of vegetable production, about 40% of fruit production, and between 20% and 30% of vegetable oil production to other Soviet republics (table 3.4). The breakup of the USSR meant that

TABLE 3.4
Azerbaijan's Export/Production Ratios for Selected Agricultural Commodities, 1987–89 and 1995–97 (in Percent)

Year	*1987–89*	*1995–97*
Vegetables	33	2
Fruits	37	3
Vegetable oil	25	7

Source: USDA/ERS (1997); Statistical Committee of Azerbaijan (various years).

Azerbaijan lost its traditional markets for agricultural products and processed food. By 1995–97 exports of vegetables, fruits, and vegetable oils accounted for about 5% of production (table 3.4).

These three factors—the catastrophic fall in production, growing financial losses and farm debts, and loss of export markets—illustrate the unsustainable nature of the collective and state farm system in Azerbaijan by the mid-1990s. The breakdown of the traditional Soviet system had emphasized by 1995 the need and urgency of reform. Other countries addressed similar transition-decline problems with gradual or halfhearted reforms, although starting much earlier. The government of Azerbaijan, starting at a much later point, when the severe difficulties could no longer be skirted, chose a more radical approach to reform—substantial dissolution of the former collective and state farm system.

Azerbaijan's Legal Framework for Reform: From Hesitation to Decisiveness

Azerbaijan declared independence on August 30, 1991, and the declaration of independence was overwhelmingly confirmed by a referendum in December of that year. As throughout the rest of the former Soviet Union, local officials and politicians in Azerbaijan recognized from the start the need for urgent economic reforms. In particular, Azerbaijan's large and formerly flourishing agriculture required substantial restructuring if it was to achieve its proven potential. Plans were drawn for ambitious privatization and other market-oriented reforms, but execution foundered, mainly due to political uncertainty, which inevitably led to lack of political will and indecisiveness. Thus, the privatization law passed in January 1993 could not be implemented, while land distribution stalled due to disagreement over the choice between private landownership and long-term leaseholding and over the distribution of agricultural equipment (Curtis, 1994). In this respect Azerbaijan did not differ from other transition countries, where land reform was the subject of vigorous parliamentary struggle between conservative and liberal forces.

Land and farm policies in Azerbaijan during the early 1990s did not extend much beyond Gorbachev-era reforms. They included augmentation of household plots, creation of marginal peasant farms, and greater decision-making flexibility for state and collective farms (box 3.1). The post-Soviet Land Code of November 1991 did not significantly alter the principles of Soviet farm structure. While it recognized private land ownership (article 10), noted the right of collective farm members (either individually or as a cooperative) to

Box 3.1. Categories of Agricultural Producers in Azerbaijan

As in other former Soviet republics, agricultural producers in Azerbaijan fell into three categories. The distinctions between these three categories can be useful even today, because each had a separate reform path. The first was that of so-called agricultural enterprises. These were primarily large state and collective farms. After independence, in 1991, these farms began to be privatized and restructured into a mixture of joint-stock companies, limited-liability partnerships, and agricultural production cooperatives. State and collective farms, along with their privatized and restructured cousins, can be referred to collectively as corporate farms. They numbered 3,014 at the end of 1990 (just before independence) and 2,241 at the end of 2004. The second category of farms, also basically inherited from the Soviet era, is here referred to as household farms. Before 1995 these were the household plots farmed by the employees of state and collective farms and the collective gardens and orchards cultivated in the countryside by urban residents. After 1995, with the dissolution of many of the state and collective farms, their owners assumed these farms as private property and land plots from dissolved state and collective farms were added to them. Household farms numbered 819,000 at the end of 2000 (excluding the occupied territories). The third category is that of so-called peasant farms. The legal basis for this fundamentally new class of farms derives from a special Law on Peasant Farms adopted in April 1992 (a similar legal framework for the establishment of peasant farms was set up at about the same time in all former Soviet republics; prior to April 1992 the 1989 USSR law on peasant farms was in force). Land for the formation of peasant farms was to be obtained from private landowners (by leasing or buying) and primarily from the municipality reserve that contained land little suitable (or totally unsuitable) for agriculture. Peasant farmers could receive or purchase reserve land for private ownership. They were also allowed to employ hired labor and had to file statistical reports with the authorities. Peasant farms in Azerbaijan numbered 66 at the end of 1990, and 36,124 at the end of 1999 (registered and nonregistered).

withdraw from large farms with land, provided the general assembly and local authorities agreed (articles 56 and 60), it neither privatized the existing state and collective farms nor called for their dissolution. The establishment in 1992 of the State Land Committee as a vehicle of land reform did not produce any tangible results either. Azerbaijan retained the traditional state and collective farm system all through the first years of independence, despite its obviously ailing performance.

The period of uncertainty and indecisiveness came to an end in June 1993, when Heydar Aliyev took over from Azerbaijan's second elected president, Abulfaz Elchibey, who resigned as Armenian forces were making serious gains in the war against Azerbaijan and local rebels were advancing on Baku (the so-called coup of June 1993) (see table 3.1). After his confirmation as president in popular elections in October 1993, Aliyev quickly negotiated a ceasefire with Armenia and Nagorno-Karabakh. The cessation of armed hostilities in 1994 allowed Aliyev to focus on economic recovery, and specifically on land reform.

Aliyev had been responsible for agriculture's spectacular growth during his tenure as first secretary of the Central Committee of the Azerbaijan Communist Party (1969–83) and in 1992 he had launched a program of agricultural reforms in the Nakhichevan enclave, where he was parliamentary chairman during a "period of exile" from central leadership. Aliyev's land reform attempts in Nakhichevan did not spread to the rest of the country, because by then Azerbaijan was embroiled in the Nagorno-Karabakh conflict, suffering from deep political instability. The situation changed radically with his election to the presidency, and from the end of 1993 onward, all land reform and farm restructuring decisions were closely associated with President Heydar Aliyev.

The general principles of the new economic system were set out in "the Aliyev Constitution" adopted by referendum in November 1995. The new constitution made a clean break with the socialist economic principles inherited from the Soviet system. It recognized private property alongside state and municipal property (Art. 13(I)), and specifically stated that both movable and immovable property (e.g., land) may be held in private ownership (Art. 29(III)). The state monopoly on land ownership that had persisted in Azerbaijan since the early 1920s was thus abolished and adherence to market principles of economic development—"for the improved well-being of the people"—was formally declared in the constitution (Art. 15(II)). Aliyev's market approach to the economy produced quick dividends in the form of what Azerbaijan calls the "contract of the century" signed in 1997 with a consortium of international oil companies for the exploration and exploitation of three offshore oil fields.

Yet at that time Azerbaijan was still a highly agrarian country and land reform was naturally regarded as one of the pillars of economic recovery. Already in December 1994 and March 1995 President Aliyev created special commissions to formulate the principles of agrarian reform (Mamedov, 2000). These commissions produced three major laws on land reform and farm restructuring in 1995–96 (table 3.5), which put in place the basic legislation for land privatization and the dissolution of collective and state farms.

TABLE 3.5
Main Legislation Related to Agrarian Reform in Azerbaijan, 1991–2007

Legislative Document	*Date*	*Content*
Land Code	9 Nov 1991	Recognizes private, collective, and state land. Includes regulations on setting up of peasant farms and withdrawal of workers from loss-making collectives. Greater decision-making freedom for collectives
Law 102 "On peasant farms"	8 Apr 1992	Elaboration of rights and responsibilities of peasant farms. Farmers may either own or lease land
Law 114 "On leasing"	30 Apr 1992	Legislative framework for land and other leasing
Law 976 "On the basis of agrarian reform"	18 Feb 1995	Outline of agrarian reform, including land distribution, farm reform, agro-industry privatization
Law 978 "On reform of state and collective farms"	18 Feb 1995	Details of collective and state farm reform
Law 155Q "On land reform"	16 Jul 1996	Land reform details
PD 716 "On ratification of the statute on the Ministry of Agriculture"	6 June 1998	Basic decree on reorganization of the Ministry of Agriculture.
Law 516IQ "On mortgage"	3 Jul 1998	Outlines procedures and regulation of mortgages (including land mortgage)
Law 587IQ "On land leasing"	11 Dec 1998	Legal basis for land leasing
Law 593IQ "On state land cadastre, land monitoring and land surveying"	22 Dec 1998	Legal basis for the state land cadastre, including monitoring and surveying of land
PD 118 "On measures to accelerate reforms in agriculture"	22 Mar 1999	Highlights problems with implementation of agrarian reform Outlines a program of post-privatization support for all agricultural producers and further reforms of agricultural enterprises
CR 49 "On concessionary sales of fuel and oil products to agricultural producers"	26 Mar 1999	Post-privatization support for agricultural producers
Law 665 IQ "On the land market"	7 May 1999	Sets minimum land prices and maximum land transaction limits, presumably aimed at preventing sweetheart land transfers

(*continued*)

TABLE 3.5
(continued)

Legislative Document	*Date*	*Content*
Land Code	25 Jun 1999	An updated codification of agrarian reform (revision of the 1991 Land Code)
PD 275 "On the State Commission for Assistance to Private Agriculture"	7 Feb 2000	Low-cost credit programs for agricultural producers
Law 208-IIQ "On vineyards and wine production"	19 Oct 2001	
Law 160-IIQ "On management of municipal land"	29 Jun 2001	Definition of municipal land, rights and land obligations of municipalities, transactions in municipal land
Law 344-IIQ "On encouragement of insurance in agriculture"	18 Jun 2002	Participation of the state in natural disaster insurance and compensation of insurance losses to insurers
CR 53 "On use of farm machinery purchased with a Japanese grant"	22 Apr 2003	First in a series of resolutions establishing state-controlled facilities for leasing of farm machinery
PD 972 "On additional measures regarding land leasing"	23 Oct 2003	Rules for leasing state and municipal land through auctions and bids
PD 468 "On additional measures for expansion of agricultural machinery leasing"	23 Oct 2004	Creation of "Agrolizing" as a state-owned company for leasing and sale of farm machinery purchased with state funds
Law 883-IIQ "On mortgage"	15 Apr 2005	Agricultural land can be mortgaged only to support agricultural production and processing; plots may not be split for purposes of mortgage
Law 926-IIQ "On family farms"	14 Jun 2005	Introduces a new category of family farms (*semeinoe krest'yanskoe khozyaistvo*) organized for farming and other agriculture-related activities on the basis of family labor and owned or leased property; provides a legal framework for the operation of household plots
CR 46 "On additional measures for livestock development"	14 Feb 2006	Improvement of veterinary services, artificial insemination, and breed selection
PD 1907 "On state support for agricultural producers"	23 Jan 2007	Reimbursement of 50% of purchase costs of fuel and fertilizers used in agricultural production

Legend: CR—Cabinet of Ministers Resolution; PD—Presidential Decree

Agrarian Reform Policies Leading to Recovery

The period of Aliyev's decisive reforms starting in 1995 can be subdivided into two stages: the first stage of land reform in 1996–97, when all the basic legislation was put in place and the overall shape of the new farm structure crystallized; and the second stage of land reform in 1998–2001, when the emphasis shifted to post-privatization farm support and elimination of bureaucratic obstacles to implementation of reform programs.

First Stage of Land Reform 1995–97

The 1995–96 laws on land and farm reform aimed at privatizing Azeri agriculture, and in the process disbanding the traditional collective and state farms. These laws defined the procedures for privatizing state-owned land and dividing up and distributing the land, livestock, and other material assets of collective and state farms to rural individuals. In addition, the reform program included privatization of much of the agro-processing sector and provision of limited post-privatization support, primarily for agricultural enterprises.

The overriding goal of land reform in 1995–96 was to define the limits of state, municipal, and private land ownership, while establishing procedures for transfer of land from state and collective ownership to the new forms of municipal and private ownership. The creation of privately owned land proceeded simultaneously on two different fronts. The first concerned the privatization of state-owned land that in 1995 was in use rights of individuals and households. This land was to be privatized—free of charge, without any payment (*besplatno*)—to the current users. Household plot operators thus became overnight owners of the land that they had been farming for years—about 3% of all agricultural land in Azerbaijan or 8% of arable land.

The second privatization direction concerned the land of collective and state farms that were slated for reorganization into new market-oriented forms and structures. As a preliminary step, this resource—97% of agricultural land and 92% of arable land in the country—had to be divided into three parts: the part that was to remain in state ownership, the part that was to be transferred to municipal ownership, and the residual that was to be made available for privatization. Once defined, the privatizable component was to be divided into equal land shares (adjusted for quality or cadastral value) and distributed to virtually everyone among the rural population. The categories of beneficiaries entitled to land shares are listed in table 3.6.

In parallel with the distribution of land shares to the rural population, the material assets of the former collective farm were to be distributed

TABLE 3.6
Who Was Entitled to a Land Share?

The 1996 Law of Land Reform defined the following list of individuals entitled to a share of privatized land in former collective and state farms:

- permanent workers of the collective or state farm;
- permanent residents in the villages associated with the collective or state farm (this basically covers all retirees as well as rural infrastructure employees, such as teachers, medical personnel, etc.);
- pensioners of the collective or state farm who currently reside in the same district or nearby town;
- peasant farmers and other individual entrepreneurs who started independent agricultural production in the villages associated with the collective or state farm before the adoption of the law.

to members and workers based on their salary and length of service. The social infrastructure of privatized state and collective farms was to be transferred into private, municipal, or state ownership. Sport facilities, nursery schools, kindergartens, and schools were to remain in joint property or to be transferred to municipalities. Communal services, such as heating, water, cafeterias, trade facilities, and businesses, could be sold, remain in joint property, or transferred to municipalities. Housing was to be transferred to the ownership of the legal occupants. Leased facilities could be sold to lessees.

The 1996 Law of Land Reform (Art. 14) explicitly specifies that "the land share is transferred into private ownership of beneficiaries *in kind*," i.e., as a physical plot, and not a paper certificate of entitlement.[1] This simultaneity of determination of land shares and their conversion into physical plots is a unique feature of land reform in Azerbaijan. Other CIS countries have generally chosen a two-stage process. The first stage involved determination of land shares and their distribution in the form of paper certificates of entitlement to unspecified parcels of land. The second stage allowed conversion of land shares into physical plots, either by special request (as in Moldova before 1998, in Ukraine before 2000, or in Russia and Kazakhstan to this day) or as part of a government-sponsored conversion program (as in Moldova and Ukraine in recent years). It took Azerbaijan substantially longer than the other CIS countries to launch its land reform program, but once the basic decision had been made the process was implemented in a much more radical manner.

Despite extensive privatization, much land relevant to agriculture was to remain in state ownership, including summer and winter grazing land, grazing camps and cattle crossings, forestland, and land of state scientific research institutes and educational institutions. Lands eligible for transfer to municipal ownership included a reserve of 5% of arable land that could be leased out to farmers. In addition, land allocated to private users before the 1996 law which exceeded the average amount of land transferred to shareholders in the state or collective farms was subject to repossession for subsequent redistribution.

Another unique provision of Azeri legislation is the immediate acceptance of the landowners' right to buy and sell land. Buying and selling of land is an emotionally charged issue in all CIS countries, and the legislators' persistent reluctance to allow these market transactions limits, not to say invalidates, the whole concept of private land ownership. Although Russia recognized private land ownership back in 1992, buying and selling of agricultural land became legally possible only after 2004. Kyrgyzstan recognized private land ownership in 1998 and immediately turned around and imposed a moratorium on buying and selling of land "for the protection of the inexperienced landowners" in 1999 (the moratorium was repealed in 2001 in response to popular pressure). Ukraine still has a moratorium on buying and selling of land, despite a tremendous increase in private land ownership through share conversion since 2000. Moldova formally allows buying and selling of land, but makes land transactions extremely costly and difficult to complete (as, incidentally, in Russia). Turkmenistan recognizes private land ownership, but quite perversely prohibits all land transactions: land is received from the state without the right to sell, sublease, give as a gift, or exchange. The Azeri law, on the other hand, clearly states that "landowners have the right . . . to lease out their land, sell it, gift it, use it as collateral, pass it in inheritance, and will it" (Law "On the basis of agrarian reform," February 1995, Art. 5; Law of Land Reform, July 1996, Art. 17).[2] It would be interesting to investigate how this legal feature of Azeri land law affected the development of land markets in Azerbaijan compared with the rest of the CIS, where land transactions are largely confined to leasing.

Privatization efforts were not limited to land and farms. Food processing facilities were to be privatized through sale or auction in an insider-type process, as in other CIS countries. Enterprises to be sold were offered first to their employees and management or to agricultural producers (as raw material suppliers). In state enterprise privatization, 15% of shares could be sold to employees and management on concessionary terms (Law 1120 "On ratification of the state program on privatization of state property for 1995–1998," September 1995). In municipal enterprise privatization, on the other hand, the controlling share of stock was to be offered to agricultural producers (farm enterprises) at a discount. Another portion of stock was to be transferred free of charge to the employees and management of the enterprise.

Municipal governments could own up to 10% of stock in food processing facilities, and the remaining stock was to be auctioned.

Finally, as part of the 1995–96 legislation, the state declared its intention to protect agricultural producers through the following policy measures (Law "On the basis of agrarian reform," February 1995, arts. 13, 14, 15):

- encouraging investment in agriculture,
- rehabilitating irrigation and land improvement facilities,
- creating a production base for agricultural producers by developing agricultural input industry,
- earmarking state budget funds for controlling livestock and plant diseases and pests,
- preparing agricultural specialists and funding agricultural research,
- funding production and social infrastructure in rural areas,
- ensuring price parity,
- funding low interest credit programs and special tax policies,
- pursuing protectionist policies for agricultural commodities.

The implementation of Aliyev's land reform required not only laws, but the sublegal acts and regulations to make the laws operational. It is an indication of resistance to the reforms that the president relied on his own State Commission for Agrarian Reform for the preparation of the sublegal acts for land reform. The government was then ordered by a special presidential decree to adopt a string of regulations prepared by the State Commission for Agrarian Reform on such key issues as land registration, surveying, parcelization, land rights, dissolution of collective and state farms, lands to be kept under state control, and rules for buying and selling land (Presidential Decree 534 "On approval of a number of legislative acts necessary for agrarian reform," January 1997).

Second Stage of Land Reform 1998–2001

By the end of 1997 the basic decrees and sublegal acts governing the farm and land reform implementation were in place, clearly defining the direction, procedures, and institutions for land and asset distribution, as well as for land titling, registration, and monitoring. Yet the actual implementation and performance of the sector were not satisfactory. For instance, land titles issued to new landowners per month in early 1997 (1,000 to 3,000) were still at the level of a trickle. By early 1998 the trickle had increased to 13,000 per month (see figure 3.2), but even this rate of issue was not sufficient for the political leadership. Second, the 1997 results in agriculture were disappointing (see table 3.2): after growing by 3% in 1996, agricultural production fell by 6% in 1997, entirely due to a sharp fall in output from corporate farms, which was not compensated fully by the growth in the individual farm sector. Furthermore, the portion of unprofitable corporate farms continued to rise. In 1997 three-quarters of enterprises were unprofitable (see table 3.3).

The second stage was aimed at accelerating the implementation of the land reform and raised another attempt at post-privatization support. The opening acts of the second phase were two presidential decrees (June 1998 and March 1999) that ordered the reorganization of the Ministry of Agriculture with the objective of eliminating its shortcomings, criticized the bureaucrats for not undertaking enough actions to "deepen" the reform, and introduced a program for post-privatization support of farms. The lack of post-privatization support measures was blamed for the fall in agricultural production in 1997, for growing losses in agricultural enterprises, and also for the halving of cotton production between 1996 and 1997 (see figure 2.8). The leadership of the State Land Committee, which was blamed for the disappointingly slow rate of land titling, was summarily replaced by the president in late 1998, and the work of both the deputy prime minister responsible for agrarian reform and the minister of agriculture was bluntly criticized. Regional governors were also criticized and urged to "rectify their mistakes."

According to the March 1999 Presidential Decree, the acceleration of the reform was to be accomplished through the traditional methods of political and organizational changes to the Ministry of Agriculture and the State Land Committee. There followed no fewer than eight decrees, laws, and resolutions from 1998 to 2000 aimed at reorganization of the Ministry of Agriculture. Decrees were issued on the topics of land cadastre, land titling, and land leasing. "Acceleration" also included legislation to regulate the distribution of land plots, touching on the topic of minimum land prices and maximum land transaction limits, which were partially aimed at preventing sweetheart land deals. The 1999 Land Code listed failure to show legitimate title and report accurately the price of land sale as grounds for refusing registration of agricultural land (article 79).

The March 1999 Presidential Decree also proposed a fairly conventional program of post-privatization support for agricultural producers. The government offered a generous package of support measures for agricultural producers, which included (1) exemption from payment of taxes for five years, except for the land tax, (2) provision of gasoline and diesel fuel at below market prices, and (3) access to low-cost credit programs available. In principle, these benefits were to be extended to farms of all organizational types—agricultural enterprises, private farms, and household plots. However, the implementation of the programs was entrusted to the Ministry of Agriculture. Although presumably slated for reorganization, the Ministry of Agriculture had only previous experience in planning implementation and control of state and collective farms under its authority. To make matters worse, the March 1999 decree held the Ministry of Agriculture accountable for the financial performance of corporate farms. Clearly, there was a fundamental knowledge gap as well as an incentive difficulty that needed to be addressed. To meet this challenge the government of Azerbaijan concluded a number of technical assistance agreements with the World Bank, borrowing funds to import the expertise for the construction of land reform support institutions (box 3.2).

Box 3.2. World Bank's Technical Assistance with Land Reform 1997–2013

The government of Azerbaijan faced very serious challenges in the implementation of the land reform and in the design of a post-privatization support program appropriate for market agriculture. The government bureaucracies had very limited capacity for implementing and controlling subordinate enterprises or designing market farm support programs. To fill the significant knowledge gap the government of Azerbaijan made ample use of borrowing from the World Bank and imported expertise to construct land reform support institutions. The World Bank assisted the government of Azerbaijan to design and implement the land reform, as well as a post-privatization program of support suitable for market agriculture. The following projects dealt directly with land and farm restructuring matters. The figures in parentheses represent the total budget costs of the projects, including the World Bank loan component, the government contribution, and the contributions of other donors.

Farm Privatization Project (FPP), 1997–2003 ($28.8 million)

The project's main objective was to accelerate the government's program for land privatization and farm restructuring of representative state and collective farms in a systematic manner and to provide models that could serve as a basis for wider geographical replicability. The project consisted of three components: (1) farm privatization support services at the national level and in the raions; (2) rehabilitation of the main irrigation water supply and drainage works; (3) a community development program.

Agricultural Development and Credit Project, 1999–2006 ($33.7 million)

The Agricultural Development and Credit Project sought to restore Azerbaijan's farming areas to former levels of productivity under a new system characterized by private family and group farms operating in private markets. The project consisted of four components: (1) a real estate registration component to support the government's national program for privatizing and titling state and collective farm land and to develop and implement the organizational and legal framework for a unified real estate cadastre system; (2) a rural finance component to establish local financial intermediaries—credit cooperatives and groups of jointly liable borrowers; (3) an information and advisory services component to increase farmers' access to information, advice, and training; and (4) a rural policy unit component to assist the government in developing an agricultural strategy.

Second Agricultural Development and Credit Project, 2006–11 ($57.7 million)

The Second Agricultural Development and Credit Project aimed to increase rural productivity and incomes by enhancing the access of farmers and small and medium rural enterprises to rural business and agricultural support services, including financial, advisory, and veterinary services.

Azerbaijan Real Estate Registration Project, 2007–13 ($38.57 million)

The objective of the Azerbaijan Real Estate Registration Project is to set up a reliable, transparent, and efficient real estate registration system supporting the real property markets, as well as suitable systems for the management and use of state-owned immovable property.

It may be premature to judge to what extent these technical assistance efforts have been successful, but it should be noted that the traditional thinking still prevails. The government approach to post-privatization support continues to emphasize subsidies and cost reimbursement to farmers. The latest example is a January 2007 Presidential Decree that ordered the government to reimburse half the farmers' costs for fuel and fertilizers (see table 3.5).

Implementation of Land Reform: Sweeping Distribution to Rural Population

The pressure applied by the president on the government bureaucrats during the second stage of land reform produced undeniable results. The titling of privatized land accelerated phenomenally in the second half of 1998 (figure 3.2). In response to the president's prodding, the number of titles issued increased from 13,000 per month in the beginning of 1998 to 80,000 per month in the last quarter of that year. Within just six months, between June–July and December 1998, fully 500,000 titles, or more than 50% of the total number of titles, were issued to the new landowners. After 1998 the titling activity slowed down considerably, simply because the task had been largely completed: there were no more rural people waiting to receive land.

According to the State Land Committee, 830,000 rural households outside Nagorno-Karabakh and other regions occupied by Armenian forces were eligible to receive land shares in the form of physical plots from land previously used by former collective and state farms. Up to August 2000, land titles were actually distributed to 807,000 households, or 97% of the entitled population. Judging by land titling, we see that the basic distribution phase of land reform in Azerbaijan took less than two years to implement.

The process of land distribution encompassed 3.2 million people (82% of the rural population in all of Azerbaijan, including Nagorno-Karabakh and the occupied districts), who received 1.3 million hectares in private ownership in a matter of three years, between 1996 and 1999. This land was allocated through privatization of land previously held by collective and state farms.

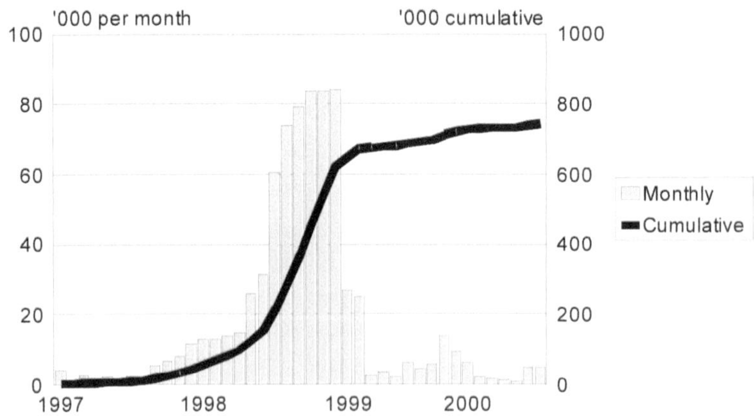

FIGURE 3.2
Land titles issued 1997–2000 (by month and cumulatively). Source: Mamedov (2000).

The universality of land distribution in Azerbaijan, as in other CIS countries, has resulted in small family holdings. The average land share turned out to be 0.43 hectares, and the average allocation per family (given four people in an average family) was around 1.7 hectares. There was considerable variability across raions, with the average land share ranging from 0.10 hectares in Lankaran to 1.26 hectares in Neftechala. The range of total family allocations was much broader, from 0.4 hectares to 5.4 hectares (again in Lankaran and Neftechala, respectively). Figure 3.3 shows the distribution of land shares and total family allocations in 52 regions.

These national data are reinforced by the World Bank survey from 2003, which confirms that land distribution in Azerbaijan was a highly egalitarian process. On a per capita basis, 70% of families received up to 0.5 hectare per person and another 25% received between 0.5 and 1.5 hectares. Among families, 83% received not more than 3.5 hectares in total. In the large, there was no evidence of favoritism in the implementation of land distribution.

Distribution of land to the rural population led to elimination of large-scale agricultural enterprises inherited from the Soviet period and dramatically increased the share of land controlled by small family farms (see chapter 4 for detailed data). This process is reflected in figure 3.4, which shows the land concentration curves for Azerbaijan and two other countries for comparison—USA as an example of an established market economy and Hungary, an advanced transition country in Central Eastern Europe.

The land concentration curves are standard Lorenz curves in which the horizontal axis is the cumulative percent of farms in each country and the vertical axis is the cumulative percent of landholdings in these farms. The diagonal line corresponds to the case of uniform or equal distribution of landholdings over farms: 50% of farms hold 50% of land and 80% of farms hold 80% of land. In reality, there is always a certain concentration of land in large farms, and the Lorenz curve bulges downward away from the diagonal. The area of the bulge is a measure of concentration or inequality (the so-called Gini index). Thus, in the USA (gray curve) 80% of farms control 40% of land, and 60% of land is concentrated in the remaining 20% of farms. In Azerbaijan, according to the 2002 agricultural census, 80% of farms control about 25% of land, and fully 75% of land is concentrated in the remaining 20% of farms. After more than five years of intensive land reform Azerbaijan was characterized by greater concentration of landholdings than the USA (with a large bulge or Gini index). Yet the concentration of land in Azerbaijan was much less than in Hungary, where 80% of farms, after 15 years of reforms, controlled about 5% of land and nearly 95% of land was in the remaining 20% of farms. We thus conclude that Azerbaijan shifted significantly toward the market curve represented by the USA, moving away from the sharply dual

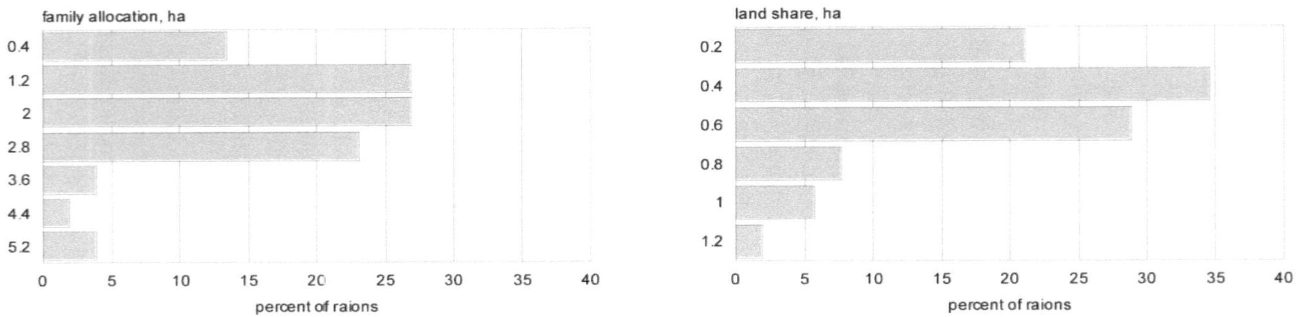

FIGURE 3.3
Distribution of land share size and total family allocation over 52 raions. Source: Mamedov (2000).

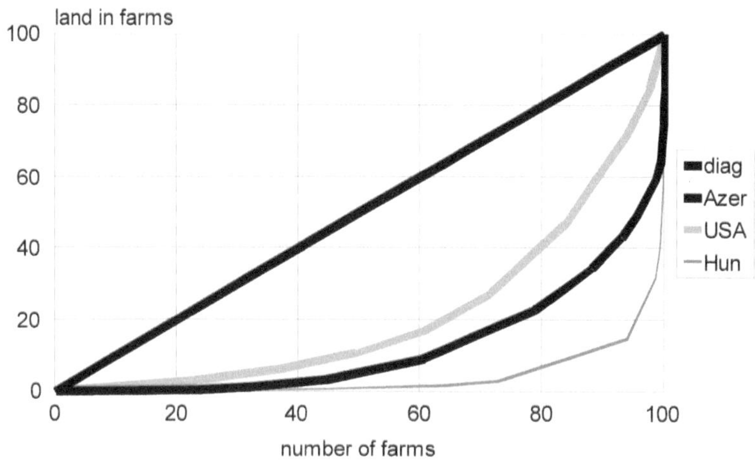

FIGURE 3.4
Concentration of agricultural land in farm holdings in Azerbaijan compared with the USA and Hungary. Source: Azerbaijan data from 2002 agricultural census; Hungary from 2003 Farm Structure Survey; USA from the Statistical Abstract of the United States.

land concentration curve that characterized the Soviet era and still prevails in Hungary (as well as other transition countries regardless of EU membership, such as Russia, Ukraine, Bulgaria, the Czech Republic, and Slovakia). The shift toward a more market-compliant farm structure is important because we expect it to produce improvements in efficiency and productivity of Azerbaijani agriculture by correcting distortions that characterized the Soviet era.

Notes

1. The State Land Committee was subsequently charged with carrying out the necessary land survey work for division of land into parcels, as well as issuing land titles (Presidential Decree 534 "On the Confirmation of a Number of Legal Acts for Agrarian Reform," 10 January 1997).

2. A legal restriction stipulated that the price of land in buy-and-sell transactions could not be less than regionally differentiated price set by the state. The State Land Committee was charged with determining the state-set price floor for land parcels (the methodology and values were later described and listed in Cabinet of Ministers Decree 158 "On determining new normative prices of land in the Azerbaijan Republic," 23 July 1998).

4

Outcomes of Reform: Transition to Individual Farming and Sector Recovery

THE IMPLEMENTATION OF THE Aliyev land reform produced a shift from collective to individual farming in an unprecedentedly short time. While most CIS countries spent a decade or longer debating and implementing share-based land distribution, land and farm assets in Azerbaijan were distributed to the rural population within four short years. In 1995–96, some 2,000 corporate farms (i.e., former collectives) controlled 4 million hectares of agricultural land; four years later, in 2000, the land managed by former collectives had dropped to 1 million hectares and the rest had shifted to individual users. The share of arable land displayed an even more dramatic shift, with individual farms increasing their holdings from 10% to 80% of arable land between 1995 and 1999. The shift in land use produced a virtually total concentration of agricultural production in individual farms, as their share in agricultural output (GAO) reached 97% of the country's total. By 2000, Azerbaijan's agriculture had totally transformed to individual agriculture.

Rapid individualization of farmland had an immediate positive impact on agricultural production. The decline in agricultural production that began in 1984 changed to growth in 1996–97, just as individualization of farming in Azerbaijan took off. Growth in agricultural production was completely attributable to growth in individual farms, and much of this was the result of increases in crop yields. Yields increased both as a result of the movement of farming from low-yield corporate farms to more productive individual farms and as a result of an overall increase in yields (in both individual and corporate farms) after 1999 due to more supportive policies for agriculture.

Changing Farm Structure: From Collective to Individual Agriculture

According to the reform laws passed in 1995–96, the traditional state and collective farms were to be restructured into any number of organizational forms—corporate farms with jointly owned land and assets run by hired managers, family farms (including newly created peasant farms and traditional household plots) operating with privately owned land and assets, and state agricultural enterprises based on state-owned land and assets. Though the state did not prescribe the legal form of future agricultural enterprises, the responsibility for carrying out farm reform was entrusted to local Agricultural Reform Committees, the chairmen of which were the heads of local government accountable directly to the president.

Many types of enterprises were to remain state property. These included scientific research facilities, education facilities, experimental farms, veterinary and phytosanitary services, hybrid seed farms, livestock selection farms, fishery enterprises, wildlife and nature preserves, important livestock and poultry concerns, irrigation and land improvement facilities, agricultural machinery producers and repair facilities, and other objects of special importance. Main irrigation and land improvement facilities were to remain state property, while facilities located within state and collective farms could be transferred to municipal property or be owned jointly by the successors to state and collective farms. State property of local importance could be transferred to municipal ownership.

In table 4.1 the new organizational forms created from former collective and state farms are shown under the heading of restructured private corporate farms. Their number increased from nil in 1990 to 2,000 in 2004. The remaining state-owned agricultural enterprises (some 300 of them after 2000) are shown under "socialized" farms. The total number of corporate farms in Azerbaijan did not change much, as former collective and state farms transformed into new private corporate farms without dismantling. Yet the agricultural land controlled by the corporate farm sector shrank dramatically in the course of reforms: from about 4 million hectares in 1990–96 to 1 million hectares after 1999 (table 4.1, figure 4.1). Corporate farms also underwent significant downsizing in the process of reform, as their average size dropped from 1,500 hectares in the early 1990s to 500 hectares after 1999 (figure 4.1).

In addition to corporate farms, table 4.1 also shows the growth in the sector of registered peasant farms created as independent family-owned units outside the former collectivist framework. Registered peasant farms (less than 3,000 in 2004) are only a small subset of some 800,000 family or household farms that comprise the individual farming sector in Azerbaijan. Based on

TABLE 4.1
Number of Farms and Agricultural Land in Use by Farms of Different Organizational Forms (End of Year)

*Farms**	*"Socialized" Farms*	*Restructured Private Corporate Farms*	*Total Number of Corporate (Registered)*	*Peasant Farms '000 ha*	*Ag Land in Corporate Farms '000 ha*	*Ag Land in Registered Peasant Farms '000 ha*
1990	3014	—	3014	66	4023	
1991	3098	14	3112	95	4040	
1992	2621	134	2755	320	4045	
1993	2495	140	2635	440	4079	
1994	2289	117	2406	815	4098	
1995	2172	315	2487	1999	4036	
1996	1867	746	2613	4110	4041	
1997	905	1280	2185	5671	2511	
1998	758	4847	5605	3721	1673	
1999	516	2795	3311	3613	1879	
2000	410	2500	2910	3248	1162	30.4
2001	249	2171	2420	2604	941	23.4
2002	321	1663	1984	2589	1131	20.1
2003	304	1839	2143	2607	1187	21.7
2004	304	1937	2241	2661	1188	25.2
2005	303	1941	2244	2681	1182	22.6

*Collective farms, state farms, and other state agricultural enterprises.
Sources: Statistical Committee of Azerbaijan (2006b, 2006f, 2007); statistical annex table A.13.

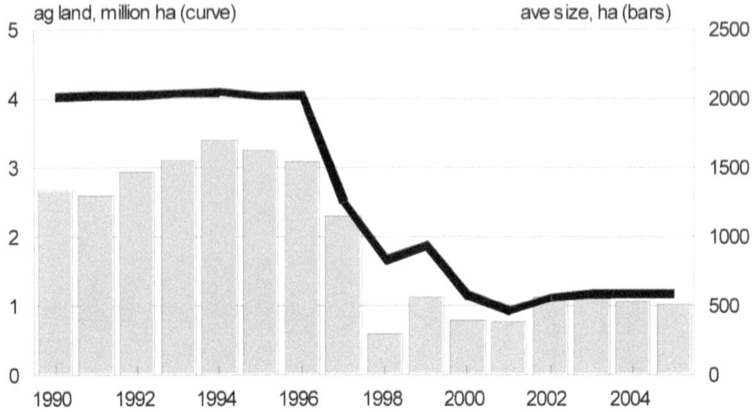

FIGURE 4.1
Agricultural land in corporate farms (curve) and average farm size (bars) 1990–2005. Source: See table 4.1.

statistics available since 2000, the average size of a registered peasant farm is around 9 hectares, which is an order of magnitude less than the size of the average corporate farm (500 hectares).

Growth of the Individual Sector: Land and Livestock

Aliyev's reforms of 1995–96 led to a spectacular increase in the amount of land in individual use, i.e., land in household plots and peasant farms. During the 1980s, when the individual sector consisted only of household plots, agricultural land in individual use moderately increased from 110,000 hectares to 130,000 hectares, generally remaining at a level of about 3% of all agricultural land in the country. The individual component of agricultural land continued increasing slowly during the early 1990s, as the new category of peasant farms began to emerge, and then showed the first signs of abrupt increase in response to the land reform legislation of 1995–96: in these two years, land in individual use jumped from 150,000 hectares to 270,000 hectares, its share doubling from 3% to 6% of agricultural land in Azerbaijan. This immediate response to the reforms of 1995–96 is clearly seen in the last two black bars in figure 4.2, despite the generally low level of land in individual use.

The land use patterns changed rapidly during the next three years 1997–99, and already in 2000, official statistics report more than 1.5 million hectares of agricultural land in individual use (gray bars in figure 4.2; household plots and peasant farms combined). Since 2000 the share of agricultural land in

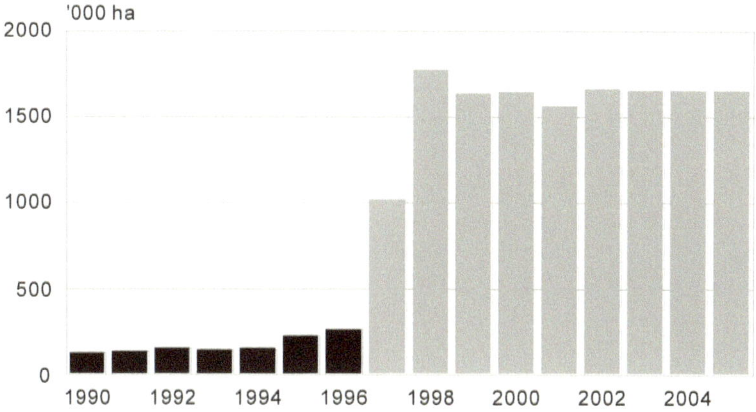

FIGURE 4.2
Agricultural land in individual use 1990–2005 (thou. ha). Source: Statistical annex table A.13.

individual use has remained at around 35%—up from 3% during the 1980s and the early 1990s (figure 4.3).

Taking 800,000 as the approximate number of rural households in Azerbaijan since 1990 (this is the number according to the 1999 population census), we obtain that during the first phase of land reform the average household plot doubled from 0.17 hectares in 1990 to 0.33 in 1996. In the next phase, after 1999, the average plot size in the individual sector reached 2.1 hectares, 12 times the size in 1990. If we moreover assume that common (municipal) land—see below—is largely used by rural households, not corporate farms, the average plot size including common land rises to 4.3 hectares.

The process of land distribution encompassed 3.2 million people (82% of the rural population in all of Azerbaijan, including Nagorno-Karabakh and the occupied districts), who received 1.3 million hectares in private ownership. This land was allocated through privatization of land previously held by collective and state farms. It was added to other individual holdings represented by household plots and land in peasant farms (about 200,000 hectares), bringing the agricultural land in individual use to over 1.5 million hectares, or nearly 40% of Azerbaijan's total agricultural land (figure 4.3).

The privatization of livestock also proceeded swiftly and decisively, but it followed a somewhat different pattern due to different initial conditions. While individual farms cultivated only 3% of land during the 1980s, the livestock herd in the household sector was always around 50% of all animals in the country. Immediately after independence, the number of animals in rural households began to grow, increasing from 1.4 million standard head, or 50%

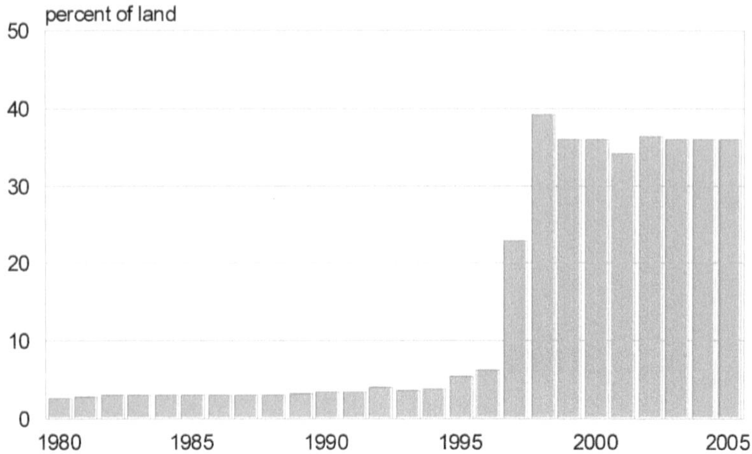

FIGURE 4.3
Share of agricultural land in individual use 1980–2005 (percent). Source: Statistical annex table A.13.

of all animals, in 1990 to 2 million standard head, or 90% of all animals, in 1996 (figure 4.4). After that the share of rural households stabilized at 97% of the total herd, although the absolute number of animals continued to increase quite steeply, exceeding 3.5 million head in 2007–08.

The overall changes in the structure of land use in Azerbaijan since 1990 are summarized in figure 4.5. This graph shows the sharp increase in the ag-

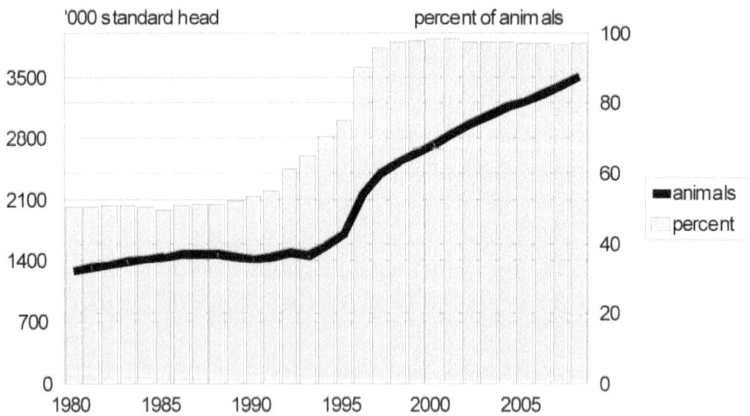

FIGURE 4.4
Livestock herd in individual farms 1980–2005 (bars—total herd in thousand standard head; curve—percent of animals in individual farms). Source: Statistical Committee of Azerbaijan (2006e).

ricultural land used by the individual sector and the correspondingly sharp decrease—almost collapse—in the agricultural land endowment of corporate farms—the successors of the Soviet-era agricultural enterprises.

Figure 4.5 also highlights another feature of agricultural land structure in Azerbaijan, namely the creation of a huge category of municipal (or common) land that accounts for 40% of all agricultural land in the country. Prior to 2000 land use was reported for individual and corporate farms, whose shares added up to 100% for a total of around 4.3 million hectares of agricultural land. Since 2000, land use is reported in three categories: corporate farms (formerly called "farm enterprises" or "agricultural enterprises"), individual farms (household plots and peasant farms combined), and a new category of land in common use, which according to the 1996 Law of Land Reform is municipally owned land.

The year-by-year data of figure 4.5 on the structure of land use by farm type are summarized in the form of averages in table 4.2, which demonstrates the change in land use patterns between 1990–96 and 2000–05: the share of corporate farms dropped from 96% to a mere 25%, while the share of individual farms on average increased from 4% to 36%. In fact this is just a lower bound on the share of land in individual farms, because as we have noted previously municipal (common) land is mostly used by rural families, not by corporate farms. Adding municipal land to individual farms, we conclude that the individual sector in fact may be using as much as 75% of all agricultural land in Azerbaijan—including both the officially allocated component and municipal land.

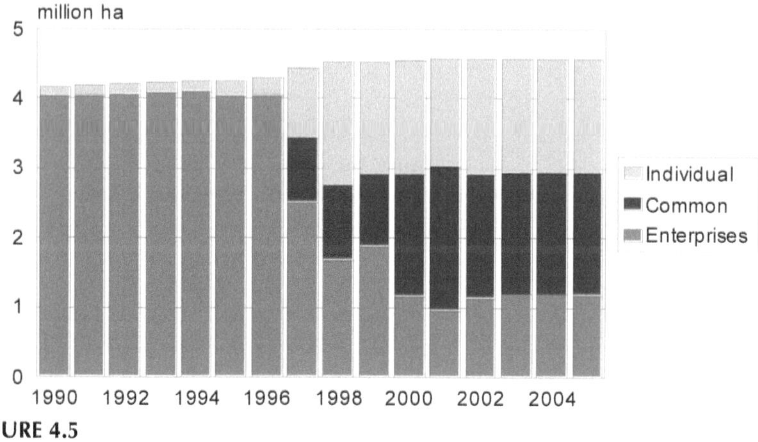

FIGURE 4.5
Agricultural land by different types of users (million hectares). Source: Statistical annex table A.13.

TABLE 4.2
Distribution of Agricultural Land by Types of Users, in Percent (Averages for 1990–96 and 2000–05)

	1990–96	*2000–05*
Corporate farms	96	25
Individual farms	4	36
Common land	0	40
Total	100	100

Source: Statistical annex table A.13.

Table 4.3 recasts basically the same data in a different format to show the structure of land use in farms of different types, separating the individual sector into peasant farms and household plots. Corporate farms rely much more heavily on pastures than either peasant farms or household plots, which mostly consist of arable land. Commons—i.e., the agricultural land component of municipally owned land—are 98% pastures and only 2% arable land.

Since individual farms—peasant farms and household plots—use mostly arable land, with very little pastures and meadows in their holdings, the share of arable land in individual use is more than double the share of agricultural land. Thus, as much as 80% of arable land is used by individual farms (black curve in figure 4.6), compared with about 40% of agricultural land (dark gray bars in figure 4.6). The share of individual farms in cropped land (i.e., land actually sown to crops) is even higher, reaching 95%–98% in recent years. This provides an early indication of the inefficiency of corporate farms, which control 20% of arable land but cultivate only 2% of sown area.

TABLE 4.3
Structure of Land Use in Farms of Different Types, in Percent (Averages for 2000–05)

	Arable Land	*Pastures*	*Orchards Vineyards Other*	*Agricultural Land*
Corporate farms	31	62	7	100
Peasant farms	78	11	11	100
Household plots	84	5	11	100
Common land	2	98	0	100

Source: Land balance tables from Statistical Committee of Azerbaijan.

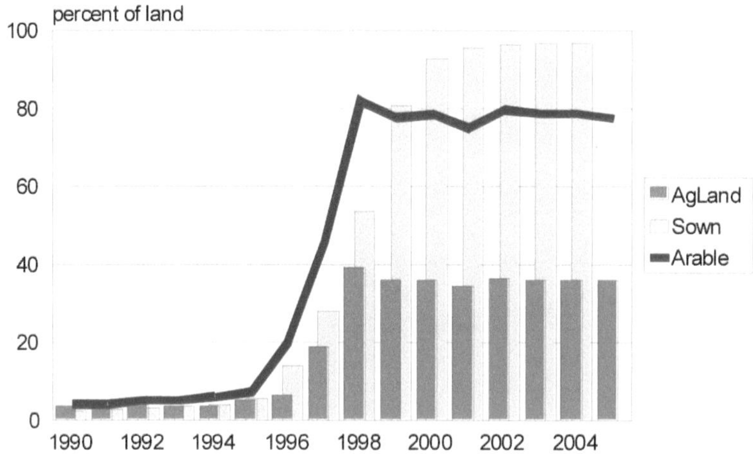

FIGURE 4.6
Share of land in individual use: Agricultural, arable, and sown land 1990–2005. Source: Statistical Committee of Azerbaijan (2006b); arable land from statistical annex table A.14.

Individualization and Recovery

The changing structure of land use had an immediate impact on the structure of agricultural production. The importance of the individual sector had been rising already during the 1980s, long before independence and land reform. The share of individual farms—just the small household plots during the Soviet era—had almost doubled from about 20% of gross agricultural output (GAO) in the early 1980s to nearly 40% in 1990. This was a huge achievement, given that the household plots at that time controlled about 3% of agricultural land in the country, but on the whole it was not different from the land–output relationship observed in other former Soviet republics. The share of individual farms continued to increase during the sluggish and half-hearted reforms in the first years of independence, reaching 60% of GAO by 1995, but it literally took off with the launching of the 1996 land reform, rising to 97% of GAO in 2000–03 (figure 4.7).

The Aliyev land reform totally changed the face of agriculture in Azerbaijan: from agriculture with predominant concentration of production and land in collective farms it quickly evolved into agriculture based almost exclusively on individual farms. This is unparalleled among the CIS countries, as even in Moldova and Ukraine, with their massive land-share conversion programs, individual agriculture contributes 60%–70% of GAO (table 4.4). Only Armenia and Georgia, Azerbaijan's Transcaucasian neighbors, match

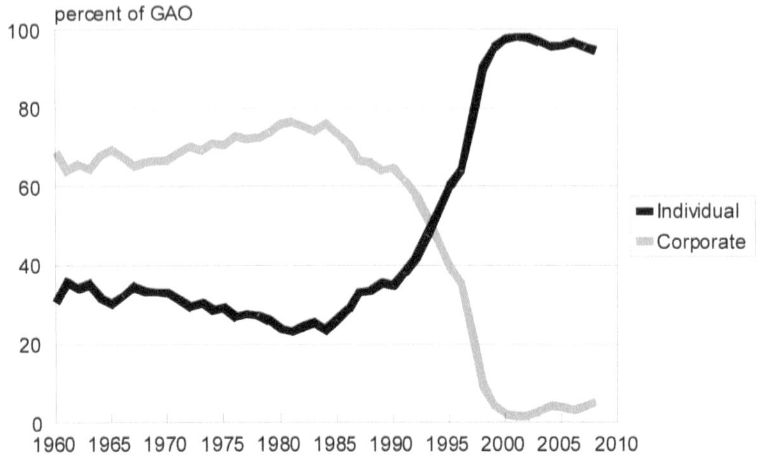

FIGURE 4.7
Share of GAO produced by individual and corporate farms 1960–2008. Source: Statistical Committee of Azerbaijan (2006b).

this level of individualization of agricultural production, but the path of land reform in these two countries was substantially different from the prevailing model in the CIS: they resolutely disbanded the collective farms back in 1992 and directly distributed land plots to the population, without resorting to any share-conversion mechanisms. Azerbaijan followed essentially the same process of land reform as Armenia and Georgia, but started much later, in 1996.

There is a clear link between the individualization of Azerbaijan's agriculture and economic recovery. The steep decline of agricultural production that began in 1984 changed to growth in 1996–97, and the upward trend has continued ever since (black curve in figure 4.8). The turning point in agriculture clearly coincides with the timing of Aliyev's land privatization efforts, when the share of agricultural land in individual farms increased rapidly from 5% in 1996 to 25% in 1998 and further to 35% in subsequent years (bars in figure 4.8).

Agricultural recovery went hand in hand with general economic recovery as manifested by GDP growth (gray curve in figure 4.8). This is not at all surprising, as we generally observe a close positive correlation between GDP growth and agricultural growth (Lerman, Csaki, and Feder, 2004). In most cases it is impossible to establish the direction of causality between the growth of these two indicators, but it is usually claimed that a favorable economic environment (GDP growth) is conducive to agricultural growth. GDP growth in Azerbaijan was made possible by the same market-oriented reform programs that energized agriculture, and individualization of land is one of the most prominent manifestations of these programs.

TABLE 4.4
Individualization of Agriculture in Azerbaijan and Selected CIS Countries (2004)

	Agricultural Land in Individual Use, %	*Arable Land in Individual Use %*	*Share of Individual Farms in GAO, %*	*GAO Produced by Individual Farms (1990=100)*	*GAO Produced by Corporate Farms (1990=100)*
Azerbaijan	38	80	97	232	5
Russia	16	18	60	136	43
Ukraine	41	41	70	140	35
Moldova	42	47	75	185	17
Armenia	34	65	96	157	n.a.
Georgia	37	46	98	65	n.a.

Sources: Statistical Committee of Azerbaijan (2006f), Statistical Committee of Russian Federation (2005), Lerman et al. (2007), Department of Statistics and Sociology of the Republic of Moldova (2004), National Statistical Service of the Republic of Armenia (2005), Ministry of Economic Development of Georgia (2005).

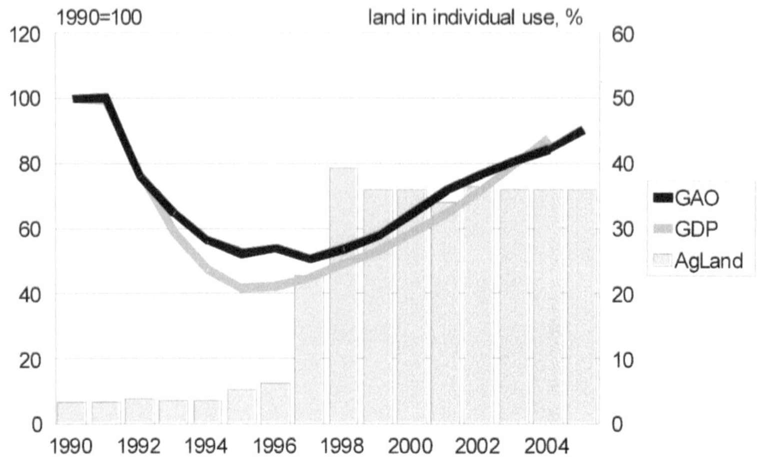

FIGURE 4.8
Economic recovery and growth of individual farming. Source: Statistical annex tables A.6 (for GDP, GAO) and A.13 (for land in individual use).

Decomposing the agricultural output index into two components—the output of the corporate farm sector and the output of the individual sector—we clearly see that the recovery after 1996–97 is entirely attributable to the growth of production in individual farms (thick black curve in figure 4.9), as the output of corporate farms continued its steady decline over the years (gray curve). The different growth behavior of the individual and corporate farms reinforces the conjecture that the recovery in agriculture is indeed linked with the progress in land reform after 1995.

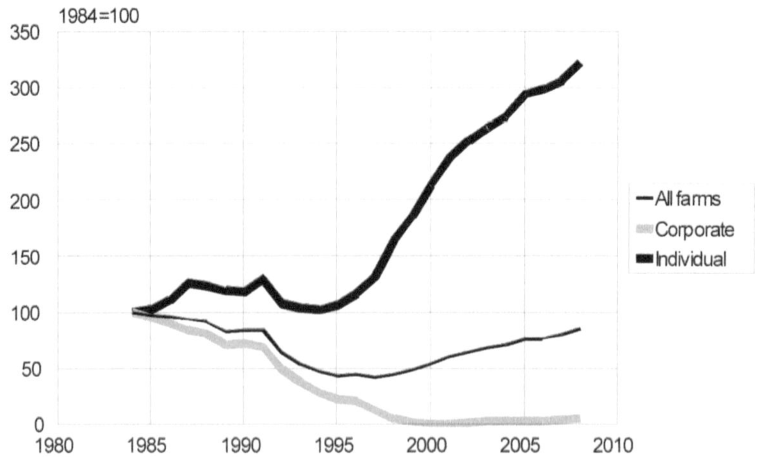

FIGURE 4.9
GAO by farm type (in percent of 1984). Source: Statistical annex table A.6.

Individualization and Productivity

An alternative view of the sectoral impacts of reform can be formed by examining the change in crop yields and in per capita food production around the 1999 watershed. The yields of all main crops—cereals, sugar beet, potatoes, melons, fruits—increased between the "pre-reform" period 1995–99 and the period since 2000 (table 4.5; the differences between the two periods are statistically significant). Vegetables are the only commodity for which the reported average yields decreased. Cotton and grapes are not included in the table: their yields also increased, but the total production volume of these commodities collapsed during the 1990s and they completely lost their importance in Azeri agriculture.

To get an overall picture of the behavior of crop yields over time, we aggregated the yields of seven major crops—cereals, cotton, sunflower, potatoes, vegetables, fruits, and grapes—separately for individual farms and corporate farms. The aggregated yields for each sector were constructed for each year between 1990 and 2005 as the sum of specific crop yields weighted by the share of the area of the specific crop in the total area for the corresponding farm sector. The aggregated yields produced by these calculations are technically expressed in centners per ha, but these are "weighted" centners aggregating seven different commodities. The aggregated yields for individual and corporate farms are shown in figure 4.10 by the two roughly parallel thick curves that seem to decline together until 1999 and rise thereafter. Throughout the entire period 1990–2005 the aggregated yields of individual farms (thick black curve) are substantially higher than the aggregated yields of corporate farms (thick gray curve).

In order to illustrate graphically the impact on yields of the transition from corporate to individual farming in Azerbaijan, we constructed a third aggregate yield series calculated as the average of the series for individual and corporate farms weighted by the percent of cropped land in corporate and individual

TABLE 4.5
Average Crop Yields for Two Consecutive Periods: 1995–99 and 2000–05 (ton/ha)

	1995–99	*2000–05*	*Change in Percent*
Grain	1.7	2.6	53
Sugar beet	10.8	26.8	148
Potatoes	9.4	11.9	27
Vegetables	15.4	13.7	-11
Melons	7.9	11.0	39
Fruits	4.4	6.2	41

Source: Statistical Committee of Azerbaijan (various years).

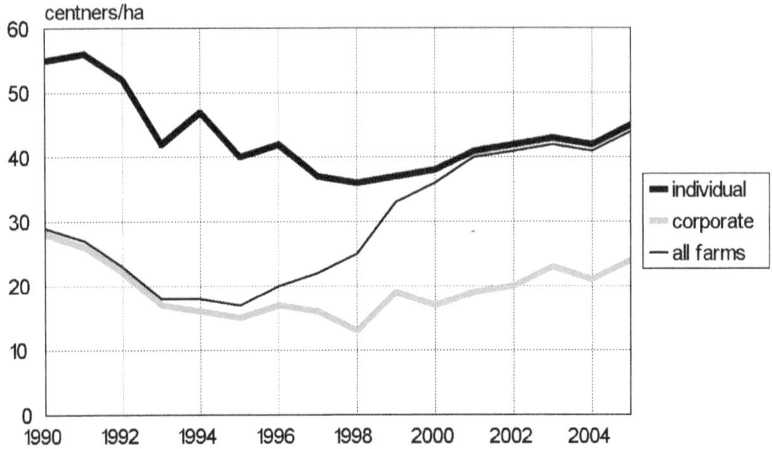

FIGURE 4.10
Aggregated crop yields for individual and corporate farms 1990–2005 (centners/ha). Source: aggregations based on reported yields in Statistical Committee of Azerbaijan (various years).

farms. The aggregated crop yields for all farms are shown by the thin black curve in figure 4.10. The aggregated crop yields for all farms rose by a factor of 2.7 between 1995 and 2005, from 17 to 44 "aggregated" centners per ha.

This extraordinary rise in yields was the result of the "double yield increase" effect combining the impact of the transition from corporate to individual farms as well as the overall increase in yields in both sectors since 1998–99. As the share of individual farms in cropped land increased from 2%–3% in the early 1990s to 98% after 2000 (see figure 4.6), the aggregated yield curve was pushed up from the lower level corresponding to yields in corporate farms to the higher level corresponding to yields in individual farms. This "farm type" effect bridging over the vertical distance between the yields curves for corporate and individual farms was further augmented by the overall increase of yields observed after 1999 in both sectors. This "double yield increase" effect was the basis for the recovery of crop production in Azerbaijan.

The robust growth in agricultural production since 2000 outstripped the fairly rapid population increase. As a result, food production per capita generally increased, as is evident from figure 4.11 that shows the percentage change between the average per capita production of selected commodities in 1995–99 and 2000–05. The per capita production of grain, potatoes, and vegetables increased particularly strongly between 1995–99 and 2000–05, but meat and milk production per capita also rose by 20%–30% between the two periods on both sides of the reform watershed.

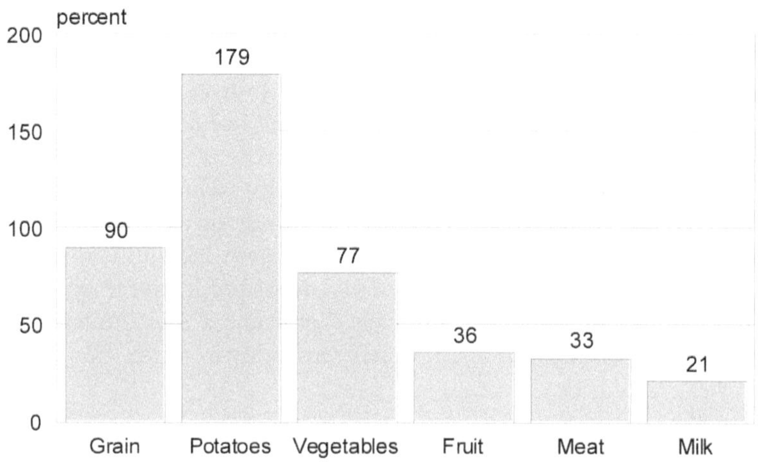

FIGURE 4.11
Change in per capita food production between the average levels in 1995–99 and 2000–05 (percent). Source: Statistical Committee of Azerbaijan (various years).

The increase in yields and in per capita production of agricultural commodities was noticed already in early 2000 by Ministry of Agriculture officials, who proudly attributed it to the new land policy. Combined with the observed link between the recovery of GAO and farm individualization (see figure 4.8), all this adds up to compelling evidence of positive impacts of land reform on agricultural performance.

The curves in figure 4.10 clearly demonstrate that individual farms had a consistent advantage in yields over corporate farms both before and after the reform. Crop yields expressed in physical units of production per hectare in effect measure the partial productivity of land. An alternative (and perhaps more conventional) way to calculate partial productivity of land is by taking

TABLE 4.6
Productivity Measures for Individual and Corporate Farms (2003 World Bank Survey)

	Number of Farm Type	*Land Respondents*	*Labor Productivity*	*TFP*
Individual farms	65	1,762	7,803	2.3
Corporate farms	15	840	3,692	1.0
All farms	80	1,589	7,032	2.1

Note: Individual farms in this table are only peasant farms, as no appropriate data were available in the survey for household plots. Definitions of productivity measures: land productivity—the value of output per ha (in thou. manats); labor productivity—the value of output per annual work unit (in thou. manats); TFP—the ratio of the value of output to total cost of inputs as reported in the survey. Source: Dudwick, Fock, and Sedik (2007).

the value of output (in money terms) per hectare. A calculation of partial productivity of land based on data from the 2003 World Bank farm survey (albeit at a single point in time) also demonstrates that individual farms on average achieve higher land productivity than corporate farms (table 4.6). Similar gaps are observed for agricultural labor productivity (calculated as the value of production per worker), as well as total factor productivity (TFP), calculated as the ratio of the value of output to the aggregated cost of all inputs reported in the survey.[1] While the partial productivity measures and total factor productivity suggest that family farms are more productive than corporate farms, the differences are not statistically significant at the 10% level due to the smallness of the samples and the large variability in survey data.

Note

1. This calculation provides a strict accounting measure of TFP equivalent to profit margin, because the denominator in this ratio is the accounting value of inputs from farm financial statements. Strictly speaking, TFP should be calculated using market prices to value production and the cost of inputs used in production. The difference between the accounting TFP shown in table 4.6 and the theoretically preferred TFP may or may not be large, depending upon how farms choose to value input use in their financial statements.

5

Outcomes of Reform: Rural Incomes and Poverty

THE BEST VINDICATION OF THE radical land reform in Azerbaijan is in its results. Chapter 4 outlined the growth in individual farming in Azerbaijan and established the link between individualization and recovery of agricultural output. In this chapter we take up the issue of the link between land reform, rural incomes, and rural poverty. How did land reform in Azerbaijan impact the welfare of rural households?

Land reform in Azerbaijan had two important effects that worked to reduce poverty in rural areas. First, it increased per capita family incomes through a one-off transfer of productive assets (land, livestock, and farm machinery) from corporate farms to households. In chapter 3 it was noted that the critical financial state of corporate farms, three-quarters of which were unprofitable in 1997, meant that wage arrears in these farms were the rule. Thus, the redistribution of the assets of these unprofitable corporate farms laid the foundations for a permanent increase in rural household incomes.

Official statistics as well as the 2003 World Bank survey indicate that land reform resulted in an increase in family holdings by approximately 2 hectares per household. We have much less reliable information on the size of the transfer of livestock per household, and virtually no information on distribution of farm machinery. A comparison of livestock holdings in the 1995 and 2001 surveys indicates a difference of a little more than one cow unit per household, though it is difficult to accept this as a precise estimate of the magnitude of the transfer. There are no survey data indicating how much farm machinery was transferred to individual households.

These one-off transfers from former collective and state farms to individual farms increased crop yields (see figure 4.10). Higher yields led to higher farm production, improving family well-being both through higher consumption (direct effect of land reform) and through additional cash income from sales of surplus products (indirect effect). The land reform in Azerbaijan, by immediately allowing buying, selling, and (most importantly) leasing of land, also contributed to the efficiency with which agricultural products were produced by redistributing production from those households that did not wish to till all owned land to those who wished to cultivate more than they owned. The latter group may be presumed to be made up of the more entrepreneurial and perhaps more efficient producers.

A second important characteristic of land reform in Azerbaijan was that distribution of land was highly pro-poor. To see this, consider the size of distributed land parcels by income level. A comparison of land distributed (per capita) to households by per capita income quintile from the 2003 World Bank survey indicates no significant differences between lower and higher income households. The lowest quintile group of households received slightly more land, though the differences were not statistically significant at the 10% level. Thus, within the survey sample, there seems to be no discernible bias in the size of land distributed based on income. This finding is consistent with further evidence from the 2003 World Bank survey that over 90% of respondents viewed the land distribution in Azerbaijan as fair.

The distribution of equal land parcels to lower and higher income households is pro-poor in the same way that an equal subsidy payment to lower and higher income households is pro-poor. A given absolute subsidy increases the income of the poor by a greater percentage than for the rich. We can construct an indicator of the "income augmentation effect" of the initial parcel distribution by comparing the ratio of the present value of the future per capita income stream to current income for poorer and richer households. This comparison shows that the income augmentation for the poorest quintile of households in Azerbaijan was three times that of the same for the richest quintile.

In sum, land reform was a principal driver of rural poverty reduction in Azerbaijan. It raised the mean consumption of rural inhabitants and effected a pro-poor change in asset distribution which can be presumed to entail a pro-poor change in income, at least in the short run. However, land reform alone was no guarantee that rural poverty fell during the period of its implementation. There were other forces that undoubtedly led to increases in rural poverty. Losses of jobs in the food processing industry led to substantial income losses for the rural population. Moreover, a significant deterioration in rural services, both in an absolute sense and when compared to urban services, led to a real deterioration in living standards in rural areas.

On balance, it is difficult to say with certainty whether poverty of rural inhabitants increased or decreased during the period of land reform considered here (1996–2003). However, three facts emerge quite clearly from the evidence. First, land reform was an important driver of poverty reduction. Second, there was a substantial decrease in rural income poverty from 2002 to 2003 and again from 2003 to 2004.[1] And last, despite improvements in income poverty, 80% of rural inhabitants in Azerbaijan reported in the 2003 World Bank survey that they had seen no substantial increase in well-being since 2000. This was at a time when production in individual households grew by 7.4% per year and when income poverty was falling rapidly. Clearly, the sharp drop in rural services and the lack of improvement thereof led people to feel a lot worse, despite substantial growth in agricultural output and (presumably) rural incomes, and a documented fall in rural income poverty.

Land Reform and Rural Incomes

How did land reform in Azerbaijan impact the incomes of rural households? The lack of comparable household surveys for the years 1995 to 2001 prevents a simple and direct answer to this question. Official statistics and cross-section household surveys with dissimilar income and expenditure aggregates, varying degrees of representativeness, and different sampling structures are the only source of information for the period of interest, 1995 to 2001 (see table A in the introduction).

A more indirect, analytical approach using cross-section survey information must be used to assess the connection between land reform and rural incomes in the crucial period from 1995 to 2001. We first demonstrate that there is a strong analytical connection between land and rural incomes by citing cross-section survey evidence showing that larger individual farms tend to have higher family incomes and higher well-being. Commercialization of individual farms is also linked with both family incomes and well-being. This cross-section evidence suggests that it is quite likely that the one-off distribution of land and livestock that was land reform in Azerbaijan raised mean per capita household expenditures in rural areas.

Land Reform Increased the Average Size of Family Holdings

One of the most immediate outcomes of land reform in Azerbaijan (as in other CIS countries) was an increase in the average size of family holdings.

TABLE 5.1
Land Ownership Before and After Reforms

	Hectares
Owned before reforms (household plot)	0.2
Total owned in 2003	2.3
Household plot in 2003	0.2
Other private land in 2003	2.1
Received against land shares during reorganization of collective farm	2.1

Note: Based on 688 respondents that provided information on distribution of land shares.
Source: 2003 World Bank survey.

We have seen in chapter 4 that, according to national statistics, the average family plot increased from 0.17 hectares in 1990 to 2.1 hectares in 1999, after the second stage of land reform. Survey data provide more details of farm size. In the 2003 World Bank survey the household plot is 0.2 hectares, which is practically identical to land owned (or used) before the reform. This essentially implies that before the reform the household plot accounted for 100% of land available to the household. In 2003, on the other hand, the household plot is a mere 10% of the land owned by the household, while the remaining 90% constitutes land received against land shares during the reorganization of the local farm enterprise (table 5.1).

The land data from the 1995 and 2001 household budget surveys show that the mean plot size for households using land increased between the two points in time (from 0.2 hectares in 1995 to 1.6 hectares in 2001). Because of differences in sample design, information from the 1995 and 2001 household budget surveys should be treated as an indicator of the trend, rather than as exact estimates of land augmentation. Yet these results are clearly consistent with evidence from both national statistics and the 2003 World Bank survey regarding the impact of land reform on farm size.

Land Leasing Allowed Farm Sizes to Grow

Land owned by rural households increased on average by a factor of 12 between the early 1990s and the early 2000s (see table 5.1). However, some households do not cultivate all the land they own, while other farmers find that their 2 hectares of owned land are not sufficient for their purposes. Land leasing provides a way for redistribution of land use allowing more enterprising and more productive land users to increase the size of their farms and those not wishing to cultivate all their land to derive an income from letting others use it. The 2003 World Bank survey showed that 10% of the additional land received by households in the process of land distribution is leased out

TABLE 5.2
Land Owned and Land Used Among Rural Families

	Household Plots			
	All Households (n = *703)*	*Households Without Leased Land* (n = *651)*	*Households With Leased Land* (n = *41)*	*Peasant Farms* (n = *80)*
Total land owned, ha	2.2	2.2	3.1	11
Total land in use, ha	2.7	1.8	15.7	151
%	100	100	100	100
Household plot, %	7	10	1	—
Other owned land, %	64	89	16	7
Leased land, %	29	0	82	93
Other, %	0	1	0	0

Source: 2003 World Bank survey.

to other farmers. Thus, land leasing is not very widespread among rural households in Azerbaijan, as only 6% of respondents in the 2003 World Bank survey use leased land. However, among those who do, leased land accounts for more than 80% of total land use, and the average farm size for those using leased land is 16 hectares, compared with 1.8 hectares for households that farm owned land only (table 5.2).

The role of leased land increases with farm size. In figure 5.1 the bottom black layer represents the owned land in household plots (in hectares), while the gray triangle on top of the black layer is the leased land (the outer

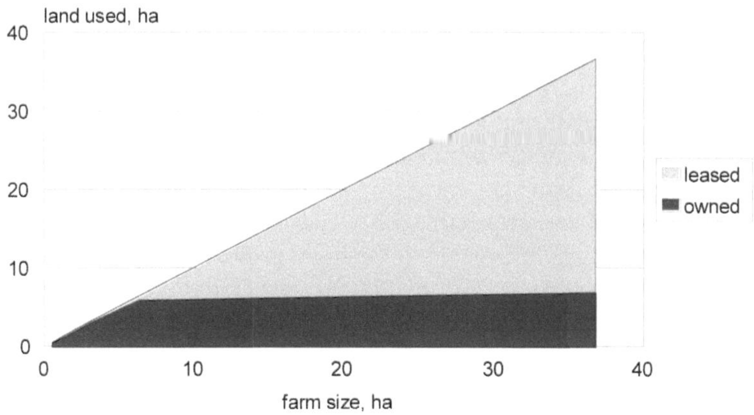

FIGURE 5.1
Use of owned and leased land in household plots. Source: 2003 World Bank survey.

boundary of the gray triangle is the total land used by the average household plot in the 2003 World Bank survey). The figure clearly shows that the share of leased land in total land used increases rapidly with the increase of farm size. There are apparently limits to the amount of land that farms can own: in figure 5.1 owned land is seen to be limited to a ceiling of about 2 hectares per household. Leasing is therefore the main mechanism that enables farmers to increase their holdings, and this mechanism is used with considerable effect in Azerbaijan. In households that lease land, total land used exceeds land owned by a large factor (16 hectares used compared with 3 hectares owned).[2] On the other hand, households that do not resort to leasing use on average less land than they own (1.8 hectares compared with 2.2 hectares owned).

Peasant farms, the second component of the individual farm sector, are substantially larger than household plots (151 hectares on average, with 11 hectares of owned land) and accordingly they make much greater use of leased land. Virtually all peasant farms lease in land (95% of peasant farms compared with only 6% of households). Leased land accounts for 93% of the holdings of the average peasant farm in the survey (compared with 29% for the average household plot and 82% for household plots with leased land). In peasant farms, the ratio of land used to land owned is 14 on average, whereas in household plots this ratio is 5.

More Land Leads to Higher Family Income

Cross-section evidence on individual farm size and family incomes from the 2003 World Bank survey shows a clear correlation between the two. Family income—both cash income and imputed income that additionally includes the value of own farm products consumed in the household—increases with the increase of farm size (figure 5.2). Farm size is measured by total land used by the family, including owned land and land leased from other owners. The average imputed income increases from 435 manat per month for smallest farms not exceeding 0.5 hectare to about 750 manat for farms larger than 5 hectares (table 5.3). The increase in family income for larger farms is mainly attributable to the rapid growth in revenue from farm sales (figure 5.3), which rises from 114 manat per month for the smallest farms to over 400 manat per month for the largest farms. The value of farm products consumed in the household also increases with farm size, but much more moderately (from 120 manat to 240 manat for the largest farms). The non-agricultural component of family income (including wages, social transfers, and other non-farm income) is independent of family size, remaining at around 150–200 manat per month across all size groups.

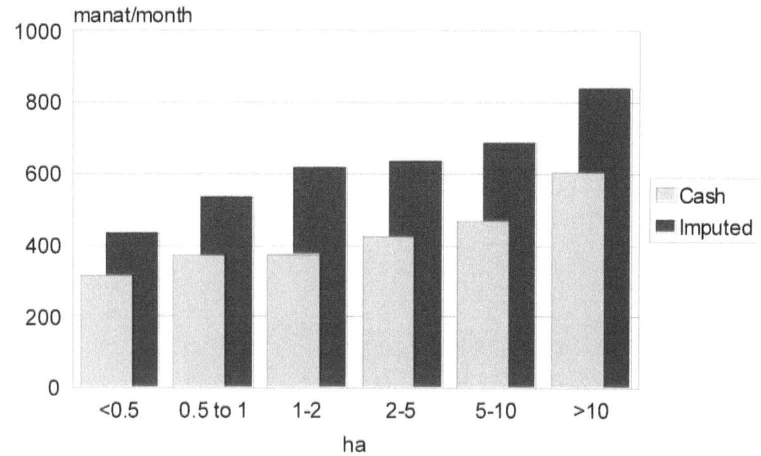

FIGURE 5.2
Family income vs. farm size (gray bars—cash income; black bars—imputed income, including value of own farm products consumed by the family). Source: 2003 World Bank survey.

As a result of these relative changes in income components, the structure of family income changes significantly with farm size (figure 5.4, table 5.3). The share of farm sales increases from 27% of income for families with the smallest farms (up to 0.5 hectare) to over 50% of income for farms larger than 10 hectares. The share of farm income (including the value of own products consumed by the family in addition to farm sales) increases from 50% to more than 80% between these extreme size categories. The share of non-agricultural income, on the other hand, diminishes from nearly 50%

TABLE 5.3
Structure of Family Income vs. Farm Size (in Percent)

	Farm Size					
	<0.5 ha	*0.5–1 ha*	*1–2 ha*	*2–5 ha*	*5–10 ha*	*>10 ha*
Farm sales	27.0	35.8	39.0	43.1	40.0	55.6
Own consumption	22.9	25.9	31.1	30.3	30.3	27.9
Wages	10.4	11.3	8.9	10.4	10.4	2.3
Social transfers	20.9	15.0	15.9	11.0	13.7	6.8
Other non-farm income	18.8	12.0	5.2	5.2	5.6	7.4
Total	100.0	100.0	100.0	100.0	100.0	100.0
Manat per month	435	532	616	636	689	842
N	167	144	134	174	55	16

Source: 2003 World Bank survey.

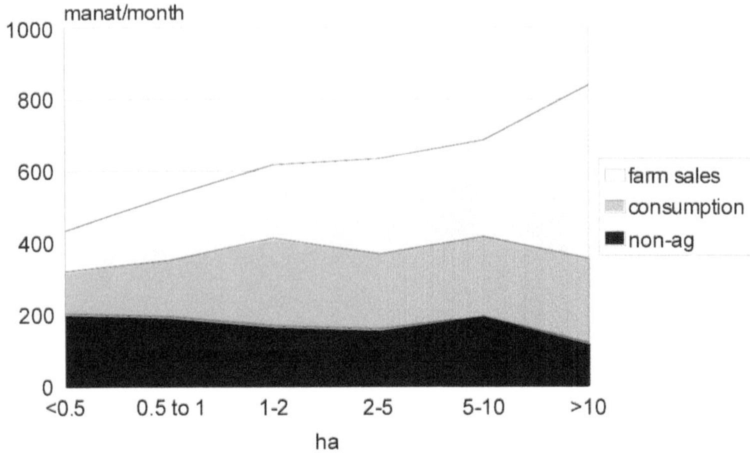

FIGURE 5.3
Components of family income vs. farm size (top layer—revenue from farm sales; middle layer—value of own products consumed by the family; bottom layer—non-agricultural income, including wages). Source: 2003 World Bank survey.

for families with the smallest holdings to less than 20% for the largest farms. The differences in farm structure are statistically significant in simultaneous comparisons between most pairs of farm size groups (by the Bonferroni test). Statistically, the differences are most pronounced between the group of smallest farms (up to 0.5 hectare) and all other groups and least pronounced

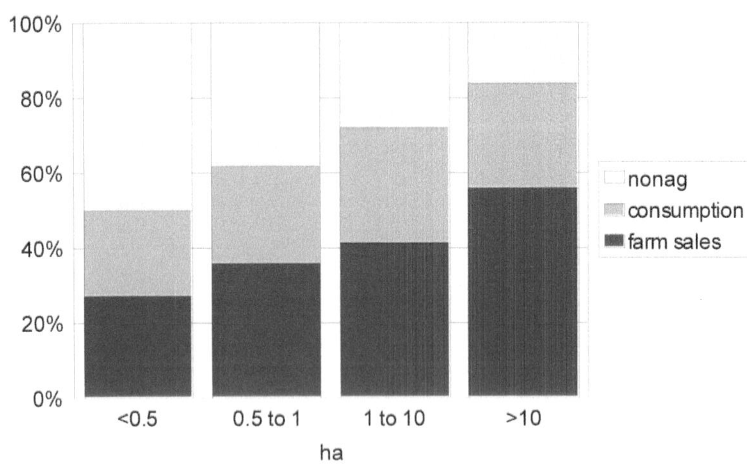

FIGURE 5.4
Structure of family income vs. farm size. Source: 2003 World Bank survey.

between the two larger groups (1–10 hectares and more than 10 hectares), primarily due to the small number of observations for farms with more than 10 hectares.

The three surveys for Azerbaijan (1995 and 2001 household budget surveys, 2003 farm survey) also provide evidence that larger landholdings increase per capita household expenditures. In addition to landholdings, these surveys had data on the number of animals, which increased from a mean of 1.9 cow units in 1995 to 3.2 cow units in 2001. Cross-section regressions of per capita expenditure (or per capita income) on a variety of independent variables for the three surveys indicate positive signs on both the size of the land plot and the number of animals (table 5.4). Moreover, in the two recent surveys (2001 and 2003) the coefficient of land plot size and herd size are significantly different from zero at 5%. Despite the differences in survey methodologies and in specific estimated models,[3] these regression results extend our view of the positive relationship between family income and asset endowment to encompass both land and livestock.

More Land Leads to Higher Family Well-Being

Evidence from the 2003 World Bank survey also shows that respondents' perception of well being increases with individual farm size. In addition to quantitative information on family incomes, the 2003 World Bank survey explored the families' perception of well-being through qualitative questions that classified the perceived standard of living into three levels: low, when family income allows nothing beyond food and daily necessities; medium, when family income is sufficient for food, daily necessities, clothing, and other consumption needs; and comfortable (or high), when in addition to the consumption needs the family can afford to purchase durables and in general does not experience material difficulties. The qualitative perception of well-being is consistent with quantitative income estimates; family income increases from low to comfortable level of well-being (table 5.5).

We have previously noted that family income increases with farm size. It is therefore not surprising that family well-being also increases with the area of land used. Households reporting a high level of well-being command significantly more land than households reporting a low or medium level of well-being (7 hectares compared with about 2 hectares only). To obtain a more rigorous relationship between well-being (a discrete variable with three values) and farm size (a continuous variable), we applied multinomial logistic regression to 2003 sample data to estimate the probability of achieving one of three levels of well-being—low, medium, high. The logistic regression produced three sets of coefficients, one for each level of well-being, and these

TABLE 5.4
Determinants of Per Capita Income: Estimated Regression Coefficient for Three Surveys
Dependent Variable: Per Capita Expenditure (1995 and 2001); Per Capita Income (2003)

Explanatory Variables	*1995* (*Quadratic*)	*2001* (*Quadratic*)	*2003* (*Logged Variables*)
Constant	96,905*	211,332*	5.852*
Household			
Size	−2,104	−18,252*	−0.540*
Squared size	−92	658*	
Head of household			
Age	−119	567^	−0.108^
Squared age	−1	−4	
Woman (relative to male head of household)	−5,036	−5,180*	−0.061
Higher education (relative to primary)	1,576	8,249*	0.123#
Secondary education (relative to primary)	3,734	4,589*	0.031
IDP or refugee		7,220^	
Agricultural assets			
Size of land plot (ha)	28,750^	7,589*	0.096*
Squared size of land plot	−3,337	−605*	
Herd size, cow units	8,230*	4,387*	0.062*
Squared herd size	−540*	−109*	
Type of farm (relative to household farm)			
Registered peasant farm		−25,083*	
Dacha plot		−11,162#	
Informally used land		−6,273^	
Number of observations	640	2471	677
R^2	0.16	0.32	0.23

* Significant at 5%; #Significant at 10%; ^Significant at 15%.

TABLE 5.5
Well-Being and Income

Level of Well-Being	*Mean Income, Manat Per Month*
1. Low (not more than food and daily necessities)	486
2. Medium (daily necessities plus clothing, etc.)	580
3. Comfortable (able to purchase durables)	627

*Statistically significant pairwise differences ($p = 0.1$): 1–3 (low-high) and 1–2 (low-medium).
Source: 2003 World Bank survey.

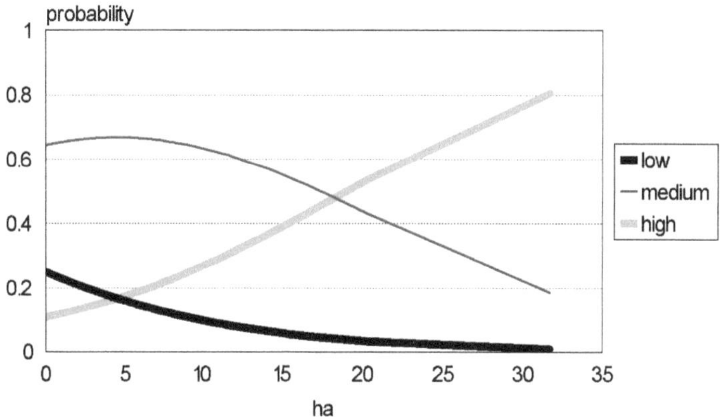

FIGURE 5.5
Estimated probability of achieving a given level of well-being (low/medium/high) as a function of farm size. Source: 2003 World Bank survey.

coefficients were used to calculate the probability of achieving the different levels. The entire process is identical to the construction of the estimated values of the independent variable in a simple linear regression with a dummy variable for categories, but in this case the regression is non-linear (a logistic model) and the outcome is a curve, not a straight line. The probabilities estimated for the three levels of well-being are presented by the three curves in figure 5.5. The probability of having a high level of well-being (gray curve) increases with the area of land used, while the probability of having the lowest level of well-being (thick black curve) decreases rapidly with farm size. This pattern is not specific to Azerbaijan: it is observed in other countries where such analyses have been undertaken, for instance, Ukraine, Moldova, and Georgia (see Lerman et al. (2007) for Ukraine; Lerman and Cimpoies (2006) for Moldova).

Commercialization of Farms Increases Family Well-Being and Income

Land is not the only factor that increases farm income and well-being. Commercialization of farm production also increases both family well-being and income. Sales of farm products contribute from 25% to 55% of family income depending on size of holdings (see table 5.3). The small household operators in the survey are not pure subsistence farmers: fully 87% of respondents report some farm sales.[4] Dichotomizing the farmers into "sellers" (those who report any sales of farm products) and "non-sellers," we see that "sellers" attain a higher level of well-being than "non-sellers" (figure 5.6). Thus,

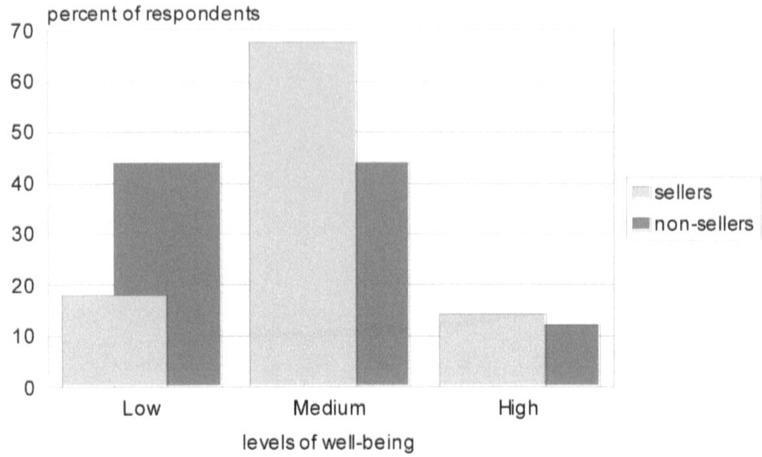

FIGURE 5.6
Well-being and commercialization. Source: 2003 World Bank survey.

the frequency of respondents who perceive their well-being as "low" is much higher among the non-sellers (44% compared with 18% among sellers). On the other hand, the frequency of those who perceive their well-being as "medium" or "high" is much higher among the sellers (82% compared with 56% among non-sellers).

The well-being results for sellers and non-sellers are consistent with the difference in family income between the two groups of respondents. Sellers achieve a higher cash income than non-sellers (390 manats per month compared with 340 manats; the difference is statistically significant). The positive income difference in favor of the sellers is entirely attributable to the additional revenue earned from sales of farm products. The non-agricultural component of family income is actually smaller among the sellers across the board—they get less in wages, receive less in social transfers, and earn less from other non-farm activities. However, farm sales more than compensate for this shortfall of non-agricultural income (figure 5.7). We observe here a kind of diversification trade-off, where non-diversifiers (those who do not generate income from farm sales) devote more time and effort to non-agricultural activities, whereas diversifiers (those who include farm sales in their income portfolio) sacrifice some non-agricultural income by devoting more time and effort to the farm, but in the end achieve higher total income.

Sellers control more land than non-sellers: the average plot size for sellers is 2.7 hectares compared with 1.8 hectares for non-sellers (the difference is statistically significant). The larger holdings enable the sellers to produce commercial surplus above the basic subsistence output. This closes the double

FIGURE 5.7
Composition of cash income for "sellers" and "non-sellers." Source: 2003 World Bank survey.

loop that describes the impact of land reform on rural incomes: land reform augments family holdings; larger holdings lead to higher farm production, improving family well being both through higher consumption (direct effect of land reform) and through additional cash income from sales of surplus products (indirect effect).

Land Reform and Rural Poverty Reduction

Reductions in poverty can emerge from increases in mean consumption, from pro-poor changes in the distribution of welfare, or from the interaction between the two (Datt and Ravallion, 1992). Evidence from cross-section surveys cited above implies that the one-off distribution of land in Azerbaijan that led to an increase of approximately 2 hectares per household most likely raised rural incomes. However, land reform had a second important effect that most likely contributed to a decrease in rural poverty in rural areas. Land reform effected a pro-poor change in asset distribution that can be presumed to entail a pro-poor change in income, at least in the short run.

Yet the financial deterioration of the Soviet economic system in rural areas simultaneously tended to reduce rural incomes and raise both income and non-income rural poverty. The financial crisis that led to loss of jobs in the food processing industry and in collective and state farms led to substantial income losses for the rural population. Moreover, a significant deterioration in rural services, both in an absolute sense and when compared to urban services, led to a real deterioration in living standards in rural areas. On balance, it is difficult to say with certainty whether poverty of rural inhabitants increased or decreased during the period of land reform considered here (1996–2003).

Land Reform Augmented Rural Assets in a Pro-Poor Way

The distribution of land in Azerbaijan seems to have been extraordinarily egalitarian. The absence of a bias toward wealthier families in land distribution can be seen by considering the size of distributed land parcels by income level. The 2003 World Bank survey provided data both on the area of land received by each household in the process of land reform and on family income at the time of the survey. Although income was observed a few years after land distribution, we had no choice but to use this information as a relevant proxy for estimating the relationship between land received and family income. The observed data on land distribution and family income were divided by the number of household members to obtain the per capita land distribution and the per capita family income for analysis.[5] The scattergram of all 684 observations plotting the land distribution per capita versus per capita family income (at the time of the survey) does not reveal any relationship between the two variables. Formally, the regression of land received per capita on income per capita is not statistically significant, with $R^2 = 0.0$.

To reduce the noise in land distribution and per capita incomes, we aggregated the data by plotting the average size of land plots received by the families in the process of reform against the average per capita household income grouped by quintiles (figure 5.8). In this way, we observed a fairly egalitarian—even progressive—distribution of plots by income level. None of the pairwise differences in average land distribution between income quintiles was statistically significant, not even the difference between the lowest quintile (quintile 1) and the quintile with the smallest land distribution value (quintile 4). To reinforce the visually discernible tendency for distribution to *decrease* with the increase of per capita income, we smoothed out the remaining noise by calculating the mean land distribution relative to the median income (a simple dichotomy instead of five quintiles). The dichotomous results indeed showed that the lower-income group received more land than the upper income group: 2.12 hectares on average for families with per capita income below the median compared with 1.87 hectares on average for families with per capita income above the median. However, the significance level of this comparison is 0.11, i.e., the difference in land distribution is not significant even at $p = 0.10$.

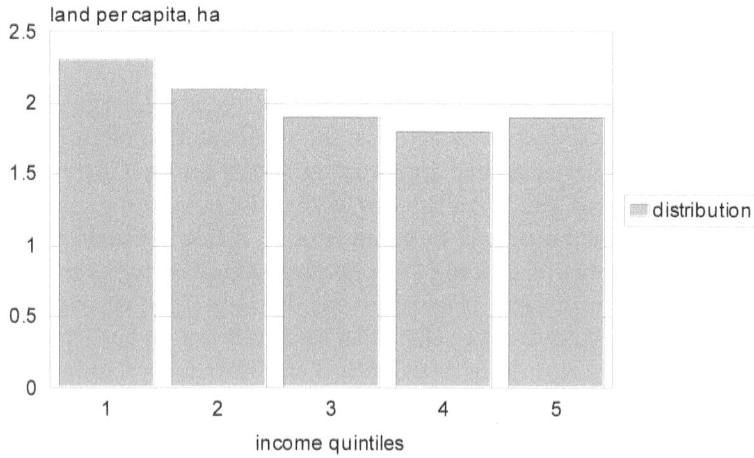

FIGURE 5.8
Land distribution and income per capita (by quintiles). Source: 2003 World Bank survey.

The 1995 and 2001 household budget surveys also provide some support for the notion that the land reform allocated land (as well as livestock assets) in a pro-poor way. To assess the changes in the distribution of land and livestock holdings across the rural population between these two points in time, we calculated the corresponding Gini coefficients for 1995 and 2001. The Gini coefficient is a standard measure of inequality of a distribution, defined as the ratio in which the numerator is the area enclosed between the Lorenz curve of the distribution and the diagonal line representing the uniform distribution, and the denominator is the area of the entire triangle under the uniform distribution line. The Gini coefficient takes values between 0 and 1, with values near 1 indicating extreme inequality of distribution, while lower values indicate more egalitarian distribution. The Gini coefficients for the distribution of land and livestock ownership were smaller in 2001 than in 1995 (table 5.6). This suggests that the distributions of both land and livestock in the 2001 survey were more equal than in 1995.

TABLE 5.6
Inequality of Agricultural Assets for Rural Households, 1995 and 2001

Year	*1995*	*2001*
Gini coefficient for the distribution of land use	0.515	0.501
Gini coefficient for the distribution of livestock herd size	0.605	0.521

Sources: Sedik et al. (2002), based on 1995 and 2001 household budget surveys

Land Distribution Was Pro-Poor and Led to a More Pro-Poor Income Distribution in the Short Run

The value of an asset should be related to the average returns that asset could bring over a period of time. Thus, the augmentation of rural household assets should have a related augmentation effect on rural incomes. This income augmentation effect can be estimated as the ratio of the value of the land received by the household to its income. As a first approximation, we can estimate the short-run value of one hectare of land by the average gross income received from farm production per hectare. This, of course, is a rough short-term estimate. The value of an asset today should be equal to the discounted present value of the asset's future income stream. However, such calculations involve assumptions about discount rates that are highly speculative. Moreover, different households will in fact derive different incomes from one hectare of land, depending on cultivation skills, other agricultural inputs employed, and the kind of crops raised. In the longer run these factors can be expected to play a greater role in shaping the income derived from distributed land. Different cultivation skills will undoubtedly lead to greater differentiation in the income received from distributed land. For these reasons we confine ourselves to making a rough estimate of the short-term "augmentation effect" on rural incomes.

The average gross income received from farm production per hectare includes both cash revenue from sale of farm product and, perhaps more importantly, the value of own farm products consumed by the family. Averaging over all rural households in the 2003 survey, we obtain about 500 manats per month for the gross farm income from one hectare of land. This number approximates the constant value of one hectare of land for all rural households (measured in manats per month).

In order to obtain the augmentation of per capita income due to land distribution, the average gross return on one hectare of land is multiplied by the number of hectares actually received per capita in the process of land reform. The results of these calculations are presented in table 5.7 (column 3). The last column in table 5.7 is the income augmentation ratio, which is calculated as the ratio of the per capita income augmentation due to additional land received by the household (in manats per month from column 3) to average per capita income (in manats per month from column 4). The income augmentation ratios are calculated by income quintile, and the falling ratio in the last column is a rough indication of the pro-poor nature of the land reform in Azerbaijan (based on the 2003 World Bank survey). The poorest households enjoyed a five–fold increase in their mean income per capita as a result of the land distribution, while the richest households enjoyed less than a two-fold increase in per capita income.

TABLE 5.7
Per Capita Income Augmentation Ratio of Land Reform in Azerbaijan

Income Quintiles	*Average "Value" of 1 ha of Land, Manat Per Month*	*Average Land Parcel Received Per Capita, ha*	*Average Income Augmentation Per Capita, Manat Per Month*	*Average Income Per Capita, Manat Per Month*	*Per Capita Income Augmentation Ratio, Times*
	(1)	*(2)*	*(3)=(1)×(2)*	*(4)*	*(3)/(4)*
1: poorest	500	0.44	220	42	5.2
2	500	0.38	190	61	3.1
3: medium	500	0.38	190	75	2.5
4	500	0.38	190	94	2.0
5: richest	500	0.57	285	165	1.7

Source: 2003 World Bank survey.

In addition to land, households also increased their livestock herd in the process of reform: it rose from 1.9 to 3.2 cow units between 1995 and 2001 (see p. 111). Unfortunately, the 2003 World Bank survey of farms did not contain information on the number of livestock distributed to households, and it was not possible to calculate by the same procedure the income augmentation effect from livestock distribution during the reform. Still, comparison of the Gini coefficients of animals in 1995 and 2001 (see table 5.6) provides limited evidence that the distribution of livestock was pro-poor as well: the distribution of animals in 2001 was substantially more egalitarian than in 1995.

To summarize, land reform had two important effects in Azerbaijan that worked to reduce rural poverty in rural areas. First, it seemed to increase per capita family incomes through a one-off asset transfer to individual households. Second, it disproportionately benefited poorer households through distribution of land and livestock. For this reason we regard land reform as the principal driver of poverty reduction in Azerbaijan.

Factors Tending to Increase Rural Poverty in Azerbaijan

Two groups of factors may act to increase rural poverty in Azerbaijan or elsewhere. One group is associated with loss of jobs and declining wages. These are monetary factors that directly contribute to income poverty of the rural population. The other group includes non-monetary factors affecting the standard of living, such as quality of rural infrastructure and access to services or facilities. These factors are responsible for non-income poverty. In this section we briefly review the evidence relating to the impacts of these factors on both income and non-income poverty.

Income Poverty: Employment and Rural Incomes

While land reform increased rural incomes and acted to reduce rural poverty, the deterioration of the Soviet economic system in rural areas depressed rural incomes and added to rural poverty. The most important negative factor for rural incomes was the loss of formal employment in both agriculture and rural industry. Official employment data on the annual average number of workers employed in former collective and state farms show a fall from 490,000 in 1995 to 24,000 in 2000 to 17,000 in 2005 (Statistical Committee of Azerbaijan, 2006a, table 19.30). These figures imply a shedding of 95% of the workforce by corporate farms in five years (1995–2000). Employment in the food processing industry in Azerbaijan most likely fell as well. Although there are no employment data for the food processing industry, employment must have fallen quite precipitously, because production in the food processing industry declined by 44% between 1995 and 2000 (Statistical Committee of Azerbaijan, 2006a, table 18.3).

Those laid off by the corporate farms and the food industry did not become unemployed: they found non-wage self-employment in the rapidly growing family farm sector, which mitigated the income-depressing effect of this massive labor shedding by the main rural employers. Those formally employed on corporate farms back in 1995 anyhow could not rely on a regular stream of wage income. Exacerbated by galloping inflation and other transition disruptions, the financial situation of the corporate farms led to mounting losses, which simply did not allow them to pay their workers regularly (see table 3.3). Wage arrears accumulated, and rural people were often left for months without being paid. Yet the shedding of so many workers in so short a time could not but exert a depressing effect on rural wages. Agricultural wages, having finally climbed to the average wage level in the economy by the mid-1980s, tumbled to roughly one-third of the average wage after 1997, just as the land reform was coming into full swing (figure 5.9).

Corporate farms and the food processing industry were traditionally the main employers in rural areas. At the household level, the fall in relative wages and in employment in these two sectors is reflected in the fall in the portion of household incomes derived from wage employment. The share of people

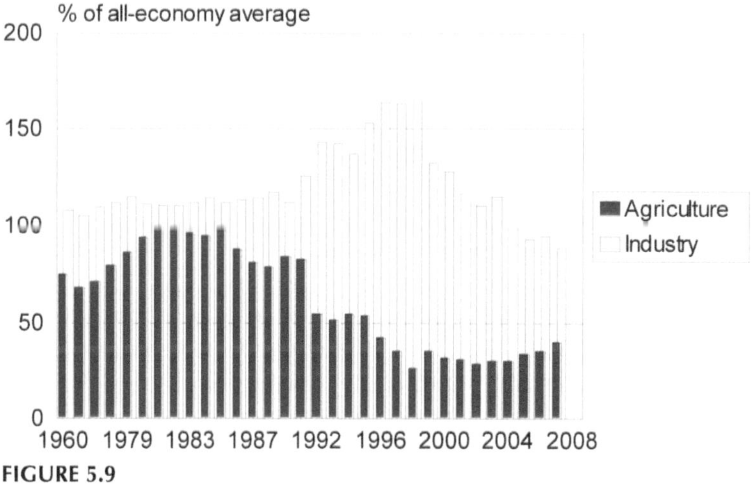

FIGURE 5.9
Relative wages in agriculture and industry 1960–2008 (in percent of all-economy average wage). Source: 1960–88 from Statistical Committee of AzSSR (1980, 1985, 1988); 1990–2007 from Statistical Committee of Azerbaijan (2006d, 2009b).

TABLE 5.8
Changes in Wage Employment and Wage Income in Rural Households, 1995–2001

	1995	*2001*
Wage earners (% of members employed aged 16–59)	39.1	18.1
Household income from wages as a portion of total expenditure (%)	46.8	31.5

Source: Sedik et al. (2002), based on 1995 and 2001 household budget surveys.

working for hire (wage earners) in rural families and the share of income derived from wages decreased markedly between 1995 and 2001, according to surveys conducted in those years (table 5.8).

Non-Income Rural Poverty: Services, Facilities, Risk

While sector performance has shown great progress in rural Azerbaijan in the years since 1996 (see chapter 4), Azeri households on the whole seem to be rather pessimistic about their well-being compared to the Soviet period. This is a surprising result, because increases in yields and growth in production can be expected to translate into the perception that things have improved. One reason for the prevailing pessimism is a continuous increase in non-income poverty in rural areas as manifested in a continuous fall in rural services since independence. The sizable perceived falls in provision of gas and electricity since Soviet times contrast with perceived improvements in Kazakhstan and Moldova as captured in the 2003 World Bank survey (table 5.9).

The deterioration in rural services as perceived by the respondents in the 2003 World Bank survey is confirmed by official statistics that show a severe decrease in gas supply per inhabitant in rural areas beginning in the late 1980s with substantial and growing differences in the level of services between urban and rural areas (table 5.10). The disparities in service provision per resident between rural and urban areas in Azerbaijan for gas, clean water, and plumbing are on the order of ten to one.

Another reason why households in Azerbaijan may be more pessimistic about their level of well-being is that household income appears to be more exposed to risk in Azerbaijan than in other countries surveyed (table 5.11). Incomes in other surveyed countries are substantially more diversified. In Azerbaijan, fully 64% of household income derived from farm production and only 11% from wage employment. In Moldova, another country with labor-intensive agriculture, 40% of household income derived from agricultural production and 33% derived from wage employment. In Kazakhstan, a country with a substantially different economic and demographic profile,

TABLE 5.9
Households' Level of Satisfaction With Provision of Basic Services

	Azerbaijan		*Kazakhstan*		*Moldova*	
	Before Reform	*At Survey Time*	*Before Reform*	*At Survey Time*	*Before Reform*	*At Survey Time*
Electricity	84.1	43.7*	68.1	86.2*	73.0	79.0*
Gas	18.4	3.5*	65.2	78.5*	35.7	37.7
Drinking water	68.9	66.7	70.0	72.6	42.5	38.6
Telephone	25.8	30.2*	48.2	55.0*	35.4	50.8*

Note: Level of satisfaction is expressed on a scale from 0 to 100 (0=not available at all; 100=always available in satisfactory quality/reliability). "Before reform" means before the dismantling of the collective/state farm.
* The difference between the two points in time is statistically significant at the 10% level.
Source: Dudwick, Fock, and Sedik (2007), based on the 2003 World Bank survey.

TABLE 5.10

The Deterioration in Public Services in Rural Areas of Azerbaijan, 1990–2003

	Piped Gas Supply Per Inhabitant (Cu. Meters Per Year)		*Piped Water Supply Per Inhabitant (Liters Per Day)*		*Piped Water Infrastructure (% of Settlements)*		*Piped Gas Infrastructure (% of Settlements)*	
Year	*Urban*	*Rural*	*Urban*	*Rural*	*Urban*	*Rural*	*Urban*	*Rural*
1990	377.1	379.9	485.9	18.8	95.7	10.8	100	80.3
1995	816.7	127.6	527.9	7.8	95.7	11.5	100	80.4
2000	385.4	31.0	350.8	3.9	95.7	11.3	100	79.2
2003	585.4	52.8	333.1	13.2				

Source: Statistical Committee of Azerbaijan (2003).

TABLE 5.11
Income Composition of Surveyed Households (Percent of Total Income in Cash and in Kind)

	Azerbaijan	*Kazakhstan*	*Moldova*
Sales of farm products	36.3	9.2	21.7
Value of farm production consumed in the family	27.4	12.9	18.5
Total salary from wage employment	10.6	45.7	32.7
Pensions and social assistance	15.5	24.1	13.5
Other non-farm income	10.2	8.1	13.2

Source: Dudwick, Fock, and Sedik (2007), based on the 2003 World Bank survey.

TABLE 5.12
Households' Perceptions of the Level of Community Life

	"Before Reform"	*At Survey Time*
Alcohol use among adults	38	28
Alcohol use among youth	44	37
Level of crime	29	25
Criminal activity among youth	28	25
Domestic abuse/violence	28	26

Note: Level of community life assessed on a scale from 0 (very low) to 100 (very high). "Before reform" means before the dismantling of the collective or state farm.
Source: Dudwick, Fock, and Sedik (2007), based on the 2003 World Bank survey.

wage employment accounted for nearly half the family income, while farm production contributed slightly over 20%.

Despite this deterioration in rural services and the high level of income risk, the quality of community life in rural Azerbaijan seems to have improved. It is generally perceived to be better than before the reforms that led to the dismantling of collective and state farms (table 5.12).

Rural Poverty in Azerbaijan Today: A Mixed Picture

Rural incomes and poverty are the touchstones by which agrarian reform in Azerbaijan should be judged. Agricultural growth, despite its importance for agriculture officials, is of little import unless it raises the welfare of those who live in rural areas. In Azerbaijan the record of agricultural and yield growth since 1996 has been nothing short of spectacular (see chapter 4). We have argued that land reform has been a principal reason for this remarkable growth.

However, the record of Azerbaijan's agrarian reform on rural welfare—rural incomes, as well as income and non-income poverty—has been surprisingly mixed. Land reform most likely raised rural incomes through the distribution of approximately 2 hectares of additional land per rural household, as well as livestock and agricultural machinery. Moreover, the distribution of land was pro-poor: poor and rich alike received nearly equal plots of land. The financial impact of such egalitarian distribution was substantially greater for the poor than for the better off. Land reform was thus a principal driving force for rural poverty reduction.

Yet the deterioration of the Soviet economic system in rural areas simultaneously reduced rural incomes and raised both income and non-income rural poverty. The loss of jobs in the food processing industry and in the reorganization of collective and state farms that characterized the period led to substantial income losses for the rural population. Moreover, a significant deterioration in rural services, both in an absolute sense and when compared to urban services, led to a real fall in living standards in rural areas. On balance, it is difficult to say with certainty whether rural poverty increased or decreased during the period of land reform between 1996 and 2003.

The dualistic trend that characterized agrarian reform in Azerbaijan continues to this day. The measure of rural income poverty in Azerbaijan has declined at an incredible pace since 2002—from 44% to 29% in just three years (World Bank, 2006). However, such indicators as the piped gas and water supply per inhabitant in rural areas have improved far less than in urban areas.

Figure 5.10 shows the substantial progress made in reduction of income poverty in Azerbaijan rural households in the years 2002 to 2004. These estimates are based on comparable household budget surveys administered by the Statistical Committee of Azerbaijan using identical questionnaires. The poverty lines used are derived from a calculation of the cost of basic needs (both food and non-food) based on observed consumption in 2003. Expressed in 2003 prices, the extreme poverty line was 131,762 manats and the poverty line was 152,144 manats (World Bank, 2006, p. 12). The incidence of rural poor in 2004 was actually less than the incidence of urban poor (for both the poor and the very poor; table 5.13).

When the national poverty line is replaced with the $2.15 per day international poverty line, rural poverty in Azerbaijan is observed to be extraordinarily low compared to other CIS countries (table 5.14). These rural poverty rates are all the more extraordinary when compared with those for the richer CIS countries. Russia, with nearly three times the average GDP per capita, has rural poverty rates four times as high. Moreover, rural poverty is substantially

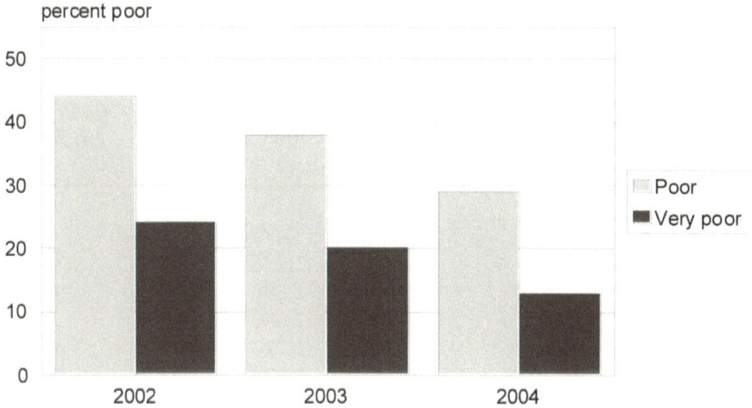

FIGURE 5.10
Reduction of rural poverty in Azerbaijan 2002–04. Source: World Bank (2006).

higher than urban poverty in most CIS countries, with Azerbaijan an exception to this pattern. While the difference between Azerbaijan and the other CIS countries in table 5.14 may reflect real poverty differences, they may also stem from differences in questionnaire design or sampling (Alam et al., 2005). Further research is needed to resolve the issue, but at present these measures of poverty are the best comparable estimates between countries available.

For all these stellar poverty results, households in rural Azerbaijan seem to remain pessimistic (compared to other countries) as to changes in their well-being. In the World Bank 2003 survey only 18% of rural households believed that well-being had improved over the past three years (table 5.15). We can

TABLE 5.13
Consumption Poverty in Azerbaijan, 2004
(Head Count and Percent, Based on National Poverty Lines)

	Azerbaijan	*Baku*	*Non-Baku Urban*	*Rural*
Population	8,295,938	2,113,398	2,341,403	3,841,137
Poor, %	27.5	17.5	34.1	29.0
Very poor, %	13.0	8.0	19.8	13.0
Share of population	100	25.5	28.2	46.3
Number of poor	2,283,872	370,533	644,588	1,113,722
Share of poor	100	16.2	28.2	48.8
Number of very poor	1,075,983	168,226	464,066	498,964
Share of very poor	100	15.6	43.1	46.4

Source: World Bank (2006).

TABLE 5.14
Poverty in CIS (2003)

Country	*Poverty Rate (Using $2.15 PPP)* Urban	Rural	*GDP Per Capita, PPP (2003 in Constant 2000 $)*	*Rural Contribution) to Poverty (Using $2.15 PPP)*
Small CIS				
Armenia	46	57	3,473	46
Azerbaijan	6	3	3,270	44
Georgia	41	62	2,538	61
Kyrgyzstan	57	77	1,646	72
Moldova	37	47	1,727	69
Tajikistan	67	76	1,034	76
Uzbekistan	34	55	1,631	73
Large CIS				
Kazakhstan	13	31	5,909	64
Belarus (2002)	2	2	5,731	25
Ukraine	1	2	5,218	44
Russia (2002)	7	14	8,373	42
Non-CIS				
Colombia	3	14	6,124	66
Turkey (2002)	18	24	6,518	46
Vietnam (1998)	14	48	2,405	92

Source: Alam et al. (2005); GDP per capita from World Bank (2007).

attribute this persistent pessimism to the meager improvements in rural infrastructure (table 5.10) and the continued riskiness of household incomes in rural Azerbaijan (table 5.11).

The example of Azerbaijan is of great import for agrarian reform in the CIS, particularly for the countries of Central Asia, which experience similar deteriorations in rural infrastructure and services. These countries, even if they implement robust land reform contributing to a substantial reduction in rural poverty, will require a great number of complementary reform mea-

TABLE 5.15
Households' Perceptions of Well-Being (Percent of Respondents)

	Azerbaijan	*Kazakhstan*	*Moldova*
Change in perceived well-being over last three years			
Improved	17.6	36.2	28.6
Unchanged	78.5	36.5	48.2
Deteriorated	3.8	27.3	23.2

Source: Dudwick, Fock, and Sedik (2007), based on 2003 World Bank survey.

sures, including large investments in rural infrastructure, in order to improve the livelihoods of rural inhabitants.

Notes

1. In this chapter we use the terms "income poverty" and "non-income poverty" to distinguish between indicators based on a measure of welfare based on a monetary aggregate and those not based on monetary aggregates. In actual use, income poverty is typically based on household expenditures as the measure, not income. However, we prefer the terms "income" and "non-income" poverty to the more awkward "expenditure" and "non-income" poverty.

2. The mean farm size is influenced by a small number of respondents who report leasing large areas, from 10 to 200 hectares each. An alternative statistics—the median—is not as sensitive as the mean to these upper-tail observations. The median farm size in the survey is just 5.2 hectares, which means that 50% of the observations in the subsample of households with leased land do not exceed 5.2 hectares while the other 50% are greater than 5.2 hectares. Still, the switch from the mean to the median does not affect our main conclusions: farms with leased land are larger than farms without leased land, and the size difference is statistically significant.

3. The dependent variable in the regression models was per capita expenditure for the 1995 and 2001 household budget surveys and per capita income (including the value of consumption of own products) for the 2003 farm survey. In the models estimated for 1995 and 2001 all continuous variables were used in absolute values as reported and the model included both linear and quadratic terms for the continuous variables (family size, age, plot size, number of animals). Outliers farther than 5 standard deviations from the mean were excluded from analysis, thus reducing the number of observations used in estimation substantially below the total number of respondents. In the model estimated for 2003 all continuous variables—both dependent and explanatory—were logged and only linear terms were used in estimation. Outliers were not censored in the 2003 survey database, but zeros reduced the number of observations from 703 to 677.

4. These findings are consistent with the results of the national household budget survey, in which over 70% of households report using their land plot for both consumption and sales (Statistical Committee of Azerbaijan, 2009b, table 145).

5. The relationship between per capita land distribution and per capita household income is not easy to estimate, because the income data are of poor quality, with many outliers stemming from the usual reluctance of respondents to disclose information about family income. We can justify our decision to use income data instead of expenditure data by the even poorer quality of expenditure information, as the corresponding question in the survey instrument was extremely complex, leading to many missing values and gross errors. On a more substantive level, income data were judged more relevant for our purpose because they included the value of own farm products consumed by the family, whereas expenditure data were strictly cash based.

6

Conclusion: Looking Beyond Agrarian Reform in Azerbaijan

IN THIS BOOK WE HAVE ANALYZED the institutional and policy changes that went into agrarian reform in Azerbaijan and illustrated their relationship with both the robust growth in agriculture and the improvement in rural incomes observed since 1996. However, the set of institutional and policy reforms that are important for rural transition and agricultural growth goes beyond agrarian reform. Land reform, interpreted in the transition context as privatization of land and restructuring of traditional large farms, is only one facet of a multidimensional process of transition to a market-oriented agriculture. Though land reform is important, successful transition requires progress in at least five dimensions, which in addition to land reform include liberalization of markets, privatization and demonopolization of services (both upstream and downstream), establishment of an institutional framework for market agriculture, and development of rural finance. The success of land privatization cannot be measured in isolation from the other dimensions. In practice, however, integrated evaluation of the process of agrarian transformation by all five dimensions is very difficult, particularly if we strive to base the evaluation on sound empirical data. So far such a multidimensional evaluation of agriculture in transition has been attempted by an "expert judgment" approach, assigning purely subjective scores to each dimension and ranking different countries by unweighted average scores (Csaki and Nash, 1998; Csaki and Kray, 2005). Conceptually similar rankings based on composite reform indices for the overall economy or society are regularly constructed by the World Bank, EBRD, Freedom House, and other international bodies.

Azerbaijan shines mainly by its achievements in the dimension of land reform, while the accomplishments in other dimensions have been less spectacular. In overall agricultural reforms Azerbaijan has seen considerable improvement since 1997, and changes have progressed faster than perhaps in any other country in the CIS. However, Azerbaijan is by no means the leader in agricultural reform in the CIS. Armenia and Kyrgyzstan score higher on general agricultural reform. Moreover, all three countries, while shining leaders in CIS, fall far below the level of agricultural reform in Central and Eastern Europe.

Azerbaijan has also seen rapid improvement since 1996 in most areas affecting the overall quality of governance and the building of market institutions. In 2009 Azerbaijan scored better than the average in the CIS countries, but again did not match the level of governance and institutional reform in Central and Eastern Europe. In the area of political reform, including democracy, corruption, and judicial framework, however, Azerbaijan scored worse than the average for CIS countries.

We start this chapter with a discussion of evidence that land and farm structure reform, specifically the shift to individual farming, is beneficial for both the agricultural sector and the rural population. We then broaden the focus to consider the impact of overall agricultural policy reforms (extending beyond land and farm structure reform) and broader still the impact of the general policy environment outside agriculture. In all instances, we observe that better agricultural performance is achieved by countries that are more advanced on the path of reform, irrespective of how we measure reform—whether by share of land in individual farming, by agriculture-related policy reforms, or by non-agricultural reform indicators.

The Impact of Land Reform: Individualization of Farming

The central hypothesis of this book is that the long-term pattern of agricultural development in the former Soviet Union and in today's CIS—with Azerbaijan one of 12 CIS members—is driven by the policy environment. Furthermore, we argue that policy changes have been at the root of agricultural recovery in the post-Soviet states.

Land Reform and Sectoral Recovery

Figure 6.1 visualizes the long-term agricultural growth trend for all 12 CIS countries in aggregate. The curve in figure 6.1 is the index of gross agricultural output (GAO) in constant prices in percent of 1965, calculated

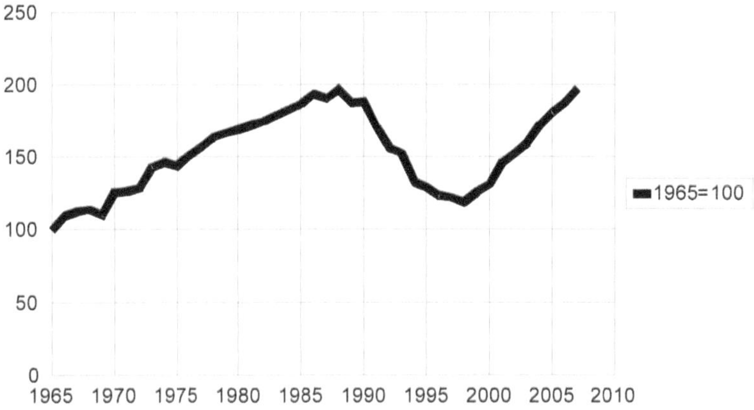

FIGURE 6.1
GAO growth 1965–2007: Average for 12 CIS countries in percent of 1965. Source: Statistical Committee of CIS (2008) with data for Georgia and Turkmenistan updated from national statistical yearbooks.

as the simple (unweighted) arithmetic average of the GAO index numbers for the 12 CIS countries. There is a striking similarity between the pattern of long-term agricultural growth for all of CIS in figure 6.1 and the pattern of growth for Azerbaijan in figure 2.1, although Azerbaijan accounts for just one-twelfth of the aggregate curve. The GAO curve in figure 6.1 clearly shows that the agricultural history of the CIS during the last 40 years, like the agricultural history of Azerbaijan in chapter 2, can be divided into four consecutive phases: (a) rapid and continuous agricultural growth between 1965 and 1985 (the Soviet period before Gorbachev); (b) stagnation going into slight decline between 1985 and 1990 (the last five years of the Soviet regime under Gorbachev); (c) steep decline during the first years of transition (1990–97); and (d) general recovery manifested in resumption of agricultural growth after 1997–98, as sustained reform efforts began to show their cumulative effects. The four phases of agricultural development are clearly linked to well-defined markers on the timeline of USSR and CIS history. This linkage is discussed in chapter 2 in connection with Azerbaijan's growth pattern (figure 2.1) and is summarized here in table 6.1.

Figure 6.2 decomposes the agricultural growth curve of the CIS into three regional curves: Transcaucasia, Central Asia, and the European CIS. The four phases of long-term agricultural development—growth, stagnation, collapse, and recovery—are clearly visible in each regional curve. The notable difference is the shift of the point where recovery starts: as early as 1991–92 in Transcaucasia, 1996–97 in Central Asia, and around 1998 in the European CIS.

TABLE 6.1
The Phases of Agricultural Development and Policy Stages in the USSR and CIS

Time Frame	*Political Regime*	*Development Phase*	*Policy Environment for Agriculture*
1965–85	Between Khrushchev and Gorbachev (Brezhnev as Party Secretary, Andropov as Prime Minister)	Soviet growth	Supportive post-Stalin policies, increased investment and reallocation of resources to agriculture
1985–90	Gorbachev, end of the Soviet Union	Stagnation going into gradual decline	Liberalization, reorganization of collectives, emphasis on household farming
1991–97	Post-Soviet independence	Steep decline	Sustained efforts to implement comprehensive market-oriented reforms
Since 1998	Established independence, growing democratization	Recovery and resumption of growth	Continuation of reforms, spreading shift to individual farming

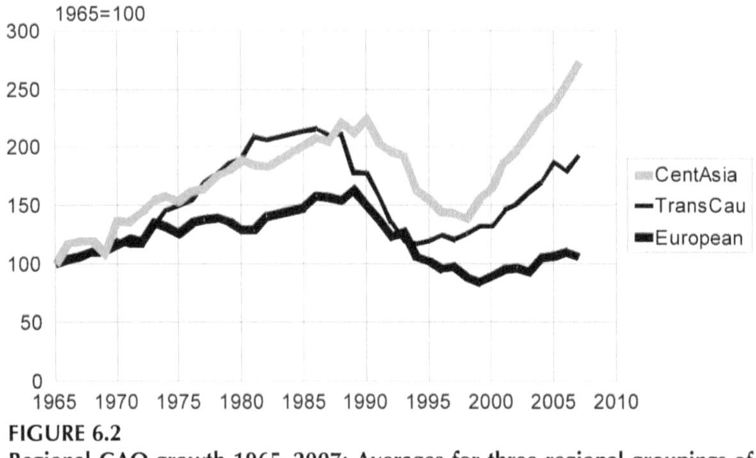

FIGURE 6.2
Regional GAO growth 1965–2007: Averages for three regional groupings of CIS countries. Source: Statistical Committee of CIS (2008) with data for Georgia (Transcaucasia) and Turkmenistan (Central Asia) updated from national statistical yearbooks.

There is a traceable link between the beginning of recovery and the implementation of significant farm structure reforms. In Transcaucasia recovery started in 1991–92, precisely when two of the three Transcaucasian countries—Armenia and Georgia—made resolute efforts to dismantle collective agriculture and distribute land to individual farms at the very beginning of transition. The rate of recovery in Transcaucasia subsequently accelerated after 1996, when Azerbaijan had adopted a farm individualization policy as part of Aliyev's reforms. It is sometimes argued that Azerbaijan's agricultural success since 1996 is simply a reflection of the booming oil revenues that fuel the overall economic growth. Armenia and Georgia do not have any oil revenues, and yet the starting point for agricultural recovery in these countries is clearly linked with the implementation of land individualization reforms. In the European CIS, recovery began around 1998, as two of the four countries—Ukraine and Moldova—began moving in earnest toward distribution of land plots to holders of paper land shares. The extent of the recovery in this group is moderate, because two other countries—Russia and Belarus—have not done much by way of actual land reform. Finally, the recovery in Central Asia began in 1996–97, when all countries moved toward implementing various reform measures in various ways. It is particularly important to note that, alongside conventional individualization of land tenure in Kyrgyzstan and Tajikistan, both Turkmenistan and Uzbekistan contributed to this recovery despite their image as "slow" reformers. In fact, these two countries allowed farm structure to shift from a collective form of organization to family leaseholding around 1998. This is basically a form of individual farming (with many restrictions), although land in family leasehold is not counted as individual tenure in official statistics and is not reflected as an advance in land reform in the formal indexes. The observed link between the beginning of recovery and the implementation of significant farm structure reforms provides further evidence of the importance of policy decisions on agricultural performance.

Land Reform in the CIS

The heart of farm structure reforms is land reform. By land reform we mean how far land tenure and farm structure have advanced from the socialist model of predominantly large-scale collective agriculture to the market model with predominance of relatively small family-operated units. This approach to land reform emphasizes individualization of agriculture—and not just privatization of land in the formal sense of ownership transfer from the state to private owners or the establishment of sophisticated land titling and registration systems. In figure 3.4 we have shown that between 1998 and 2002

Azerbaijan moved toward a farm structure that is closer to market economies than to the dual Soviet model. This shift in farm structure clearly sets Azerbaijan apart from some other transition countries in CIS and Central Eastern Europe. Table 6.2 summarizes the different forms of land tenure and farm structure that have emerged across the CIS countries as a result of differences in the implementation of land reform.

The qualitative patterns of land reform in table 6.2 can be quantified by the so-called ECA Land Reform Index, which measures the progress from the socialist model of land use to the market model.[1] Table 6.3 gives for each country the ECA Land Reform Index for 2004—the last year when such estimates were published by the World Bank. Alongside with the Land Reform Index, table 6.3 also reports the broader ECA Agricultural Policy Index, which in addition to the evaluation of land reform includes four other dimensions relevant for the transition in agriculture: liberalization of agricultural markets, privatization and demonopolization of agricultural services (both upstream and downstream), establishment of an institutional framework for market agriculture, and development of rural finance. The ECA reform indexes are constructed on a scale from 1 to 10, where 1 corresponds to a command economy and 10 to an economy with completed market reforms. Countries with a reform index below 6 are characterized as slow reformers, whereas countries with a reform index of 6 and higher are moderate (6–7) or advanced (above 7) reformers.

Table 6.3 linking the qualitative land reform patterns of table 6.2 with the ECA Land Reform Index reveals a concrete regional differentiation of the 12 CIS countries on the scale of reforms. The Transcaucasia region, which includes Azerbaijan as well as Armenia and Georgia, has achieved the greatest progress in land reform among the CIS countries, and it accordingly has the highest Land Reform Index, averaging 8.3 out of 10. In each of the other two regions—European CIS and Central Asia—we clearly distinguish two subregions: good reformers and laggards. In the European CIS, Ukraine and Moldova have virtually completed the conversion of land shares to plots and their farming structure is characterized by a very strong presence of individual farms. The average Land Reform Index for these two countries is 6.5 and they are characterized as "advanced" reformers. The other two countries in this region—Russia and Belarus—are relative laggards, with continued predominance of large-scale corporate farms and marginal allocation of land in the form of physical plots. Their average land reform index is 3.5—much lower than for Ukraine and Moldova. A similar dichotomy is observed in Central Asia, where Kyrgyzstan and Tajikistan appear to be much more advanced on the path of reform than Kazakhstan, Uzbekistan, or Turkmenistan: the average Land Reform Index is 7 for the two former countries and 4 for the three "slow" reformers.

TABLE 6.2
Differences in the Implementation of Land Reform in CIS

	Potential Private Land Ownership	*Allocation Strategy*	*Transferability*	*Farm Organization*	*Watershed Date for Individualization*
Armenia	All	Plots	Buy/sell, lease	Individual	1992
Georgia	All	Plots	Buy/sell, lease	Individual	1992
Azerbaijan	All	Plots	Buy/sell, lease	Individual	1996
Moldova	All	Shares to plots	Buy/sell, lease	Individual + corporate	1998
Ukraine	All	Shares to plots	Buy/sell, lease	Individual + corporate	2000
Kyrgyzstan	All	Shares to plots	Buy/sell, lease	Individual + corporate	1998
Kazakhstan	All	Shares to plots*	Buy/sell, lease	Individual + corporate	2003
Russia	All	Shares	Buy/sell, lease	Corporate + individual	**
Tajikistan	None	Shares to plots	Use rights	Individual + corporate	1999
Turkmenistan	All	Leasehold	None	Individual leaseholds	1998
Uzbekistan	None	Leasehold	None	Individual leaseholds	1996
Belarus	Household plots only	None	None	Corporate + individual	**

*The June 2003 Land Code practically annulled the permanent rights associated with land shares and forced the shareholders either to acquire a land plot from the state (by outright purchase or by leasing) or to invest the land share in the equity capital of a corporate farm.

**In Russia and Belarus individual farms began to be created in 1992, but the process of individualization has not taken off as in other countries

TABLE 6.3
Regional Classification of CIS Countries by Progress in Land Reform

	Region	*ECA Land Reform Index (2004)*	*ECA Agricultural Policy Index (2004)*	*Status of Land Reform*
Armenia	Transcaucasia	9	7.8	"Advanced"
Georgia	Transcaucasia	7	6.0	"Advanced"
Azerbaijan	Transcaucasia	9	6.6	"Advanced"
Moldova	European CIS	7	6.0	"Advanced"
Ukraine	European CIS	6	6.2	"Advanced"
Russia	European CIS	5	6.2	"Slow"
Belarus	European CIS	2	2.6	"Slow
Kyrgyzstan	Central Asia	8	7.4	"Advanced"
Tajikistan	Central Asia	6	5.2	"Advanced"
Kazakhstan	Central Asia	5	6.2	"Slow"
Uzbekistan	Central Asia	5	4.0	"Slow"
Turkmenistan	Central Asia	2	1.8	"Slow"

Source: ECA indexes from Csaki and Kray (2005).

Land Reform as Individualization

We emphasize individualization of agriculture, i.e., the extent of transition from collective to individual farming, as a measure of success in transition countries, because we find fairly convincing evidence that both sectoral performance and rural well-being generally increase with the shift to individual farming. Let us review the evidence. On the sectoral level, we observe that CIS countries with a higher share of land in individual use have achieved greater recovery in agriculture since 1996. For 9 of the 12 CIS countries, a strong positive association is observed between the degree of individualization and agricultural growth (figure 6.3; the coefficient of correlation is 0.83). There are only three curious outliers—Georgia, Moldova, and Ukraine: these countries have a high share of land in individual use and yet display relatively sluggish growth performance (possibly because of slower progress in other dimensions of agricultural policy reform: compare the ECA Land Reform Index with the ECA Agricultural Policy Index in table 6.3). A similar trend demonstrating faster agricultural growth for countries with more land in individual use has been previously noted for all 23 transition countries including both CIS and Central Eastern Europe (Lerman, Csaki, and Feder, 2004).

On the household level, independent individual farmers are better off and more optimistic than employees of large corporate farms, and rural family incomes grow (in both absolute and per capita terms) with the increase of land endowments under individual farming (see, e.g., Lerman (2004); Lerman and Cimpoies (2006); Lerman et al. (2007)). Thus, distribution of land

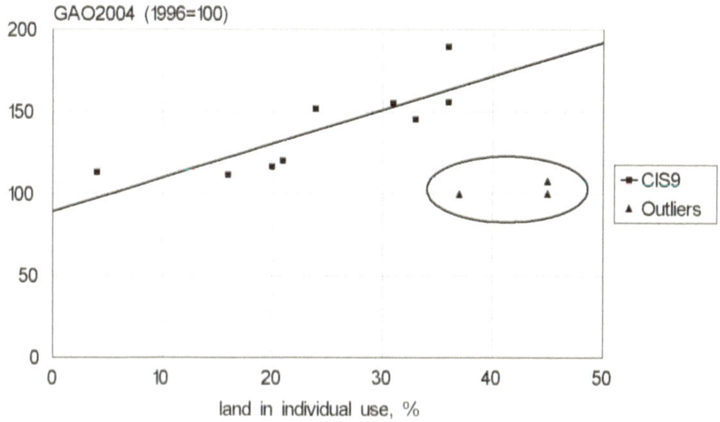

FIGURE 6.3
Agricultural growth vs. land in individual use in CIS. Outliers: Georgia, Moldova, Ukraine. Source: Authors' calculations based on data from Statistical Committee of CIS (2008).

to rural households, i.e., individualization of farming, has an immediate impact on poverty alleviation. Recent farm surveys for both Moldova (Lerman and Sutton, 2008) and Russia (Brock et al., 2008) indicate with considerable confidence that small family farms ("household plots") achieve higher levels of total factor productivity and technical efficiency than large corporate farms that succeeded the former collectives.[2] Regional data for Russia also produce higher estimates of technical efficiency for regions with a higher level of individualization (Lerman and Schreinemachers, 2005).

Outside the transition space, Lipton (2006) argues that the observed increase in the share of land cultivated by small farms over time is positive evidence of their efficiency and competitiveness by market tests. Ahearn et al. (2002), using a time series of labor and capital in US farms for 1978–96, show that in the United States small farms in fact achieve higher total factor productivity than large farms. This result is analogous to that for Moldova, where TFP calculated from a 2000 farm survey is found to decrease with increasing farm size, demonstrating "diseconomies of size" (Lerman and Sutton, 2008).

Individual farming acts as a labor sink that prevents the spread of rural unemployment and rural-to-urban migration. This is demonstrated by regional data from Russia and Poland, where individual farms attract more labor per unit of land than former collectives and the new corporate farms (Lerman and Schreinemachers, 2005). This is a highly desirable effect in the relatively poor transition countries that cannot afford adequate unemployment relief programs and must strive to avoid the "East-German syndrome" that drove two-thirds of the labor force out of agriculture in the interest of improving agricultural labor productivity (Koester and Brooks, 1997). Lipton (2006) in fact notes that the higher intensity of labor in small family farms is a universal phenomenon, which is furthermore conducive to the poverty alleviation effect that he associates with small farms.

Because of the labor sink effect, partial productivities of land and labor sometimes give contradictory results for small individual farms: the productivity of land is always found to be higher in small farms, while the productivity of labor is sometimes lower. Reports of lower productivity of labor for small farms in CIS countries have always been used as ammunition by opponents of reform, who conveniently ignored the opposite evidence of land productivity and never bothered with total factor productivity. Yet in a recent study of Russia's 80 regions, those with a higher level of individualization were observed to achieve higher productivity of agricultural labor, despite the fact that they employ relatively more workers in agriculture due to the labor sink effect discussed above (Lerman and Schreinemachers, 2005). Rizov (2005) shows for 15 transition countries in Central Eastern Europe and the CIS (using panel data for 1990–2001) that the shift to individual land use has positively contributed to labor productivity (despite the labor sink effect).

It is for these reasons that, in our view, the first measure of success is individualization of agriculture—and not privatization of land in the formal sense of ownership transfer from the state to private owners or the establishment of sophisticated land titling and registration systems. Of course individualization of agriculture is not a sufficient condition of success in transition, as some counter-examples show, and evidence from market economies suggests that individual farms are only one—albeit dominant—component of the established farming structure. Yet individualization of agriculture is the measure that has the most direct impact on the rural population and without which agricultural policy reforms in all other dimensions are likely to have a much attenuated impact. It is this measure that is most likely to have sustainable long-term effects on growth and we accordingly use it to justify our contention that Azerbaijan is an obvious example of successful agrarian reform among the CIS countries.

Overall Agricultural Policy Environment

We have argued that land and farm reform are crucial in setting a foundation for growth in agricultural production, largely because they represent a critical first-level constraint for growth of agricultural production and rural incomes. However, policy reforms along these lines alone are not sufficient to guarantee recovery of the sector or rural income growth. A program of other enabling reforms within the agricultural sector, the macroeconomy, and the institutions of policy making and implementation are also important in order to support market agriculture. The differences in productivity between individual and corporate farms drove the one-off increase in productivity after 1996, when the Azeri agriculture was rapidly individualized. However, the yields continued to increase after 2000 (see figure 4.10), when the initial impact of individualization had long since worn out. Average growth of GAO from 1996–2001 was 8% per year, while from 2001 to 2004 growth averaged 14% per year. The persistent increase in yields and accelerated growth in agriculture were the result of additional factors, primarily the attention to the policy environment.

During the crucial period from 1997 to 2004 Azerbaijan made dramatic progress in the general enabling environment for agriculture. This is evident from table 6.4, which reflects the change in agricultural reform policies of Azerbaijan and other transition countries using the World Bank's ECA Policy Reform Index (for details see the discussion around table 6.3 above). Though not near the level of the Central and East European countries that entered the EU in 2003, Azerbaijan was considerably above the CIS average in 2004. It also outstripped other CIS countries by the percentage change in its reform status index between 1997 and 2004. Furthermore, we see from table 6.4 that the progress with policy reform in Azerbaijan clearly continued beyond the 1996 watershed, which probably explains the economic recovery and the increases in yields in recent years (see chapter 4). Policy reforms, with land reform as one component of a comprehensive bundle, clearly exhibit a positive association with agricultural performance. This conclusion is borne out by previous analyses for all transition countries (see, e.g., Lerman, Csaki, and Feder, 2004).

TABLE 6.4
Status of Agricultural Policy Reforms in Selected Transition Countries 1997–2004: World Bank ECA Policy Reform Index

Country	*1997*	*2000*	*2004*	*Change from 1997 to 2004, %*
Azerbaijan	5.0	6.4	6.6	32
Average CIS	4.8	5.1	5.5	15
New EU members in CEE	7.8	8.6	9.2*	18

*2003.
Source: Csaki and Nash (1998); Csaki and Kray (2005).

Disaggregating the composite policy reform index into its five dimensions, we notice that Azerbaijan's progress has been quite uneven (figure 6.4). The progress with land reform has been nothing short of spectacular: the land reform index in 2004 is 9, compared with the benchmark of 10 for the status of completed market reforms. Yet the achievements in other dimensions have been less spectacular. Agro-processing and rural supply lag behind with a score of 6 out of 10, while the score for institutional development is particularly low at 5 out of 10. Still, figure 6.4 clearly shows that Azerbaijan has maintained the momentum of agricultural reforms in all five dimensions since 1997: the policy reform index increased between 1997 and 2004 in all areas.

In sum, despite progress, particularly in land reform, the reform experience in Azerbaijan has been far from an absolute success. Food processing reforms, for example, were little different than in other CIS countries and have not resulted in a dynamic food processing industry. Instead, disorganized agricultural supply chains, a poor business environment, high transaction costs for market coordination and trade, poor public services and institutional capacity and inadequate public investment in infrastructure has hampered the formation of robust agricultural marketing chains in Azerbaijan. Furthermore, reforms in the areas of agricultural institutions and rural finance have been slow and much remains to be done.

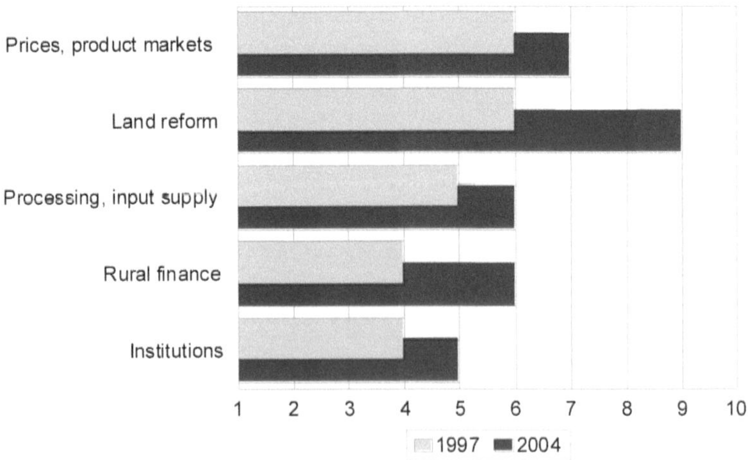

FIGURE 6.4
The five components of the World Bank Policy Index for Azerbaijan between 1997 and 2004. Source: See table 6.4.

Overall Governance and Institutions

The World Bank's ECA Index is geared specifically to agricultural reforms in transition economies. It does not include progress of general economic policies or building of market institutions outside agriculture. Good governance or "institutional quality" has long been viewed as a fundamental ingredient of sustained economic development. Governance consists of the traditions and institutions by which authority in a country is exercised. This includes the process by which governments are selected, monitored, and replaced; the capacity of the government to effectively formulate and implement sound policies; and the respect of citizens and the state for the institutions that govern economic and social interactions among them (Kaufman, Kraay, and Zoido-Lobaton, 1999). Indicators of governance, institutional quality, democratization, and other social dimensions in transition countries are regularly estimated by the World Bank Worldwide Governance Indicators (WGI) research project and by Freedom House (Boston, USA).

WGI has published estimates of institutional good governance in 212 countries since 1999 (Kaufman, Kraay, and Mastruzzi, 2007). WGI estimates of the quality of governance cover six areas. Each area estimate is an index on a scale of 0 to 100 that is a weighted average of a number of independently produced indices of perceptions of governance. Table 6.5 presents four indicators of governance in Azerbaijan from WGI for the two years 1996 and 2006 focusing on the capacity of the government to effectively formulate and implement sound policies: regulatory quality, rule of law, control of corruption, and government effectiveness. These are specifically "non-political" indicators of governance quality with no necessary connection to the degree of democratic quality of the country. *Regulatory quality* measures the ability of the government to formulate and implement sound policies and regulations that permit and promote private sector development. *Rule of law* measures the extent to which agents have confidence in and abide by the rules of society, and in particular the quality of contract enforcement, the police, and the courts, as well as the likelihood of crime and violence. *Control of corruption* measures the extent to which public power is exercised for private gain, including both petty and grand forms of corruption, as well as "capture" of the state by elites and private interests. *Government effectiveness* measures the quality of public services, the quality of the civil service and the degree of its independence from political pressures, the quality of policy formulation and implementation, and the credibility of the government's commitment to such policies.

TABLE 6.5
General Indicators of Institutional Quality in Azerbaijan, 1996–2006

	Regulatory Quality		*Rule of Law*		*Control of Corruption*		*Government Effectiveness*	
	1996	*2006*	*1996*	*2006*	*1996*	*2006*	*1996*	*2006*
Azerbaijan	16	34	18	22	13	15	17	28
Percent of CEE average	26	52	31	42	26	27	32	44
Percent of CIS average	88	121	73	112	73	68	81	105

Source: WGI (2007).

Table 6.5 illustrates that the quality of policy-making and implementation institutions in Azerbaijan has improved on average during the ten years from 1996 to 2006. Regulatory quality and government effectiveness have improved most significantly, while there has been little improvement in control of corruption in Azerbaijan. The improvement in governance in Azerbaijan has exceeded the average improvement in both CEE and CIS countries in all but the area of control of corruption. This can be seen by the increase in the scores for Azerbaijan as a percentage of the scores for the CEE and CIS averages (table 6.5, lines 2 and 3). It is also significant that governance quality in Azerbaijan in the areas of regulatory quality, rule of law, and government effectiveness exceeded that in the mean of all CIS countries in 2006.

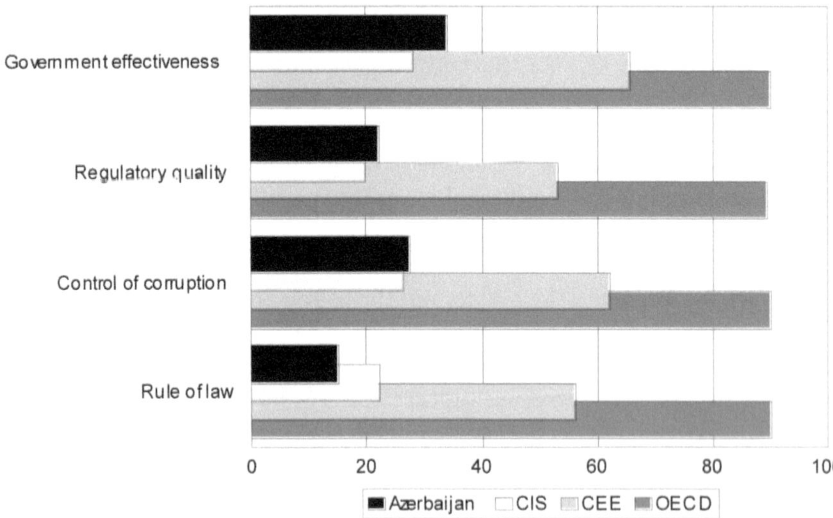

FIGURE 6.5
General governance indicators in Azerbaijan, CIS, CEE, and OECD countries, 2006 (on a scale of 0 to 100). Source: WGI (2007).

Despite improvements, all CIS countries, including Azerbaijan, have a long way to go until the quality of their institutions reaches the level of the CEE countries, and there is an enormous chasm between the quality of institutions in the CIS and the OECD countries (figure 6.5). In fact, viewed in comparison to OECD and CEE countries, institutions in Azerbaijan do not seem to differ much from the institutions in other CIS countries.

Despite progress on "non-political" indicators of institutional quality, Azerbaijan, as most CIS countries, has seen a worsening in more general indicators of democracy. However, despite studies that indicate a correlation between indicators of democracy and corruption and economic growth, there appears to be little connection for Azerbaijan in the period covered. To see this, consider the Freedom Index published annually by Freedom House in the United States. The Freedom Index includes assessment of democratization, corruption, and governance in transition countries.[3] The various indicators annually estimated by a panel of experts are described in table 6.6.

TABLE 6.6
Indicators Estimated for the Freedom House Freedom Index

Democratic Governance. Considers the democratic character and stability of the governmental system, the independence effectiveness and accountability of legislative and executive branches, and the democratic oversight of military and security services
Electoral Process. Examines national executive and legislative elections, electoral processes, the development of multiparty systems, and popular participation in the political process
Civil Society. Assesses the growth of nongovernmental organizations (NGOs), their organizational capacity and financial sustainability, and the legal and political environment in which they function; the development of free-trade unions; and interest group participation in the policy process
Independent Media. Addresses the current state of press freedom, including libel laws, harassment of journalists, editorial independence, the emergence of a financially viable private press, and Internet access for private citizens
Judicial Framework and Independence. Highlights constitutional reform, human rights protections, criminal code reform, judicial independence, the status of ethnic minority rights, guarantees of equality before the law, treatment of suspects and prisoners, and compliance with judicial decisions
Corruption. Looks at public perceptions of corruption, the business interests of top policy makers, laws on financial disclosure and conflict of interest, and the efficacy of anti-corruption initiatives

Source: www.freedomhouse.org.

The Freedom Index scores are assessed on a scale from 1 to 7, where 1 is "best" (i.e., maximum democratic progress) and 7 "worst" (least democratic progress). Table 6.7 shows a general deterioration in democratic attitudes in Azerbaijan between 1999 and 2009: the scores for judicial framework and corruption deteriorated, while the governance score remained unchanged. As a result, the composite democracy score deteriorated by 12% between 1999 and 2009. This pattern of general deterioration of democratic governance institutions in Azerbaijan is repeated in the average scores for the CIS countries, with one notable difference: while Azerbaijan at least showed no deterioration in governance, the average governance score for the CIS countries deteriorated quite strongly (by 17%) with all the other indicators. Compared with scores of around 6 for Azerbaijan and the CIS countries, the new EU members achieve scores of 2–3. Their democratic governance institutions thus receive much better evaluations. Moreover, table 6.7 shows an improvement in most scores of the new EU members, contrary to the general deterioration in the CIS and in Azerbaijan.

Ideally, one would like to observe more robust economic growth in countries with better governance, less corruption, better judiciary, and greater democracy. This would provide an ultimate justification for the entire set of governance and institutional reforms implemented with such huge efforts by all transition countries. Unfortunately, neither WGI nor Freedom House links their governance-oriented indicators with measures of economic growth. The early volumes of Freedom House's *Nations in Transit* analyzed this link and established the existence of a strong positive correlation between economic growth and the level of political and economic reform (Karatnycky et al., 1997, 1999). This conclusion is confirmed by another analysis based on 1992–99 growth data in transition countries (Lerman, Csaki, and Feder, 2004), which found a positive association between composite policy reform

TABLE 6.7
Freedom Index Scores for Azerbaijan, the CIS, and the New EU Members in Central Eastern Europe

	Governance		*Judicial Framework*		*Corruption*		*Democracy**	
	1999	*2009*	*1999*	*2009*	*1999*	*2009*	*1999*	*2009*
Azerbaijan	6.25	6.25	5.50	5.75	6.00	6.50	5.58	6.25
CIS average	5.38	6.29	5.27	5.88	5.85	6.10	5.31	5.92
New EU countries average	2.60	2.78	2.33	2.28	3.33	3.25	2.41	2.39

*The Democracy Score is the average of the ratings for Governance, Judicial Framework, and Corruption, as well as Electoral Process, Civil Society, and Independent Media.
Source: www.freedomhouse.org.

indices[4] and ranks reflecting a range of performance measures (GDP and GAO growth, changes in agricultural employment and agricultural labor productivity). In general, higher values of policy indices were found to be associated with higher growth (or more moderate decline) in GDP and with improvement in productivity of agricultural labor. In other words, a country's economic performance improves as it achieves greater progress in implementing a broad mix of market-oriented institutional and policy reforms (in the rural sector and throughout the rest of the economy). Though the above studies have indicated a correlation between indicators of democracy and corruption and economic growth, it is clear that GDP and GAO have grown in Azerbaijan since 1996 despite deterioration in these indicators, just as has been the case in the CIS as a whole.

Our final attempt to link agricultural performance with policy reform is based on another non-agricultural measure of reform. This is the so-called Sachs-Warner Openness Indicator, which dichotomizes countries into "open" and "closed" by a trade-based measure incorporating three dimensions: tariffs, non-tariff barriers, and black-market premium on foreign exchange.[5]

Prior to 1994, all CIS countries were classified as closed. In 1994 only two CIS countries were classified as open: Moldova and Kyrgyzstan. Four more countries "opened up" between 1994 and 1996: Armenia, Georgia, Azerbaijan, and Tajikistan. Russia and Ukraine were classified as closed even in 1999 (as were Belarus, Kazakhstan, Uzbekistan, and of course Turkmenistan). It may be of interest to note that the open countries are "small" while the closed countries are "large."

We have calculated the cumulative growth in both GDP and GAO between 1990 and 1994 (the early reform phase) and then between 1994 and 2004 (the agricultural recovery phase). It turns out that the "open" countries did much worse than the "closed" countries in the early transition period 1990–94 by both GDP growth and GAO growth. In fact, the "open" countries dropped much more than the "closed" countries during the initial decline phase. But then their rebound was much stronger in 1994–2004: the "open" countries overtook the "closed" countries by a very wide margin by both GDP and GAO. These results are summarized in table 6.8.

* * *

This last chapter has been about the implications and limits of reform in Azerbaijan. The evidence assembled is certainly not conclusive, but it adds up fairly convincingly to a clear result: better agricultural performance is achieved by countries that are more advanced on the path of agricultural reform, irrespective of how we measure it—whether by share of land in individual farming or by agriculture-related policy reforms (as in the ECA index). Land

TABLE 6.8
Growth and Openness in CIS Countries: The Decline Period 1990–1994 and the Recovery Period 1994–2004

	Cumulative GDP Growth		Cumulative GAO Growth	
Openness Status as of 1999	*1990–94*	*1994–2004*	*1990–94*	*1994–2004*
Open: Armenia, Azerbaijan, Georgia, Kyrgyzstan, Moldova, Tajikistan	−55.7	65.0	−35.1	43.3
Closed: Belarus, Russia, Ukraine, Kazakhstan, Turkmenistan, Uzbekistan	−31.8	40.6	−22.9	5.0

**Note*: All CIS countries were "closed" before 1994. The "open" countries changed their status between 1994 and 1996.

and farm reform are crucial in setting a foundation for growth in agricultural production, largely because they represent a critical first-level constraint for growth of agricultural production and rural incomes. Policy reforms along these lines alone are not sufficient to guarantee recovery of the sector or rural income growth. A program of other enabling reforms within the agricultural sector, the macroeconomy, and the institutions of economic policy making and implementation are also important in order to support market agriculture. However, the critical first-level constraint is still land reform. Progress on this issue should come first; other issues are secondary.

When we expand our view to include non-agricultural reform indicators (Freedom Index or the Openness Indicator) our judgments become far more speculative. For a crosssection of countries the weight of the cumulative evidence seems to support our initial hypothesis that the long-term pattern of agricultural development in transition countries, including Azerbaijan, is driven by the policy environment (figure 6.5, tables 6.7 and 6.8). However, in the case of Azerbaijan the record over time has been one of improvements in the economy while indicators of democracy have deteriorated.

Notes

1. ECA is an acronym for "Europe and Central Asia," referring to the post-socialist transition countries in this region. The ECA Land Reform Index was introduced in 1997 (Csaki and Nash, 1998) and subsequently updated on an annual basis. For latest updates see Csaki and Kray (2005).

2. In these studies, total factor productivity (TFP) is calculated using production function methodology, whereas technical efficiency is calculated by production frontier analysis.

3. For further details about the Freedom Index methodology and selected data see the Freedom House web site www.freedomhouse.org. *Nations in Transit* is a print report with comprehensive tables of the Freedom Index annually published by Freedom House since 1997.

4. The composite policy reform indices in this study included the World Bank Agricultural Policy Reform Index for 1999 and an Aggregate Policy Index for 1997–98 calculated as simple average of five policy-oriented indices: the World Bank Agricultural Policy Reform Index, the Freedom House Freedom Index, the World Bank Liberalization Index, the *Euromoney* Creditworthiness Index, and the World Bank Country Policy and Institutional Assessment (CPIA) Index. For details see Lerman, Csaki, and Feder (2004, p. 190, table 5.6).

5. The openness indicator was introduced by Sachs and Warner (1995); some fascinating update work was done by Wacziarg and Welch (2003).

Statistical Annex

List of Tables

TABLE A.1
Population: Total and Rural 1979–2008 (End of Year)

	Total Population, Thousands	*Rural Population, Thousands*	*Rural Population, %*	*Population 1979=100*	*Rural Population 1979=100*
1913	2339.2	1783.3	76.2		
1926	2313.7	1664.2	71.9		
1938	3205.2	2048.4	63.9		
1958	3697.7	1930.4	52.2		
1959	3815.7	1980.5	51.9		
1964	4509.5	2270.7	50.4		
1969	5117.1	2552.5	49.9		
1970	5227.0	2594.7	49.6		
1971	5338.9	2632.0	49.3		
1972	5444.0	2667.0	49.0		
1973	5543.8	2689.7	48.5		
1974	5644.4	2723.1	48.2		
1975	5733.7	2740.4	47.8		
1976	5828.3	2762.9	47.4		
1977	5924.0	2795.8	47.2		
1978	6028.3	2828.0	46.9		
1979	6114.3	2866.8	46.9	100.0	100.0
1980	6206.7	2905.2	46.8	101.5	101.3
1981	6308.8	2952.9	46.8	103.2	103.0
1982	6406.3	2999.3	46.8	104.8	104.6
1983	6513.3	3053.5	46.9	106.5	106.5
1984	6622.4	3097.9	46.8	108.3	108.1

1985	6717.9	3129.9	46.6	109.9	109.2
1986	6822.7	3171.4	46.5	111.6	110.6
1987	6928.0	3205.4	46.3	113.3	111.8
1988	7021.2	3215.3	45.8	114.8	112.2
1989	7131.9	3284.6	46.1	116.6	114.6
1990	7218.5	3360.2	46.5	118.1	117.2
1991	7324.1	3439.7	47.0	119.8	120.0
1992	7440.0	3511.5	47.2	121.7	122.5
1993	7549.6	3578.7	47.4	123.5	124.8
1994	7643.5	3637.9	47.6	125.0	126.9
1995	7726.2	3691.7	47.8	126.4	128.8
1996	7799.8	3742.0	48.0	127.6	130.5
1997	7876.7	3794.2	48.2	128.8	132.3
1998	7953.4	3889.1	48.9	130.1	135.7
1999	8016.2	3929.8	49.0	131.1	137.1
2000	8081.0	3973.5	49.2	132.2	138.6
2001	8141.4	4011.3	49.3	133.2	139.9
2002	8202.5	4048.2	49.4	134.2	141.2
2003	8265.7	4011.4	48.5	135.2	139.9
2004	8347.3	4049.0	48.5	136.5	141.2
2005	8436.4	4079.8	48.4	138.0	142.3
2006	8532.7	4135.1	48.5	139.6	144.2
2007	8629.9	4165.1	48.3	141.1	145.3
2008	8730.3	4210.8	48.2	142.8	146.9

Source: Statistical Committee of Azerbaijan (200[redacted]a, 2009b).

TABLE A.2
Total and Agricultural Employment

	Total Number of Employed, Thousands	*Employed in Agriculture, Thousands*	*Share of Employed in Agriculture, %*	*Agricultural Employment, Percent of 1980*	*Agricultural Employment, Percent of 1965*
1965		570.1			100.0
1966		570.5			100.1
1967		570.9			100.1
1968		571.3			100.2
1969		571.7			100.3
1970		572.0			100.3
1971		584.7			102.5
1972		588.2			103.2
1973		609.5			106.9
1974		640.4			112.3
1975		664.2			116.5
1976		669.5			117.4
1977		709.8			124.5
1978		725.3			127.2
1979		740.9			129.9
1980	2299.5	756.4	32.9	100.0	132.7
1981	2366.5	778.9	32.9	103.0	136.6
1982	2428.2	799.5	32.9	105.7	140.2
1983	2503.1	830.6	33.2	109.8	145.7
1984	2559.4	850.0	33.2	112.4	149.1

1985	2619.2	865.3	33.0	114.4	151.8
1986	2671.1	879.6	32.9	116.3	154.3
1987	2749.5	920.4	33.5	121.7	161.4
1988	2761.3	899.0	32.6	118.9	157.7
1989	2880.9	904.8	31.4	119.6	158.7
1990	3703.4	1144.4	30.9	150.6	199.9
1991	3732.0	1186.1	31.8	156.1	207.1
1992	3722.0	1291.5	34.7	170.1	225.6
1993	3714.6	1203.5	32.4	158.4	210.2
1994	3631.3	1143.9	31.5	150.6	199.9
1995	3613.0	1112.8	30.8	146.6	194.5
1996	3686.7	1172.4	31.8	154.5	205.0
1997	3694.1	1071.3	29.0	141.1	187.2
1998	3701.5	1139.6	30.8	150.7	199.9
1999	3702.8	1566.3	42.3	207.1	274.7
2000	3704.5	1517.2	41.0	200.6	266.1
2001	3715.0	1482.0	39.9	195.9	259.9
2002	3726.5	1495.0	40.1	197.6	262.2
2003	3747.0	1497.0	40.0	197.9	262.6
2004	3809.1	1502.7	39.5	198.7	263.6
2005	3850.2	1510.0	39.2	199.6	264.8
2006	3973.0	1547.2	38.9	204.5	271.4
2007	4014.1	1550.7	38.6	205.0	272.0
2008	4056.0	1553.1	38.3	205.3	272.4

Sources: 1965–79 from Statistical Committee of USSR (various years), adjusted upward by an estimate of self-employed in agriculture (about 25% of all employed); 1980–89 from Statistical Committee of CIS (2008); 1990–2008 from Statistical Committee of Azerbaijan (2006d, 2009a)

TABLE A.3
Wages in Agriculture and Industry Relative to the Average Wage in the Economy

Year	Agriculture	Industry	Petroleum Sector*
1960	74.6	108.4	
1965	67.7	105.3	
1970	71.1	109.8	
1975	79.5	111.9	
1979	86.4	115.0	
1980	93.9	111.3	
1981	99.1	110.6	
1982	99.0	110.7	
1983	95.8	112.1	
1984	94.5	114.1	
1985	97.8	111.9	
1986	87.8	114.0	
1987	80.7	114.1	
1988	78.3	117.6	
1990	84.1	112.3	
1991	82.1	125.8	
1992	54.4	143.7	
1993	51.3	142.3	
1994	54.2	137.1	
1995	53.7	153.0	
1996	42.3	163.6	
1997	35.0	163.3	
1998	26.1	164.5	
1999	35.3	132.4	341.8
2000	31.2	128.3	367.6
2001	30.4	116.6	419.5
2002	28.5	110.6	409.1
2003	29.9	115.1	373.4
2004	30.0	98.8	453.9
2005	33.6	93.3	408.7
2006	35.2	94.3	425.3
2007	40.2	88.3	391.8

*Petroleum appeared as a separate economic sector (mining) after the change of the statistical classification in 1999. Prior to that it was presumably included in industry.

Source: 1960–88 from Statistical Committee of AzSSR (1980, 1985, 1988); 1990–2007 from Statistical Committee of Azerbaijan (2006d, 2009b).

TABLE A.4
Sectoral Structure of GDP

Year	*Agriculture*	*Industry*	*Petroleum and Natural Gas*	*Non-Oil Industry*	*Other Sectors*
1980	28.0	44.8			27.2
1981	29.3	43.3			27.5
1982	28.9	43.0			28.1
1983	30.8	40.7			28.5
1984	31.7	39.0			29.3
1985	32.7	42.8			24.5
1986	31.7	41.5			26.8
1987	30.4	43.5			26.2
1988	29.7	41.4			29.0
1989	30.7	43.2			26.1
1990	37.5	34.8			27.7
1991					
1992					
1993	27.1	24.9			48.0
1994	32.4	20.4			47.2
1995	25.3	27.3	16.3	11.0	47.4
1996	24.9	25.8	13.7	12.1	49.3
1997	20.0	25.3	15.4	9.9	54.7
1998	18.0	22.0	13.5	8.5	60.0
1999	18.2	28.2	20.3	7.9	53.6
2000	15.9	36.0	27.6	8.4	48.1
2001	14.7	37.6	29.6	8.0	47.7
2002	14.0	37.4	28.8	8.6	48.6
2003	12.2	37.2	27.5	9.7	50.6
2004	10.8	38.3	29.0	9.3	50.9
2005	9.0	47.5	39.4	8.1	43.5
2006	6.7	57.3	50.9	6.4	36.0
2007	6.4	59.5	53.7	5.8	34.1
2008	5.7	57.4	52.5	4.9	36.9

Note: The gap in data in 1991–92 is attributable to the shift from the system of Soviet national accounts, based on socialist concepts of gross social product and net material product (NMP), to the internationally accepted system of national accounts, based on gross domestic product (GDP). The data for the Soviet period 1980–90 are based on NMP series in current prices from Statistical Committee of CIS (2008; the data for the post-Soviet period 1993–2005 are based on GDP series as reported in Statistical Committee of CIS (2008) for 1993–94 and Statistical Committee of Azerbaijan (2005, 2007, 2009a) for 1995–2008. Petroleum sector data began to be published as a separate category only after the change in industry classification in 1999; the petroleum data for 1995–98 are estimates from Ministry of Economic Development (2001).

TABLE A.5
GDP and GAO Growth 1965=100

		GAO			Share of Individual Sector in GAO, %
	GDP	All Farms	Corporate	Individual	
1965	100.0	100.0	100.0	100.0	30.4
1966		102.0	99.0	108.6	32.4
1967		108.8	102.2	124.0	34.7
1968		115.0	109.7	126.9	33.6
1969		107.6	103.1	117.9	33.3
1970	133.0	126.7	121.7	138.3	33.2
1971	139.0	126.0	124.4	129.8	31.3
1972	145.0	130.4	132.0	126.6	29.5
1973	157.0	148.6	148.3	149.5	30.6
1974		174.1	178.1	165.1	28.8
1975	184.9	169.3	172.3	162.6	29.2
1976	202.2	192.0	201.5	170.3	27.0
1977	215.5	198.5	206.2	181.0	27.7
1978	231.4	215.7	225.0	194.3	27.4
1979	244.7	231.5	246.1	198.1	26.0
1980	271.3	260.0	284.0	205.1	24.0
1981	293.9	278.7	307.2	213.4	23.3
1982	301.9	283.0	307.2	227.5	24.5
1983	311.2	285.4	305.0	240.6	25.6
1984	327.2	307.7	335.5	244.3	24.1
1985	343.1	301.0	321.1	250.3	26.2
1986	348.6	295.7	304.3	271.1	28.9
1987	362.4	290.6	282.6	308.7	33.3
1988	364.8	282.8	273.2	302.5	33.7
1989	342.5	257.6	241.5	291.7	35.7
1990	315.3	260.1	244.2	289.2	35.1
1991	313.1	260.8	233.0	316.3	38.3
1992	242.5	198.8	166.7	264.8	42.0
1993	186.4	168.2	127.1	254.5	47.8
1994	149.8	146.9	98.2	250.3	53.8
1995	132.1	136.5	78.4	260.6	67.3
1996	133.7	140.7	72.8	286.0	67.3
1997	141.6	132.1	44.2	321.3	74.1
1998	155.8	140.2	19.3	401.7	93.3
1999	167.1	150.1	9.5	454.6	96.0
2000	185.7	168.3	5.6	520.6	97.7
2001	204.0	186.9	5.4	580.4	98.2
2002	225.8	198.9	6.0	616.9	98.1
2003	251.0	210.0	10.2	642.4	97.0
2004	268.5	219.6	12.4	667.9	95.7

(continued on next page)

	GDP	GAO			Share of Individual Sector in GAO, %
		All Farms	Corporate	Individual	
2005	339.4	236.1	12.9	718.9	96.0
2006	456.5	238.3	12.7	729.3	96.8
2007	570.6	247.7	17.9	748.6	95.7
2008	632.3	262.8	21.5	788.1	94.6

Source: Statistical Committee of Azerbaijan (various years); GDP updates for recent years from Statistical Committee of CIS (2008) and National Bank of Azerbaijan (2009).

TABLE A.6
GDP and GAO Growth 1984=100

Year	GDP	GAO		Individual
		All Farms	Corporate	
1984	100.0	100.0	100.0	100.0
1985	104.9	97.8	95.7	102.5
1986	106.5	96.1	90.7	111.0
1987	110.8	94.4	84.2	126.4
1988	111.5	91.9	81.4	123.8
1989	104.7	83.7	72.0	119.4
1990	96.4	84.5	72.8	118.4
1991	95.7	84.8	69.4	129.5
1992	74.1	64.6	49.7	108.4
1993	57.0	54.7	37.9	104.2
1994	45.8	47.7	29.3	102.5
1995	40.4	44.4	23.4	106.7
1996	40.9	45.7	21.7	117.1
1997	43.3	42.9	13.2	131.5
1998	47.6	[illegible]	5.7	164.4
1999	51.1	48.8	2.8	186.1
2000	56.8	54.7	1.7	213.1
2001	62.3	60.7	1.6	237.6
2002	69.0	64.6	1.8	252.5
2003	76.7	68.2	3.0	263.0
2004	82.1	71.4	3.7	273.4
2005	103.8	76.7	3.9	294.3
2006	139.6	77.4	3.8	298.6
2007	174.5	80.5	5.3	306.4
2008	193.3	85.4	6.4	322.6

Source: See table A.5.

TABLE A.7
Growth of Crop and Livestock Production 1990=100

Year	Crop Production			Livestock Production		
	All Farms	*Corporate*	*Individual*	*All Farms*	*Corporate*	*Individual*
1990	100	100	100	100	100	100
1991	102.0			97.3		
1992	75.2			78.6		
1993	62.9			67.7		
1994	52.5			63.6		
1995	46.6	32.1	84.3	62.7	23.6	94.5
1996	48.3	33.4	96.4	64.2	19.1	100.7
1997	41.4	21.7	105.2	67.1	7.5	115.5
1998	43.0	9.5	151.7	72.9	3.4	129.3
1999	47.0	4.4	185.0	76.3	2.3	136.4
2000	56.3	2.1	231.8	79.2	2.9	141.1
2001	65.4	1.7	271.7	82.4	3.8	146.5
2002	70.0	1.5	291.5	86.9	5.5	153.5
2003	73.7	1.3	307.8	92.3	13.8	157.5
2004	76.6	1.4	320.1	97.6	17.5	164.4
2005	84.6	1.6	353.7	101.1	17.9	170.5
2006	83.9	1.6	351.3	104.1	17.4	176.3
2007	85.9	1.9	359.0	110.4	25.3	181.8
2008	92.1	2.9	382.8	114.9	29.4	186.5

Source: Statistical Committee of Azerbaijan (2006b, 2009b).

TABLE A.8
Share of Individual Sector in Crop and Livestock Production

Year	*Share of Individual Sector in GAO, %*	*Share of Individual Sector in Crop Production, %*	*Share of Individual Sector in Livestock Production, %*
1985	26.2	14.1	51.6
1990	35.1	23.6	55.2
1995	67.3	53.4	86.8
1996	67.3	53.4	86.8
1997	74.1	63.4	89.5
1998	93.3	89.8	98.6
1999	96.0	93.8	99.0
2000	97.7	97.1	98.6
2001	98.1	97.9	98.3
2002	98.2	98.6	97.6
2003	97.0	98.7	94.4
2004	95.7	98.5	91.7
2005	96.0	98.6	92.6
2006	96.8	98.6	94.4
2007	95.7	98.7	90.7
2008	94.6	98.6	87.9

Source: Statistical Committee of Azerbaijan (2006b, 2008, 2009a).

TABLE A.9
Structure of Agricultural Production:
Shares of Crop and Livestock Production in GAO by Farm Type

	Share of Livestock Production in GAO, %			*Share of Crop Production in GAO, %*		
Year	*All Farms*	*Corporate Farms*	*Individual Farms*	*All Farms*	*Corporate Farms*	*Individual Farms*
1980	25			75		
1981	30			70		
1982	31			69		
1983	29			71		
1984	30			70		
1985	32			68		
1986	34			66		
1987	35			65		
1988	36			64		
1989	39			61		
1990	36			64		
1991	35			65		
1992	31			69		
1993	46			54		
1994	34			66		
1995	41	17	53	59	83	47
1996	41	17	53	59	83	47
1997	41	17	50	59	83	50
1998	39	8	41	61	92	59
1999	43	11	44	57	89	56
2000	42	26	42	58	74	58
2001	39	35	39	61	65	61
2002	39	52	39	61	48	61
2003	41	75	40	59	25	60
2004	41	79	39	59	21	61
2005	43	80	41	57	20	59
2006	43	75	42	57	25	58
2007	38	81	36	62	19	64
2008	37	83	34	63	17	66

Source: 1980–89 from Statistical Committee of CIS (2008); 1990–2005 from Statistical Committee of Azerbaijan (2006b, 2009a).

TABLE A.10
Agricultural and Arable Land (thousand ha)

						Land Used by Farms		
Year	*Agricultural Land*	*Arable Land*	*Perennials*	*Pastures Meadows*	*Irrigated Ag Land*	*Ag Land*	*Arable*	*Perennials*
1965	4145.7	1341.8	190.0	2234.7	1278.0	3918.4	1335.4	191.0
1966	4131.1	1333.6			1244.0	3931.6	1326.9	203.6
1967	4228.6	1385.4			1224.0	3992.2	1361.9	214.5
1968	4221.1	1353.5			1176.0	4012.3	1329.7	225.0
1969	4228.2	1350.1			1142.0	4014.6	1325.8	238.6
1970	4253.0	1339.3	264.2	2279.6	1128.0	4032.4	1320.1	278.7
1971	4254.2	1376.2			1130.0	4035.6	1362.9	291.5
1972	4265.6	1388.7			1132.5	4045.2	1373.5	313.0
1973	4268.4	1380.4			1140.5	4044.8	1365.8	302.4
1974	4267.4	1394.8			1148.5	4043.9	1379.3	313.5
1975	4273.6	1423.3	312.9	2327.3	1156.5	4049.1	1407.2	333.8
1976	4274.1	1401.8			1165.2	4059.3	1386.0	353.0
1977	4274.5	1392.6			1176.2	4059.7	1379.5	369.5
1978	4275.5	1380.3			1189.2	4063.5	1365.2	379.7
1979	4277.4	1371.2			1198.2	4066.5	1357.1	403.3
1980	4282.0	1360.9	404.8	2335.4	1212.0	4067.6	1346.6	414.6
1981	4289.6	1394.3			1249.6	4075.0	1378.9	420.9
1982	4306.4	1419.3			1277.5	4089.6	1404.5	422.4
1983	4318.0	1427.4			1298.6	4096.9	1412.6	430.4
1984	4319.6	1448.5			1316.7	4098.1	1434.0	437.6
1985	4327.0	1454.3	416.6	2369.3	1334.6	4112.3	1441.0	419.4

1986	4338.3	1532.3			1347.5	4123.8	1518.6	365.2
1987	4360.7	1555.1			1362.7	4139.8	1541.6	347.3
1988	4364.3	1562.2			1387.8	4141.8	1548.4	344.7
1989	4369.0	1572.4			1407.3	4149.0	1560.2	340.9
1990	4382.9	1589.0	347.4	2365.7	1418.5	4160.6	1576.7	330.7
1991	4448.7	1615.8	326.9	2421.2	1435.7	4180.8	1599.8	320.5
1992	4446.2	1612.3	310.3	2431.4	1448.8	4208.3	1598.6	287.0
1993	4456.7	1620.4	310.5	2430.3	1453.2	4227.2	1606.5	276.5
1994	4486.0	1623.2	308.7	2453.7	1449.1	4252.6	1609.1	244.5
1995	4489.1	1628.4	309.5	2435.3	1449.5	4260.0	1614.7	226.9
1996	4526.2	1672.2	262.9	2478.5	1450.0	4312.9	1659.6	185.9
1997	4588.7	1695.7	260.8	2526.7	1437.7	4350.8	1673.1	161.8
1998	4682.1	1735.5	250.0	2622.4	1439.0	4342.9	1708.9	121.2
1999	4692.4	1761.6	236.9	2630.6	1429.1	4349.0	1728.7	108.5
2000	4740.4	1766.8	236.8	2678.0	1423.0	4557.0	1743.2	102.7
2001	4745.6	1775.9	227.0	2682.9	1418.1	4578.2	1753.6	99.6
2002	4744.9	1783.2	225.9	2681.7	1422.9	4570.0	1759.5	100.2
2003	4754.6	1785.6	225.8	2690.3	1422.9	4579.0	1764.4	99.8
2004	4754.9	1790.8	222.8	2691.4	1428.1	4580.0	1769.9	101.4
2005	4758.6	1797.6	221.5	2693.9	1429.7	4584.8	1776.6	105.5
2006	4756.0	1795.5	221.1	2693.9	1429.1	4581.9	1774.5	118.9
2007	4756.5	1808.4	224.7	2677.8	1429.6	4582.2	1787.8	126.8
2008	4756.7	1818.4	227.5	2669.0	1429.5	4523.9	1659.7	134.1

Source: Statistical Committee of Azerbaijan (2006b, 2009b).
Note: Perennials include fruit orchards, vineyards, and tea plantations.

Table A.10A. Agricultural and Arable Land: Definitions

Agricultural land is the sum of three main components: land designated as arable (i.e., land for field crops and horticulture), land designated for perennials (orchards, vineyards, tea plantations), and land designated as meadows and pastures for grazing. The average structure of agricultural land since 2000 is shown in figure A.1. This structure is fairly representative of the entire period since 1965 although the area of agricultural land increased from 4.2 million ha to 4.8 million ha during this time.

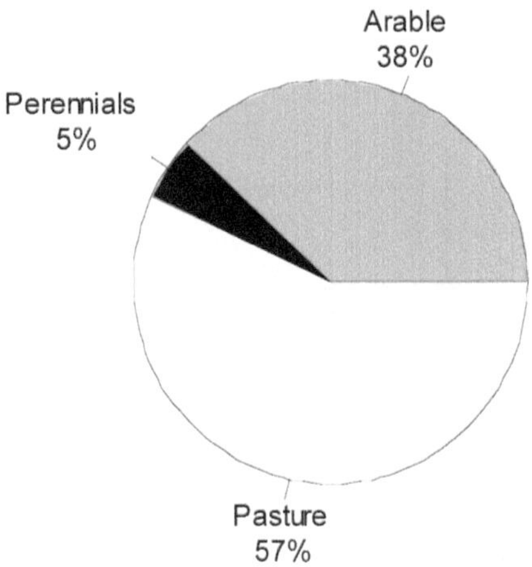

FIGURE A.1
Average structure of agricultural land 2000–08. Total area of agricultural land 4.8 million hectares. Source: Table A.10.

There are two series of data for agricultural land and its components: a series based on land mapping surveys that record the stock of land in each category and a series based on actual use of land in farms. The difference between the two series for agricultural land has been remarkably stable over time (a gap of about 5%). The gap for arable land has been even smaller. However, the situation is different for land under perennials: here the two series—land stock and land use—were virtually identical up to 1992 and then they diverged widely (figure A.2). Although the stock of land under perennials decreased over time as land was reclassified, the actual cultivation of fruit trees, vineyards, and tea plantations declined dramatically faster as trees and vines were uprooted due to changing economic conditions (see also chapter 2, box 2.4). The process of destruction of perennial plantations seems to have been arrested in 2000, but land actually under perennials had dropped to less than 50% of the land stock in the corresponding category. Land used for perennials has shown some improvement since 2005, approaching 60% of the land stock in 2008.

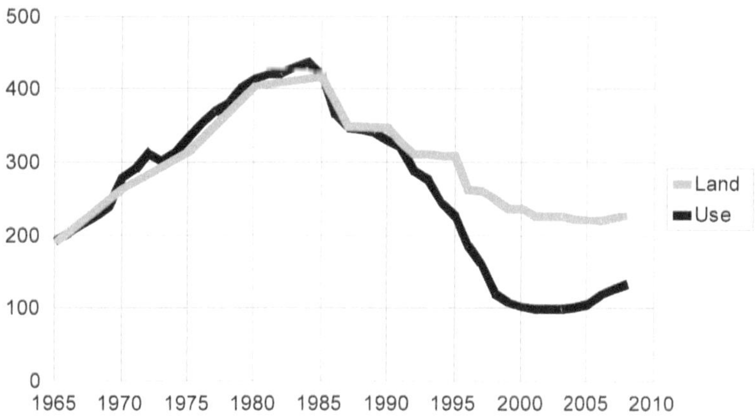

FIGURE A.2
Perennials: land stock and actual land use 1965–2008. Source: Table A.10.

TABLE A.11
Cropping Pattern: Field Crops and Perennials

	Cultivated, '000 ha	*Field Crops, %*	*Perennials, %*	*Fruit, %*	*Grapes, %*	*Tea, %*
1965	1341.3	85.8	14.2	49.8	46.9	3.4
1966	1415.6	85.6	14.4	49.6	47.2	3.2
1967	1432.3	85.0	15.0	48.7	48.0	3.4
1968	1430.2	84.3	15.7	47.8	48.9	3.3
1969	1410.5	83.1	16.9	46.7	50.1	3.2
1970	1474.7	81.1	18.9	53.5	43.6	2.8
1971	1420.2	79.5	20.5	51.5	45.7	2.8
1972	1587.7	80.3	19.7	48.7	48.7	2.6
1973	1560.0	80.6	19.4	47.9	49.7	2.4
1974	1589.9	80.3	19.7	46.8	50.6	2.6
1975	1643.9	79.7	20.3	44.1	53.4	2.5
1976	1665.7	78.8	21.2	42.1	55.4	2.5
1977	1678.2	78.0	22.0	39.8	57.6	2.6
1978	1667.7	77.2	22.8	37.9	59.5	2.7
1979	1679.3	76.0	24.0	36.2	61.4	2.4
1980	1678.5	75.3	24.7	34.1	63.4	2.5
1981	1710.4	75.4	24.6	32.3	65.1	2.6
1982	1777.2	76.2	23.8	32.2	65.1	2.7
1983	1792.8	76.0	24.0	31.6	65.6	2.9
1984	1817.4	75.9	24.1	32.1	64.9	3.0
1985	1790.7	76.6	23.4	33.0	63.9	3.2
1986	1683.4	78.3	21.7	37.7	58.7	3.7
1987	1753.6	80.2	19.8	39.4	56.7	3.9
1988	1812.5	81.0	19.0	39.5	56.7	3.8
1989	1637.3	79.2	20.8	40.7	55.4	3.8
1990	1793.2	81.6	18.4	41.1	54.9	4.0
1991	1793.3	82.1	17.9	42.5	53.4	4.1
1992	1644.1	82.5	17.5	44.5	51.0	4.6
1993	1671.3	83.5	16.5	44.5	50.7	4.8
1994	1507.3	83.8	16.2	49.5	45.1	5.4
1995	1434.8	84.2	15.8	51.9	43.1	5.0
1996	1393.3	86.7	13.3	50.7	44.8	4.5
1997	1239.7	86.9	13.1	54.6	41.0	4.4
1998	1041.6	88.4	11.6	65.7	29.0	5.4
1999	941.2	88.5	11.5	76.0	18.9	5.1
2000	1144.2	91.0	9.0	80.9	13.8	5.3
2001	1261.9	92.1	7.9	84.5	11.5	3.9
2002	1323.1	92.4	7.6	87.4	8.9	3.7
2003	1319.3	92.4	7.6	88.6	7.7	3.7
2004	1395.2	92.7	7.3	88.5	7.9	3.6
2005	1433.4	92.6	7.4	88.2	9.1	2.7
2006	1445.2	91.8	8.2	91.2	7.3	1.5
2007	1450.6	91.2	8.8	89.9	8.8	1.3
2008	1634.0	91.8	8.2	89.4	9.9	0.7

Source: Statistical Committee of Azerbaijan (2006b); 2006–08 private communication (July 2009)

TABLE A.12
Cropping Pattern: Field Crops

	Field Crops, '000 ha	*Grain, %*	*Technical Crops, %*	*Of Which: Cotton, %*	*Vegetables, %*	*Feed crops, %*
1965	1150.3	57.2	20.1	18.7	4.6	18.0
1966	1212.0	57.6	19.4	18.0	4.4	18.6
1967	1217.8	55.5	18.6	17.3	4.5	21.4
1968	1205.2	54.0	18.3	16.9	4.5	23.2
1969	1171.9	51.5	18.3	16.9	4.6	25.5
1970	1196.0	52.0	17.6	16.1	4.8	25.7
1971	1128.7	43.7	19.7	18.2	5.0	31.6
1972	1274.7	50.9	16.8	15.4	4.7	27.6
1973	1257.6	48.9	17.2	15.8	5.1	28.8
1974	1276.4	48.8	17.9	16.4	5.1	28.2
1975	1310.1	46.7	17.6	16.1	5.0	30.7
1976	1312.7	47.7	18.0	16.5	5.4	28.9
1977	1308.7	46.8	18.2	16.7	5.5	29.6
1978	1288.0	44.9	19.0	17.4	5.4	30.7
1979	1276.0	41.8	20.5	18.9	5.3	32.4
1980	1263.9	38.8	21.5	19.7	5.5	34.2
1981	1289.5	36.5	23.7	21.9	5.5	34.4
1982	1354.8	37.8	24.4	22.6	5.3	32.6
1983	1362.4	37.1	24.2	22.3	5.5	33.3
1984	1379.8	36.3	23.3	21.5	5.5	34.9
1985	1371.3	36.0	23.2	21.5	5.1	35.6
1986	1318.2	31.3	24.5	22.8	5.3	38.9
1987	1406.3	32.8	23.3	21.6	5.1	38.8
1988	1467.8	36.7	21.9	20.4	5.0	36.5
1989	1296.4	30.4	22.9	21.6	5.8	40.9
1990	1462.5	39.9	19.3	18.0	5.1	35.7
1991	1472.8	44.2	18.0	16.7	4.9	32.9
1992	1357.1	46.7	18.7	17.2	4.4	30.2
1993	1394.8	50.9	17.5	16.0	4.0	27.6
1994	1262.8	50.4	18.3	17.0	4.4	26.8
1995	1207.9	50.5	18.8	17.4	4.1	26.7
1996	1207.4	53.0	19.3	17.7	5.1	22.6
1997	1077.9	61.2	21.1	19.6	5.9	11.9
1998	920.4	64.6	18.5	16.9	8.4	8.5
1999	832.7	62.4	12.6	11.3	12.9	12.1
2000	1041.5	62.2	11.3	9.7	13.1	13.3
2001	1162.3	65.4	8.5	7.2	13.0	13.0
2002	1222.9	67.2	6.3	5.0	13.0	13.5
2003	1219.5	63.7	7.3	5.5	13.5	15.6
2004	1293.8	63.0	7.6	6.0	13.5	15.9
2005	1327.9	60.4	9.9	8.5	13.5	16.1
2006	1326.3	59.2	9.5	7.8	13.3	18.1
2007	1323.9	55.9	7.3	5.7	14.0	22.9
2008	1499.9	59.6	4.7	3.2	5.4	23.2

Source: Statistical Committee of Azerbaijan (2006b. 2009b); 2008 private communication (July 2009)

TABLE A.13

Agricultural Land by Users: Corporate and Individual Farms

		Land in Farms, '000 ha				Structure of Land in Farms, %		
Year	*Ag Land, '000 ha*	*All Farms*	*Corporate*	*Individual*	*Common Land*	*Corporate*	*Individual*	*Common Land*
1965	4145.7	3918.4	3846.2	72.2		98.2	1.8	
1966	4131.1	3931.6	3855.8	75.6		98.1	1.9	
1967	4228.6	3992.2	3907.1	85.1		97.9	2.1	
1968	4221.1	4012.3	3925.6	86.7		97.8	2.2	
1969	4228.2	4014.6	3926.5	88.1		97.8	2.2	
1970	4253.0	4032.4	3943.8	88.6		97.8	2.2	
1971	4254.2	4035.6	3946.6	89.0		97.8	2.2	
1972	4265.6	4045.2	3955.7	89.5		97.8	2.2	
1973	4268.4	4044.8	3955.2	89.6		97.8	2.2	
1974	4267.4	4043.9	3954.1	89.8		97.8	2.2	
1975	4273.6	4049.1	3959.3	89.8		97.8	2.2	
1976	4274.1	4059.3	3969.4	89.9		97.8	2.2	
1977	4274.5	4059.7	3969.4	90.3		97.8	2.2	
1978	4275.5	4063.5	3972.8	90.7		97.8	2.2	
1979	4277.4	4066.5	3975.6	90.9		97.8	2.2	
1980	4282.0	4067.6	3976.0	91.6		97.7	2.3	
1981	4289.6	4075.0	3976.0	99.0		97.6	2.4	
1982	4306.4	4089.6	3990.1	99.5		97.6	2.4	
1983	4318.0	4096.9	3996.5	100.4		97.5	2.5	

1984	4319.6	4098.1	3996.7	101.4		97.5	2.5	
1985	4327.0	4112.3	4010.5	101.8		97.5	2.5	
1986	4338.3	4123.8	4020.1	103.7		97.5	2.5	
1987	4360.7	4139.8	4036.1	103.7		97.5	2.5	
1988	4364.3	4141.8	4033.5	108.3		97.4	2.6	
1989	4369.0	4149.0	4035.6	113.4		97.3	2.7	
1990	4382.9	4160.6	4022.6	138.0		96.7	3.3	
1991	4448.7	4180.8	4039.5	141.4		96.6	3.4	
1992	4446.2	4208.3	4045.4	162.9		96.1	3.9	
1993	4456.7	4227.2	4079.0	148.2		96.5	3.5	
1994	4486.0	4252.6	4098.0	154.6		96.4	3.6	
1995	4489.1	4260.0	4035.6	228.2		94.6	5.4	
1996	4526.2	4312.9	4041.0	271.9		93.7	6.3	
1997	4588.7	4350.8	2511.3	1013.2	917.7	56.5	22.8	20.7
1998	4682.1	4342.9	1673.0	1772.2	1079.2	37.0	39.2	23.9
1999	4692.4	4349.0	1879.2	1630.0	1025.5	41.4	35.9	22.6
2000	4740.4	4557.0	1162.5	1640.3	1754.2	25.5	36.0	38.5
2001	4745.6	4578.2	941.3	1560.0	2076.9	20.6	34.1	45.4
2002	4744.9	4570.0	1130.6	1661.0	1778.4	24.7	36.3	38.9
2003	4754.6	4579.0	1187.3	1648.0	1743.7	25.9	36.0	38.1
2004	4754.9	4580.0	1188.0	1648.1	1743.9	25.9	36.0	38.1
2005	4758.6	4584.8	1182.2	1648.1	1754.5	25.8	36.0	38.2

Source: Land balance tables from Statistical Committee of Azerbaijan.

Table A.14
Arable Land by Users: Corporate and Individual Farms

Year	Arable Land, '000 ha	Land in Farms, '000 ha				Structure of Land in Farms, %		
		All Farms	Corporate	Individual	Common Land	Corporate	Individual	Common Land
1965	1341.8	1335.4	1300.7	34.7		97.4	2.6	
1966	1333.6	1326.9	1291.3	35.6		97.3	2.7	
1967	1385.4	1361.9	1322.4	39.5		97.1	2.9	
1968	1353.5	1329.7	1289.9	39.8		97.0	3.0	
1969	1350.1	1325.8	1285.3	40.5		96.9	3.1	
1970	1339.3	1320.1	1279.3	40.8		96.9	3.1	
1971	1376.2	1362.9	1321.9	41.0		97.0	3.0	
1972	1388.7	1373.5	1332.3	41.2		97.0	3.0	
1973	1380.4	1365.8	1324.6	41.2		97.0	3.0	
1974	1394.8	1379.3	1338.2	41.1		97.0	3.0	
1975	1423.3	1407.2	1365.9	41.3		97.1	.9	
1976	1401.8	1386.0	1344.6	41.4		97.0	3.0	
1977	1392.6	1379.5	1338.5	41.0		97.0	3.0	
1978	1380.3	1365.2	1323.9	41.3		97.0	3.0	
1979	1371.2	1357.1	1315.5	41.6		96.9	3.1	
1980	1360.9	1346.6	1303.7	42.9		96.8	3.2	
1981	1394.3	1378.9	1331.4	47.5		96.6	3.4	
1982	1419.3	1404.5	1356.9	47.6		96.6	3.4	
1983	1427.4	1412.6	1364.4	48.2		96.6	3.4	
1984	1448.5	1434.0	1385.1	48.9		96.6	3.4	

1985	1454.3	1441.0	1391.8	49.2		96.6	3.4	
1986	1532.3	1518.6	1469.0	49.6		96.7	3.3	
1987	1555.1	1541.6	1491.2	50.4		96.7	3.3	
1988	1562.2	1548.4	1495.9	52.5		96.6	3.4	
1989	1572.4	1560.2	1505.0	55.2		96.5	3.5	
1990	1589.0	1576.7	1514.0	62.7		96.0	4.0	
1991	1615.8	1599.8	n.a.	n.a.		96.0	4.0	
1992	1612.3	1598.6	n.a.	n.a.		95.0	5.0	
1993	1620.4	1606.5	n.a.	n.a.		95.0	5.0	
1994	1623.2	1609.1	n.a.	n.a.		94.0	6.0	
1995	1628.4	1614.7	1497.0	117.7	0.0	92.7	7.3	0.0
1996	1672.2	1659.6	1556.8	102.8	0.0	93.8	6.2	0.0
1997	1695.7	1673.1	905.6	763.0	4.5	54.1	45.6	0.3
1998	1735.5	1708.9	303.3	1402.9	2.7	17.7	82.1	0.2
1999	1761.6	1728.7	380.2	1340.8	7.6	22.0	77.6	0.4
2000	1766.8	1743.2	368.6	1368.5	5.9	21.1	78.5	0.3
2001	1775.9	1753.6	336.8	1314.4	102.4	19.2	75.0	5.8
2002	1783.2	1759.5	263.1	1401.9	94.5	15.0	79.7	5.4
2003	1785.6	1764.4	371.7	1389.0	3.7	21.1	78.7	0.2
2004	1790.8	1769.9	372.0	1389.0	4.0	21.1	78.7	0.2
2005	1797.6	1776.6	392.0	1369.5	8.4	22.1	77.4	0.5

Source: Land balance tables from Statistical Committee of Azerbaijan.
Note: No breakdown of arable land by farm type is available for 1991–94. The shares of corporate and individual farms in arable land for these lands were estimated by interpolation between the data points for 1990 and 1995.

TABLE A.15
Livestock (Thousand Head, End of Year)

Year	Cattle	Cows	*Sheep Goats*	Pigs	Poultry	*All Animals**
1965	1460.3	576.3	4034.9	85.2	6850.5	1940.8
1966	1583.2	616.3	4371.8	106.7	7713.3	2108.2
1967	1678.9	651.4	4713.1	101.2	8427.9	2244.6
1968	1671.4	648.1	4708.3	91.9	8038.6	2231.8
1969	1560.3	615.0	3960.6	89.8	8623.8	2051.6
1970	1576.8	605.1	4371.2	113.1	8780.8	2113.0
1971	1576.1	594.5	4478.3	122.3	8846.2	2124.6
1972	1564.7	591.8	4692.3	129.3	10585.8	2152.7
1973	1637.4	620.1	5078.6	142.8	12446.1	2284.0
1974	1652.9	623.3	5163.8	151.2	13227.5	2316.7
1975	1666.9	621.9	5128.4	135.3	12487.2	2318.1
1976	1645.7	614.3	5144.5	141.3	13626.0	2310.5
1977	1691.5	631.3	5254.7	169.2	14806.1	2382.0
1978	1720.6	646.3	5257.8	167.0	17184.8	2434.9
1979	1768.8	663.6	5306.4	187.6	18552.3	2503.7
1980	1806.2	675.8	5361.6	183.1	20687.6	2567.5
1981	1851.6	699.2	5471.2	179.8	23152.6	2648.2
1982	1887.1	723.1	5332.4	184.4	24470.0	2683.5
1983	1941.1	738.5	5396.4	190.0	25925.5	2759.0
1984	1985.4	747.4	5491.9	211.9	28455.3	2840.3
1985	2025.6	746.3	5595.1	224.3	30010.6	2907.6
1986	2025.1	749.3	5640.9	235.6	30785.5	2920.6
1987	2012.2	743.4	5705.2	229.5	30786.7	2913.5
1988	1979.0	742.7	5747.7	213.4	31361.5	2888.7
1989	1915.5	716.3	5513.6	202.1	30343.2	2790.5
1990	1831.6	710.7	5418.7	156.7	29050.8	2679.6
1991	1826.2	733.7	5292.3	137.3	27665.0	2645.8
1992	1730.9	738.0	4901.3	66.9	21704.3	2444.8
1993	1621.3	711.7	4539.0	47.9	17032.2	2250.3
1994	1632.8	742.5	4557.6	33.4	14417.8	2236.1
1995	1681.7	772.6	4644.4	30.4	13333.4	2282.5
1996	1779.9	826.7	4922.0	23.4	12030.7	2394.7
1997	1843.5	862.9	5267.0	21.0	13234.0	2504.6
1998	1913.2	895.0	5511.9	26.1	13873.7	2605.7
1999	1961.4	925.8	5773.8	19.7	14711.1	2687.9
2000	2021.6	958.9	6085.7	18.6	14740.0	2779.4
2001	2097.9	1001.7	6558.9	16.9	15351.2	2909.0
2002	2178.6	1042.3	6986.4	19.8	17137.5	3050.6
2003	2241.8	1075.7	7280.1	20.4	17545.0	3147.3
2004	2315.8	1117.0	7488.8	22.9	18253.3	3249.5
2005	2380.0	1151.3	7698.7	22.9	19035.9	3342.5
2006	2445.0	1183.6	7868.4	21.3	18800.0	3422.0
2007	2511.8	1216.8	8109.7	18.7	20800.0	3532.6
2008	2569.6	1242.1	8276.2	10.3	22352.9	3621.8

* Thousand standard head, calculated using the following weights for head by species: 1 for cattle; 0.1 for sheep and pigs; 0.01 for poultry.
Source: Statistical Committee of Azerbaijan (2006e, 2009b); 2008 private communication (July 2009).

TABLE A.16
Livestock by Farm Type:
Share of Animals in Individual Farms (Percent of Total by Species)

Year	*Cattle*	*Cows*	*Sheep, Goats*	*Pigs*	*Poultry*	*All Animals**
1965	51.1	63.6	32.3	23.1	76.6	48.0
1966	53.9	66.3	36.0	29.3	76.3	50.9
1967	56.5	68.4	39.3	26.2	74.4	53.4
1968	56.5	69.4	40.8	19.3	73.6	53.6
1969	55.3	68.2	42.8	16.3	72.4	53.4
1970	53.2	66.6	41.3	19.7	70.1	51.3
1971	52.2	66.7	41.0	21.7	62.3	50.1
1972	51.8	66.5	41.5	22.9	66.8	50.1
1973	52.9	66.8	42.0	26.1	69.5	51.2
1974	52.5	66.5	41.2	26.3	66.8	50.7
1975	52.1	66.3	40.5	22.0	68.0	50.2
1976	51.2	65.3	38.6	17.5	64.9	49.0
1977	51.9	66.1	38.8	22.8	66.5	49.7
1978	51.8	66.5	38.2	18.9	67.2	49.7
1979	51.8	66.8	38.0	17.1	67.8	49.8
1980	52.1	67.6	38.1	13.5	69.7	50.3
1981	52.3	67.6	38.3	10.5	67.1	50.4
1982	52.7	68.3	37.4	12.0	65.8	50.6
1983	52.7	68.0	39.2	13.3	63.7	50.8
1984	51.9	67.5	40.1	11.1	60.2	50.2
1985	51.3	67.5	40.8	10.7	57.4	49.6
1986	52.5	67.6	42.6	10.1	56.6	50.7
1987	52.8	67.9	43.8	9.5	56.5	51.1
1988	53.1	68.2	44.6	8.4	55.1	51.3
1989	53.3	67.6	46.8	12.2	56.6	52.1
1990	54.5	68.7	47.4	11.4	58.1	53.2
1991	56.5	70.5	48.6	10.9	59.4	55.0
1992	63.1	75.7	52.9	10.6	68.2	61.3
1993	66.7	78.3	54.2	13.4	81.6	65.2
1994	72.2	81.6	58.2	23.4	90.7	70.4
1995	77.5	81.0	62.5	29.3	93.5	75.3
1996	92.2	94.1	82.2	43.2	95.3	90.3
1997	97.4	97.9	90.4	67.6	96.9	95.9
1998	98.6	99.0	93.3	70.1	97.0	97.4
1999	99.0	99.3	95.4	79.2	96.0	98.0
2000	99.1	99.3	95.7	84.9	96.0	98.2
2001	99.2	99.4	96.4	87.0	92.3	98.2
2002	99.2	99.4	96.5	77.3	81.1	97.6
2003	99.2	99.4	97.1	73.0	75.7	97.4
2004	99.1	99.3	96.6	65.5	77.6	97.3
2005	99.1	99.3	96.4	68.6	74.7	97.0
2006	99.0	99.3	96.5	69.5	70.2	96.9
2007	99.0	99.2	96.5	72.2	66.3	96.5
2008	99.0	99.2	96.6	56.2	66.3	97.0

Source: Calculated from Statistical Committee of Azerbaijan (2006e, 2009b) (see previous table); 2008 private communication (July 2009)

TABLE A.17
Inflation Rate and Consumer Price Index 1992–2008 (December to December)

	Inflation Rate	*CPI 1994=100*	*CPI 1995=100*	*CPI 1992=100*
1992				100
1993	1293.8			1394
1994	1786.8	100.0		26298
1995	84.6	184.6	100.0	48523
1996	6.8	197.2	106.8	51808
1997	0.4	197.9	107.2	51960
1998	−7.6	182.9	99.1	48001
1999	−0.5	182.0	98.6	47754
2000	2.2	186.0	100.8	48758
2001	1.3	188.4	102.1	49397
2002	3.3	194.6	105.4	51022
2003	3.6	201.6	109.2	52858
2004	10.4	222.6	120.6	58356
2005	5.4	234.6	127.1	61507
2006	11.4	261.4	141.6	68518
2007	16.7	305.0	165.2	79961
2008	15.3	351.7	190.5	92195

Source: National Bank of Azerbaijan (2009); Statistical Committee of Azerbaijan (2003, 2006a, 2008); the CPI series from 1992 calculated by splicing at 2000.
Note: The inflation rates in this table (December to December) are different from the inflation rates in table 3.3, which are calculated as changes in year-to-year averages.

TABLE A.18
Nominal and Real Exchange rates 1992–2008

	Exchange Rate		Real Exchange Rate Index (December to December)	
	Old Manat, AZM/US$, (December)	New Manat, AZN/US$ (Average for the Year)	Dec 1992 = 100	Dec 2000 = 100
1992	41.5		100.0	
1993	123.9		22.0	
1994	3941.0		38.1	
1995	4440.0	0.8828	23.9	
1996	4122.6	0.8605	21.4	
1997	3894.0	0.7973	20.5	
1998	3880.3	0.7738	22.5	
1999	4374.4	0.8236	26.2	
2000	4562.3	0.8948	27.6	100
2001	4804.1	0.9313	26.8	97.2
2002	4439.1	0.9722	24.0	86.9
2003	3900.8	0.9821	20.8	75.2
2004	3659.0	0.9827	20.5	74.2
2005	4201.9	0.9459	23.7	85.8
2006	4106.1	0.8927	24.6	89.0
2007	3896.2	0.8581	26.3	95.1
2008	4566.9	0.8216	33.7	121.8

Note: The first manat (AZM) was introduced in 1992, replacing the Russian ruble at a rate of ten rubles to one manat. The new ("national") manat (AZN) was introduced on January 1, 2006, at a value of 5,000 old manats.

Source: National Bank of Azerbaijan (2009); the old manat exchange rates after 2000 calculated by splicing.

References

Ahearn, M., Yee, J., and Huffman, W. (2002): "The Effect of Contracting and Consolidation on Farm Productivity," paper presented at the Economics of Contracting in Agriculture Workshop, Annapolis, MD (July).

Alam, A., Muthi, M., Yemtsov, R., Murrugarra, E., Dudwick, N., Hamilton, E., and Tiongson, E. (2005): *Growth, Poverty and Inequality in Eastern Europe and the Former Soviet Union* (Washington, DC: World Bank).

Brock, G., Grazhdaninova, M., Lerman, Z., and Uzun, V. (2008): "Technical Efficiency in Russian Agriculture," in Z. Lerman, ed., *Russia's Agriculture in Transition: Factor Markets and Constraints on Growth* (Lanham, MD: Lexington Books).

Csaki, C., and Kray, H. (2005): *The Agrarian Economies of Central-Eastern Europe and the CIS: An Update on Status and Progress in 2004*, ECSSD Working Paper No. 40 (Washington, DC: World Bank).

Csaki, C., and Nash, J. (1998): *The Agrarian Economies of Central-Eastern Europe and the CIS: Situation and Perspectives 1997*, World Bank Discussion Paper No. 387 (Washington, DC: World Bank).

Curtis, Glen E., ed. (1994): *Azerbaijan: A Country Study* (Washington, DC: Library of Congress) [http://lcweb2.loc.gov/frd/cs/aztoc.html].

Datt, G., and Ravallion, M. (1992): "Growth and Redistribution Components of Changes in Poverty Measures: A Decomposition with Applications to Brazil and India in the 1980s," *Journal of Development Economics*, vol. 38, pp. 275–295.

Department of Statistics and Sociology of the Republic of Moldova (2004): *Agriculture of the Republic of Moldova* (Chisinau).

Diamond, D., Bettis, L., and Ramsson, R. (1983): "Agricultural Production," in A. Bergson and H.S. Levine, eds., *The Soviet Economy: Toward the Year 2000* (London: Allen and Unwin).

Dudwick, N., Fock, K., and Sedik, D. (2007): *Land Reform and Farm Restructuring in Transition Countries. The Experience of Bulgaria, Moldova, Azerbaijan and Kazakhstan*, World Bank Working Paper No. 104 (Washington, DC: World Bank) [http://go.worldbank.org/2W17PBZ490].

Easterly, W., and Fischer, S. (1995): "The Soviet Economic Decline," *World Bank Economic Review*, vol. 9, no. 3, pp. 341–372.

Economist (1977): "The Dutch Disease," *The Economist*, pp. 82–83 (November 26).

Economist Intelligence Unit (2007): "Boom and Gloom" [Economist.com] (March 8).

Energy Information Administration (2004): *International Energy Annual* [www.eia.doe.gov/iea/wep.html].

Encyclopedia Britannica (2004): *Encyclopedia Britannica*, CD edition.

Encyclopedia Britannica Online (2007): [www.britannica.com/eb/article-9108701/Azerbaijan>Economic regions].

European Bank for Reconstruction and Development (2001): *EBRD Transition Report* (London: EBRD).

FAO (2007): FAOSTAT Online Statistical Database [http://faostat.fao.org/].

Government of Azerbaijan (2004). *State Program on Social-Economic Development of Regions of Azerbaijan Republics for the Years of 2004–2008* (Baku) [www.un-az.org/undp/povrep.php].

Hanson, P. (2003): *The Rise and Fall of the Soviet Economy: An Economic History of the USSR from 1945* (London: Longman).

Index Mundi (2008): Azerbaijan oil: Proved reserves as of 1 January 2008 [http://www.indexmundi.com/azerbaijan/oil_proved_reserves.html].

Karatnycky, A., Motyl, A., and Graybow, C. (1999): *Nations in Transit 1998: Civil Society, Democracy and Markets in East Central Europe and the Newly Independent States* (New Brunswick, NJ, and London: Transaction Publishers).

Karatnycky, A., Motyl, A., and Shor, B. (1997): *Nations in Transit 1997: Civil Society and Markets in East Central Europe and the Newly Independent States* (New Brunswick, NJ, and London: Transaction Publishers).

Kaufman, D., Kraay, A., and Mastruzzi, M. (2007): *Governance Matters VI: Aggregate and Individual Governance Indicators, 1996–2006*, World Bank Policy Research Working Paper 4280 (Washington, DC: World Bank).

Kaufman, D., Kraay, A., and Zoido-Lobaton, P. (1999): *Governance Matters*, World Bank Policy Research Working Paper 2196 (Washington, DC: World Bank).

Koester, U., and Brooks, K. (1997): *Agriculture and German Reunification*, World Bank Discussion Paper No. 355 (Washington, DC: World Bank).

Lerman, Z. (2004): "Policies and Institutions for Commercialization of Subsistence Farms in Transition Countries," *Journal of Asian Economics*, vol. 15, pp. 461–479.

Lerman, Z., and Cimpoies, D. (2006): "Land Consolidation as a Factor for Rural Development in Moldova," *Europe-Asia Studies*, vol. 58, no. 3, pp. 439–455.

Lerman, Z., Csaki, C., and Feder, G. (2004): *Agriculture in Transition: Land Policies and Evolving Farm Structures in Post-Soviet Countries* (Lanham, MD: Lexington Books).

Lerman, Z., Csaki, C., and Sotnikov, S. (2000): *Farm Debt in CIS: A Cross-Country Analysis*, World Bank Discussion Paper No. 424 (Washington, DC: World Bank).

Lerman, Z., Kislev, Y., Kriss, A., and Biton, D. (2003): "Agricultural Output and Productivity in the Former Soviet Republics," *Economic Development and Cultural Change*, vol. 51, no. 4, pp. 999-1018.

Lerman, Z., and Schreinemachers, P. (2005): "Individual Farming as a Labor Sink: Evidence from Poland and Russia," *Comparative Economic Studies*, vol. 47, no. 4, pp. 675–695.

Lerman, Z., Sedik, D., Pugachov, N., and Goncharuk, A. (2007): *Rethinking Agricultural Reform in Ukraine*, Studies in the Agricultural and Food Sector in Central and Eastern Europe, Vol. 38 (Halle, Germany: IAMO—Leibniz Institute of Agricultural Development in Central and Eastern Europe).

Lerman, Z. and Sutton, W. (2008): "Productivity and Efficiency of Small and Large Farms in Transition: Evidence from Moldova," *Post-Soviet Studies*, vol. 24, no. 2, pp. 97–120.

Liefert, W., and Swinnen, J. (2002): *Changes in Agricultural Markets in Transition Economies*, Agricultural Economic Report No. 806 (Washington, DC: U.S. Department of Agriculture, Economic Research Service).

Lipton, M. (2006): "Can Small Farmers Survive, Propse or Be the Key Channel to Cut Mass Poverty?" *eJADE—Electronic Journal of Agricultural and Development Economics*, vol. 3, no. 1, pp. 58–85 [http://www.fao.org/es/esa/en/ejade.htm].

Maddison, A. (1995): *Monitoring the World Economy, 1820–1992* (Paris: OECD).

Mamedov, G. (2000): *Zemel'naya reforma v Azerbaidzhane* [in Russian] (Baku: Elm).

Millar, J. R. (1990). *The Soviet Economic Experiment* (Urbana: University of Illinois Press).

Ministry of Economic Development of Azerbaijan (2001): "The oil sector," *Economic Trends Azerbaijan July-September 2001* (Baku).

Ministry of Economic Development of Georgia (2005): *Agriculture of Georgia* (Tbilisi).

Ministry of Finance (1914): *Narodnoe khoziaistvo v 1913 g.* (Petrograd: Ministerstvo Finansov).

National Bank of Azerbaijan (2009): [www.nba.az].

National Statistical Service of the Republic of Armenia (2005). *Statistical Yearbook of Armenia* (Yerevan).

Richardson, E. (1999): *The Struggle for Sobriety: Anti-Alcohol Campaigning under Gorbashev and Yeltsin*, Research Papers in Russian and East European Studies ResPREES 99/1, Centre for Russian and East European Studies, University of Birmigham (March).

Rizov, M. (2005): "Does Individualization Help Productivity of Transition Agriculture?" *Agricultural Economics*, vol. 33, pp. 215–227.

Rosenberg, C., and Saavalainen, T. (1998): *How to Deal with Azerbaijans Oil Boom? Policy Strategies in a Resource-Rich Transition Economy*, IMF Working Paper WP/98/6 (Washington, DC: International Monetary Fund).

Sachs, J., and Warner, A. (1995): "Economic Reform and the Process of Global Integration," *Brookings Papers on Economic Activity*, 1, pp. 1–118.

Sedik, D. (1993): "A Note on Soviet Per Capita Meat Consumption," *Comp. Econ. Studies*, vol. 35, no. 3, pp. 39-48 (Fall).

Sedik, D., Fock, K., Davis, D., Trento, S., and Molinari, B. (2002): *Azerbaijan Rural Poverty Assessment*, mimeo (Washington, DC: World Bank).
Sedik, D., Sotnikov, S., and Wiesmann, D. (2003): *Food Security in the Russian Federation*, FAO Economic and Social Development Paper No. 153 (Rome: FAO).
Service, R. (2005): *Stalin* (London: Pan Books), p. 198.
Shend, J. Y. (1993): *Agricultural Statistics of the Former USSR Republics and the Baltic States*, Statistical Bulletin No. 863 (Washington, DC: USDA Economic Research Service) [data tables downloadable from www.ers.usda.gov/data/archive/93009].
Soviet Encyclopedia (1967): *Bol'shaya Sovetskaya Entsiklopedia*, 3rd ed. (Moscow).
Statistical Committee of AzSSR (1980): *Narodnoe khoziaistvo Azerbaidzhanskoi SSR za 60 let, iubileinyi statisticheskii sbornik* (Baku).
——— (1985): *Narodnoe khoziaistvo Azerbaidzhanskoi SSR v 1984 godu, statisticheskii ezhegodnik* (Baku).
——— (1988): *Narodnoe khoziaistvo Azerbaidzhanskoi SSR v 1988 godu, statisticheskii ezhegodnik* (Baku).
Statistical Committee of Azerbaijan (2001): *Azerbaijan in the XX Century*, v. 1, 2 (Baku).
——— (2003): *Statistical Yearbook of Azerbaijan 2003* (Baku).
——— (2005): *Statistical Yearbook of Azerbaijan 2005* (Baku).
——— (2006a): *Statistical Yearbook of Azerbaijan 2006* (Baku).
——— (2006b): *The Agriculture of Azerbaijan 2006* (Baku).
——— (2006c). *Families in Azerbaijan 2006* (Baku).
——— (2006d). *Labor in Azerbaijan 2006* (Baku).
——— (2006e). *Number of Livestock and Poultry 2006* (Baku).
——— (2006f). *Azerbaijan in Figures 2006* (Baku) [www.azstat.org].
——— (2007). *Azerbaijan in Figures 2007* (Baku) [www.azstat.org].
——— (2008): *Statistical Yearbook of Azerbaijan 2008* (Baku) [http://www.azstat.org/publications/yearbook/SYA2008/en/index.shtml].
——— (2009a). *Azerbaijan in Figures 2009* (Baku) [www.azstat.org].
——— (2009b). Online statistical information by directions [www.azstat.org/indexen.php].
Statistical Committee of CIS (2008): *Official Statistics of the Countries of the Commonwealth of Independent States*, CD-ROM 2008–13 (Moscow).
Statistical Committee of Russian Federation (2005): *Rossiya v tsifrakh* (Moscow).
Statistical Committee of USSR (1969): *Narodnoe khoziaistvo SSSR v 1968 g., statisticheskii ezhegodnik* (Moscow: Statistika).
——— (1972): *Narodnoe khoziaistvo SSSR 1922–1972, statisticheskii ezhegodnik* (Moscow: Statistika).
——— (1982): *Narodnoe khoziaistvo SSSR 1922–1982, statisticheskii ezhegodnik* (Moscow: Finansy i statistika).
——— (1987): *Narodnoe khozyaistvo za 70 let, statisticheskii ezhegodnik* (Moscow: Finansy i statistika).
——— (1988): *Sel'skoe khoziaistvo SSSR, Statisticheskii sbornik* (Moscow: Finansy i statistika).

——— (1989): *Narodnoe khoziaistvo SSSR v 1988 g., statisticheskii ezhegodnik* (Moscow: Finansy i statistika).

——— (1991): *Narodnoe khoziaistvo SSSR v 1990 g., statisticheskii ezhegodnik* (Moscow: Finansy i statistika).

Wacziarg, R., and Welch, K. (2003): *Trade Liberalization and Growth: New Evidence*, National Bureau of Economic Research, Working Paper 10152 (December) [http://www.nber.org/papers/w10152].

WGI (2007): *World Wide Governance Indicators, 1996–2006* (Washington, DC: World Bank) [http://info.worldbank.org/governance/wgi2007/home.htm].

World Bank (2006): *Azerbaijan Extended Poverty Profile, 2002–2004* (Washington, DC).

World Bank (2007): *World Development Indicators* [http://go.worldbank.org/3JU2HA60D0].

USDA/ERS (1997): *Agricultural Trade of NIS and Baltic States* (Washington, DC: USDA Economic Research Service) [http://www.ers.usda.gov/data/archive/97003/].

Index

About the Authors

Zvi Lerman is professor and Sir Henry d'Avigdor Goldsmid Chair in Agricultural Economics at the Hebrew University of Jerusalem. He is author of *Agriculture in Transition: Land Policies and Evolving Farm Structures in Post-Soviet Countries.*

David J. Sedik is Senior Agricultural Policy Officer responsible for the Europe and Central Asia region in the Food and Agriculture Organization of the UN. His duties combine policy related research on current issues of the region with the rendering of policy advice to member countries.

www.ingramcontent.com/pod-product-compliance
Ingram Content Group UK Ltd.
Pitfield, Milton Keynes, MK11 3LW, UK
UKHW012040150926
475560UK00001B/113

9 780739 143162